FROM CONTRABAND
TO FREEDMAN

RECENT TITLES IN
CONTRIBUTIONS IN AMERICAN HISTORY

FROM CONTRABAND TO FREEDMAN

Federal Policy Toward Southern Blacks
1861-1865

★

Louis S. Gerteis

CONTRIBUTIONS IN AMERICAN HISTORY
NUMBER 29

GREENWOOD PRESS, INC.
Westport, Connecticut ● London, England

Library of Congress Cataloging in Publication Data

Gerteis, Loùis S
    From contraband to freedman.

    (Contributions in American history, no. 29)
    Bibliography: p.
    1. United States—History—Civil War—Negroes.
2. Slavery in the United States—Emancipation.
3. Freedmen. I. Title.
E453.G47   973.7'15'0396073075   72-801
ISBN 0-8371-6372-2

Library of Congress Catalog Number: 72-801

ISBN: 0-8371-6372-2

First published in 1973

Greenwood Press, Inc., Publishing Division

51 Riverside Avenue, Westport, Connecticut 06880

Manufactured in the United States of America

For My Father and in Memory of My Mother,
Helen Saxton Gerteis

Contents

PART III
THE MISSISSIPPI VALLEY

Preface

The nature and scope of this study imposes difficult problems of organization. The description of developing federal policies requires a chronological narrative, while the distinct political and geographical features of the areas under federal occupation demand separate discussion. These conflicting requirements cannot be entirely resolved. For analytical purposes, I have chosen to emphasize regional variations in the occupied South. Chronological developments, therefore, necessarily overlap. It has seemed to me to be more important that the necessities of war determined the course of federal policy. Since the war cannot be separated from the regions in which it was fought, I have discussed federal policy toward Southern blacks as it emerged in the several areas under Union control.

In the process of completing the research for this work, I have enjoyed the assistance and goodwill of several librarians and archivists. Sarah Jackson and Elaine Everly of the National Archives went out of their way to bring significant documents and collections to my attention. Mrs. Jackson has long guided scholars through the massive and complex Civil War Military Command Records, and I could not have used that collection efficiently or thoroughly without her aid. I am similarly indebted to Dr. Clifton H. Johnson, Director of the Amistad Research Center, Dillard University. Dr. Johnson has organized and cataloged the rich American Missionary Association Archives, making that collection easily accessible and extremely useful to scholars of varied interests.

Among my colleagues, I owe particular thanks to Professor Richard Sewell of the University of Wisconsin who served as my dissertation advisor and in whose seminar this study began. I am thankful as well

ix

for the assistance of Professor Joseph Logsdon of Louisiana State University at New Orleans. Professor Logsdon led me to a number of essential sources and freely shared with me his detailed knowledge of New Orleans during the Civil War and Reconstruction. I extend my thanks as well to Professor Ira Berlin of Federal City College, Washington, D.C., for his willingness to read and criticize the manuscript at several stages of its development. Similarly, I am indebted to Professor Gilman Ostrander of the University of Waterloo, Ontario, who read the entire manuscript and shared with me his skills as a historian and writer.

Finally, without timely financial support from several sources, this study would have been exceedingly difficult to complete. I am appreciative of the assistance provided by the Regents of the University of Wisconsin in the form of a graduate fellowship for the year 1968-1969, and by the Curators of the University of Missouri in the form of a summer research grant in 1970. I am deeply indebted to my wife Gretchen who provided financial support during my graduate years, and who prevented me from completely forsaking youth and sunshine for the appealing gloom of libraries and archives.

List of Abbreviations

AGO   Adjutant General's Office, Record Group
94, National Archives

—AFIC   Letters Received, 1861-1870, American
Freedmen's Inquiry Commission Records

—DCT   Division of Colored Troops

—GP   General's Papers

—MSR   Military Service Records

AMA Archives   American Missionary Association Archives,
Amistad Research Center, Dillard University,
New Orleans, Louisiana

BRFAL   Bureau of Refugees, Freedmen, and Abandoned
Lands, Record Group 105, National Archives

—GSC   General Superintendent of Contrabands

CWPR   Civil War Pension Records, Record Group 15,
National Archives

CWSAR   Records of Civil War Special Agencies, Treasury
Department, Record Group 366, National Archives

LC   Library of Congress

OR   R.N. Scott, et al. (eds.), *War of the*
                  Rebellion: a Compilation of the Official
                  Records of the Union and Confederate Armies,
                  130 vols. (Washington, D.C., 1880-1901)

QMG   Records of the Office of the Quartermaster
                  General, Record Group 92, National Archives

SHSW   State Historical Society of Wisconsin,
                  Madison, Wisconsin

USCC   Records of the United States Army
                  Continental Commands, 1821-1920, Record
                  Group 393, National Archives

—DG   Department of the Gulf

—DT   Department of the Tennessee

—DVa-NC   Department of Virginia and North
                  Carolina

FROM CONTRABAND
TO FREEDMAN

Introduction

★

I

Intent on righting the wrongs of historical "racism," current historians
of the Civil War era have largely discredited and dismissed traditional
evaluations of the sectional conflict and its aftermath. Southern blacks,
traditionally portrayed merely as the ignorant dupes of unscrupulous
and fanatical Radical Republicans, now receive fuller and more sympathetic treatment from historians dedicated to the cause of racial
equality. Consciously anti-racist historians have focused attention on
the long neglected Negro, thereby enriching with new materials the
period's historiography.[1]

The desire to do justice to blacks has changed the values with which
contemporary historians are interpreting the past. But the traditional
theoretical context for historical analysis of the Civil War era remains
substantially intact despite changing points of view. By and large, historians continue to accept the postulation that the Civil War and
Reconstruction wrought dramatic and fundamental changes in the society and economy of the South. In part, the presumption of basic
upheaval reflects an understanding of the unavoidable dislocations produced by war. But it emerges as well from an evaluation of abolitionist
and Radical influence and motives. In the past, historians contended
that antislavery men sought to destroy the social and economic order
of the South. Historians of liberal sentiments have continued to maintain that abolitionists and Radicals attempted to achieve fundamental
and sweeping changes in the South. From both points of view, emancipation, the Freedmen's Bureau, and Radical Reconstruction seemed
to open the way for basic social change.[2]

Egalitarian values now dominate the historical literature. But the

3

victory has been a superficial one, achieved in large measure simply by upending traditional arguments. Historians once lamented the disorder and violence of the Civil War era as unnecessary and therefore tragic. The same turmoil is now described as symptomatic of fundamental social change. Similarly, the singleminded abolitionists and Radicals, formerly denounced as irresponsible fanatics, are now placed at the vanguard of a social revolution. Yet, the presumption of radical social change raises more questions than it answers. If emancipation marked the beginning of a social revolution, why did the bright hopes raised by Union victory fade so completely and so quickly during Reconstruction? Where had the revolution failed? What had gone wrong? Some historians have placed the blame on congressional Radicals. The Radicals, thought to be the dominant political group early in 1866, evidently failed to consolidate their wartime victories. Other historians have charged individuals with malice, weakness, and cowardice in the protection of blacks. In any case, Northern whites seemed to abandon blacks and betrayed the revolution.[3]

Yet, had a revolution actually occurred? Certainly the war produced social and economic dislocation. Certainly there were reformers during the war working in the South to uplift and liberate the former slaves. But there is no compelling reason to accept the proposition that the legal transition from slavery to freedom for four million blacks (as dramatic as it sounds) involved social revolution. Nor is it necessary to assume that the war and emancipation destroyed or dramatically altered antebellum forms of economic and social organization in the South. We have not yet asked the most important questions about the Civil War and its effects. Perhaps we have been misled by our current values and concerns. As a number of recent studies illustrate, it is not difficult to prove that blacks have been and continue to be oppressed by whites. But to concentrate on "racism" and on the gross signs of racial oppression is to overlook the possibility of discrete and subtle change. Indeed, if one views slavery simply as an extreme form of racial subordination, the war and emancipation seem almost insignificant. If, as David Potter observes, "Racial subordination was the essence, and slavery was only an overt form," what difference did the Civil War make?[4]

As Eugene Genovese has demonstrated, slavery involved far more than racial subordination. It underlaid the development of a slave civilization.[5] Its collapse must have produced significant, if not dramatic, changes. We have not been wrong to expect change; we have simply misunderstood the context within which change could occur in the postwar South. Whatever changes might have occurred as a result of the war, federal authorities took care to see that they would not be revolutionary. The details of federal labor policies and the wartime failure of Radical reforms indicate that emancipation did not involve specific changes either in the status of the former slaves or in the conditions under which they labored.

II

Federal policy toward Southern blacks pursued two major objectives: the mobilization of black laborers and soldiers, and the prevention of violent change. Conservative Republicans as well as Radicals understood that Southern blacks constituted a vital resource in the midst of civil war. If federal authorities failed to mobilize blacks and neglected to encourage their defection from Rebel territory, slave labor would strengthen the Confederacy and prolong the war. Moreover, if the victorious Union army did not regulate blacks and oversee the operations of plantations within federal lines, the unavoidable dislocations of war might stimulate "servile insurrection" and leave the South's cotton economy in ruins. Thus, while the Union's military needs required the swift mobilization of black laborers and, later, soldiers, the federal government imposed labor policies designed to prevent violent and fundamental changes in the society and economy of the crumbling Confederacy.[6]

To the extent that blacks were concerned, Reconstruction did not begin in a climate of hope. The Civil War did not create the necessary conditions for sweeping reforms. In December 1866 the abolitionist and former slave Frederick Douglass surveyed the effects of the Civil War. He considered the prospects for social reconstruction in the South without enthusiasm. "The stern logic of events," Douglass believed, determined that the interests of the nation were "identical with and inseparable from those of the Negro." But unless blacks possessed "the power to protect themselves," the long arm of the federal government would prove to be "far too short to protect the

rights of individuals in the interior of distant States.'' Douglass' fears
were prophetic. Reconstruction did not address itself to what Kenneth
Stampp has called the ''sociology of freedom.'' Laws alone could not
protect an ''economically dependent class.''[7]

Antislavery men, their goals subordinated to the Union's military
needs, were unable to advance reforms in the midst of war. Efforts
to provide land for blacks were quickly isolated and defeated. Even
the moderate, paternalistic goal of improving the black man's intellectual and moral character ran counter to the military needs of the
federal government. William Tecumseh Sherman, who despised blacks
and secessionists equally, scornfully dismissed Northern humanitarian
concerns with the freedmen's welfare. ''But the nigger?'' Sherman
asked as he marched north toward Virginia after his devastating Georgia campaign. ''Why in God's name can't sensible men let him
alone?'' ''Don't military success imply the safety of Sambo?''[8]

The failure of reform could be traced partly to the scope of the
war and partly to the contradictory sentiments with which Northerners
responded to it. Despite Douglass' faith in the ''stern logic of events,''
the Civil War aroused passions that hardly promoted the interests of
blacks. While the abolitionist Robert G. Shaw led a regiment of black
troops in a valiant and bloody assault on Fort Wagner near Charleston
harbor in July 1863, draft rioters burned, bludgeoned, and lynched
their way through the black section of New York City. The war and
emancipation seemed to inflame rather than cool Northern anti-Negro
prejudice. Although abolitionists extolled the freedmen's bravery in
battle, black soldiers were given little reason to believe that the Union
army valued or promoted their freedom. Army regulations maintained
the subordination of blacks. An anonymous black conscript in
Louisiana, angered by the brutal treatment he received, warned that
black men would not long fight the battles of the ''union master.''[9]

III

For blacks, Reconstruction began in 1861 when Union forces
occupied positions in Tidewater Virginia and in the Sea Islands of
South Carolina. Early in 1862, western armies advanced to capture
Confederate defenses on the Tennessee and Mississippi rivers and to
occupy portions of western Tennessee, Arkansas, and northern Missis-

sippi. New Orleans fell in May 1862; Vicksburg, in July 1863. From the outset of the war, Union army officers and government officials faced the fundamental question of the black man's status as a freedman. The decisions made during the war concerning the treatment, organization, and employment of Southern blacks shaped postwar policies toward the freedman and in large measure precluded the possibility of radical social reconstruction in the South.

PART I

VIRGINIA
AND THE CAROLINAS

★

1

Emancipation as a

War Necessity

Wherever federal troops occupied slave territory, slavery as an institution crumbled and collapsed. While Northerners generally displayed little interest in liberating blacks, federal authorities lacked the will and the ability to maintain or restore the slave system. Emancipation was inevitable, although its details were uncertain and equivocal. At Fortress Monroe, Virginia, where Union forces occupied Confederate territory at the outset of the war, the federal government took its first reluctant and halting steps toward emancipation.

Nowhere was American slavery older than in the area of Fortress Monroe. In 1619, a Dutch man-of-war sold its cargo of Africans to English settlers at Jamestown and for two and a half centuries thereafter a slave system expanded and matured, providing at last the foundation and justification for Southern nationalism, secession, and a confederation of slave states. The Civil War had hardly begun in May 1861 when General Benjamin F. Butler sailed into Hampton Roads to occupy a portion of the seceded state of Virginia. There were as yet few signs of war in the Tidewater country. Butler landed his modest force of Massachusetts volunteers without opposition, securing a base at Fortress Monroe for future military operations on the Yorktown peninsula.

Despite the inexperienced general's good fortune in avoiding a fight, Butler was dissatisfied with his new post. The future significance of Fortress Monroe concerned him less than his isolation from centers of political power. He sought wider responsibility and thought he should have it. His troops had been the first to answer Lincoln's call-to-arms, and the first to arrive in the vulnerable and apprehensive federal capital. His assignment to eastern Virginia therefore struck him as a form of exile, an undeserved hardship to be overcome as quickly as possible.[1] Butler worked to make his influence felt in Washington once more and soon found that the issue of slavery provided him with the means. As a Union commander surrounded by disloyal slaveholders, Butler developed the first official justification for emancipation as a war necessity.

Butler arrived at Fortress Monroe on May 22, 1861, and set about securing the area from Rebel attack. On May 23 a federal patrol scouted the countryside around the village of Hampton. On every estate they encountered disconcerted whites and exhilarated but cautious slaves. The soldiers, after all, had not come to deliver the slaves from bondage, and it was not yet clear to the troops, the slaves, or the local slaveholders what effects federal occupation would have. But seeing their masters in obvious disarray, the slaves welcomed the invaders and gathered around the Yankee troops at every opportunity. As evening approached, the soldiers returned to Fortress Monroe, and, with nightfall, three black men made their way to the Union pickets, offering their services to the Yankees and seeking protection from their masters.[2]

Recent experiences had prepared Butler for the situation he encountered the following morning. In his march from Annapolis to Washington a month earlier, Butler had promised Maryland's governor that his troops would enforce slave discipline and protect slave property. He was anxious, he said then, to quiet fears of Negro insurrection. His troops would not interfere with the laws of the state of Maryland and would cooperate with local forces "in suppressing most promptly and effectually" any slave uprising. But Butler's solicitude toward Maryland slaveholders did not increase his popularity in the new Republican administration, and he received a stern rebuke from Massachusetts Radical governor, John A. Andrew. The general quickly discovered, moreover, that the immediate threat to public order in Maryland came not from the slaves but from pro-secession whites, who attacked Butler's troops as they marched through Baltimore.[3] Nevertheless, Butler justified his position on the grounds that Maryland had remained loyal to the Union and therefore required federal protection for her slave property.

Smarting from his exile to Hampton Roads, Butler did not intend to treat Virginia slaveholders with the same consideration he had shown Marylanders. He therefore decided to keep the three fugitives who had entered his lines, and ignored the entreaties of a Virginia militia officer who demanded their return under the provisions of the federal Fugitive Slave Law. Butler now argued that since Rebels in the Hampton area were using blacks to erect fortifications in support of the Rebellion, the slave property in his possession was contraband, liable to confiscation by the laws of war. The Virginia officer withdrew without his property, and Butler immediately explained his position to the War Department, requesting instructions for future action.[4]

II

Benjamin Butler was no abolitionist, and his reasons for declaring the Hampton fugitives contrabands of war were legal and practical rather than moral. "I am credibly informed," he wrote his superior, "that the negroes in this neighborhood are now being employed in the erection of batteries." Under the circumstances, Butler thought that Union forces were justified in appropriating slave property for their own uses. "I had great need for labor," he explained, adding that a receipt for the confiscated slaves had been sent to the owner. Butler did not question the sanctity of slave property, only its uses.[5]

Although he tried to limit the effects of his contraband decision, Butler was soon overwhelmed by the magnitude of slave defection. A few days after the initial contraband decision, Butler acknowledged that the question of slave property involved matters of a "very serious magnitude" which he had not anticipated. The number of blacks escaping to federal lines increased steadily, and the blacks, fearing family separation, arrived more frequently with entire families and groups of relatives. While Butler's contraband decision justified the confiscation of slave property useful to the enemy, the care of dependent blacks involved entirely new considerations. As a "military question," Butler thought it necessary to deprive Rebel masters of their able-bodied slaves, but to do so required the acceptance of large numbers of women and children. The commander had no doubt, he wrote his superior, that humanitarian considerations demanded the care and protection of dependent blacks as well as the able-bodied. Accordingly, he soon appointed a superintendent to administer to their needs. But the whole matter involved political questions which Butler prudently chose not to judge.[6]

Politically, the situation was very sensitive indeed. Two months would pass before Congress expressed its opinion, in the form of a House Resolution, that federal officers *need not* enforce the fugitive slave act. Not until March 1862 did both houses positively forbid the return of fugitive slaves. Butler therefore followed a cautious course. As soon as he had informed General Winfield Scott of his actions, he judiciously tested the acceptability of his decision with the anti-abolitionist Postmaster General, Montgomery Blair. Blair quite agreed with Butler that "secession niggers" should be confiscated as contrabands of war, although he hoped Butler would take in only the able-bodied, leaving to the Rebels the burden of caring for non-productive blacks. The matter came before the entire Cabinet on the morning of May 30, 1861. Afterwards, Blair reported that Lincoln referred laughingly to "Butler's fugitive slave law," regarding it, however, as a very serious matter since the number of Negroes likely to come under federal control was extremely large. At any rate, the Cabinet chose to take no action to restrict Butler, as much, thought Blair, from the administration's desire to "escape responsibility from acting at all at this time" as from any enthusiasm for liberating slaves.[7]

In the absence of any clear congressional or executive policy, Butler's contraband decision proved quite useful to the federal war effort. Under the circumstances, however, the official sanction Butler soon received from Secretary of War Simon Cameron was painfully complex. Since, as Cameron noted, the government could not recognize the rejection of federal obligations by any state, it could likewise not fail to perform its federal obligations toward the states. But while the enforcement of the Fugitive Slave Law was a responsibility of the federal government, the "suppressing and dispersing" of "armed combinations" represented a higher federal obligation. Thus, while the Union army would not interfere "with the relations of persons held to service under the laws of any State," commanders should "refrain" from surrendering fugitives to "alleged masters," lest this slave property contribute to the armed rebellion. Cameron directed Butler to employ fugitive blacks as best he could, keeping an account of their labor and "the value of it." The expense of their maintenance would also be recorded so that a "final disposition" of the blacks could readily be made at some future date.[8]

Butler's contraband policy, as sanctioned by Cameron, was a long way from emancipation, but it was a first step in that direction. By maintaining the fugitive's status as property, Butler's policy won the acceptance of men like Blair who were as yet firmly opposed to general emancipation. As Edward L. Pierce, Butler's superintendent of contraband labor, observed, there was "often great virtue" in such technical phrases as "contraband of war" for shaping public opinion. Pierce, a young Massachusetts army private and friend of Charles Sumner and Salmon P. Chase, supervised contraband labor for Butler at Fortress Monroe during the summer of 1861 before undertaking a more important task as Treasury superintendent of confiscated cotton plantations in South Carolina's Sea Islands. Pierce recognized the limitations of Butler's policy, but thought it an important first step. "The venerable gentleman, who wears gold spectacles and reads a conservative daily," he thought, "prefers confiscation to emancipation." Those who were fearful of emancipation and recoiled from abolitionist arguments would yield gracefully to arguments of military necessity.[9]

In July 1861 Butler began using large numbers of contrabands to construct breastworks around the town of Hampton. There were more than 850 blacks under Union control in the Fortress Monroe area by that time and nearly 300 of them were men between the ages of eighteen and forty-five.[10] Under Pierce's direction, the men worked nine hours a day, beginning at dawn to avoid the hottest portion of the afternoon. The blacks worked willingly, Pierce found, although a few feared that their masters would punish them for serving the Yankees, and one inquired suspiciously why Union officers recorded the names of their owners. Pierce sought to calm their fears of re-enslavement, but was not altogether confident himself that government policy would uphold their emancipation. To urge the men forward, Pierce told them that slaveholders charged their race with indolence, and that he hoped to return North to report that blacks "were as industrious as whites." Pierce shortly left the Hampton Roads area, later to become involved in more extensive efforts in South Carolina to prove that blacks would work as free men.[11]

As the depths of the secessionist crisis became evident, Congress looked with increasing favor on efforts to use blacks to the advantage of the Union cause. Emancipation came, as Pierce noted, not from humanitarian zeal but from military necessity. Congress remained ambivalent toward slavery, but moved haltingly toward a policy of mobilizing the labor of Southern blacks. Early in July 1861 the House of Representatives passed a resolution introduced by Illinois abolitionist Owen Lovejoy, expressing the opinion that "it is no part of the duty of the soldiers of the United States to capture and return fugitive slaves." While the measure lacked the binding effect of law and could not prevent commanders from returning slaves, it tended to justify the contraband policy already inaugurated by Butler. Similarly, a federal defeat at Bull Run on July 21 did not mark an increase in emancipation sentiment, while it did strengthen congressional resolve to deprive Rebels of their slave property. Immediately after the rout at Manassas Junction, both houses of Congress passed a resolution declaring that the North had no intention of disturbing the institution of slavery in the South. It was with no sense of contradiction that Congress then passed the first Confiscation Act which provided the opening wedge for emancipation as a war necessity.[12]

Because the Confiscation Act did not disturb the legal status of slaves, its supporters evidently felt a troublesome issue had been skirted. By the terms of the act, all property (including slaves) used to aid the Rebellion was subject to confiscation. Thus Southern blacks were not declared free, but were simply confiscated from their Rebel owners. The act provided a needed legal sanction for Butler's policies at Fortress Monroe. Thereafter, Secretary Cameron moved quickly to clarify federal policy toward fugitive blacks.[13]

It was clear, by act of Congress, that federal officers might confiscate the slaves of disloyal and rebellious persons, but the status of fugitives from loyal masters remained uncertain. Army officers, as Cameron realized, could not in practice determine the legal status of every fugitive black entering their lines. Nor did the secretary believe that the independent claims of allegedly loyal masters should be taken as final proof of ownership. Under the circumstances, Cameron argued, the "substantial rights" of loyal masters would be best protected by army acceptance of all fugitives until the restoration of domestic tranquility. While under the care of the federal government, advised Cameron, blacks should be employed by officers as usefully as possible.[14]

While federal authorities developed this policy of practical emancipation, abolitionists advanced plans of their own for the Fortress Monroe contrabands. Boston abolitionist James Redpath, who welcomed the contraband decisions, urged the secretary of war to collect all "living contraband articles" in a central camp, employ those useful to the army, and ship the rest to Haiti. Redpath proposed to act as agent for the enterprise, without cost to the government. Since the number of contrabands would soon become too large for useful employment by the army, Redpath warned, blacks would become an "embarrassment" to the troops unless efforts were made to remove them. Cameron replied without enthusiasm, promising to give the proposal consideration at his leisure.[15]

Veteran abolitionist Lewis Tappan, a leading figure in the American Missionary Association (which during the war became the largest organization devoted to the aid and improvement of freedmen), suggested directly to Butler that some contrabands might be removed to the North. The contraband decision, said Tappan, had filled the hearts of many "friends of freedom" with thankfulness, although he himself feared that the number of contrabands entering Union lines might prove an embarrassment to commanders and a detriment to the blacks. If surplus contrabands could be shipped North, private benevolence could more easily provide for their physical, intellectual, and moral improvement, and the refugees could find employment on the farms and in the workshops of loyal Northern citizens.

Butler, however, thought the plan wrong-minded and potentially harmful to the blacks. To send large numbers of agricultural laborers North where their labor was not wanted seemed to him unwise. They

were more cheaply and effectively cared for in the South, Butler
insisted, where the climate was warm and where there was considerable abandoned property to accommodate them. If the American Missionary Association wished to aid the blacks, Butler suggested that
they send quantities of substantial, cheap clothing for the coming
winter. But Tappan remained skeptical of government intentions
toward fugitives. If he and other philanthropists could be certain "that
the fugitives will never be remanded back into slavery," there would
be a great willingness to supply clothing and other goods for their
relief in the South. The government had not yet adopted a firm policy,
Tappan reminded Butler, and the tenure of individual commanders
remained uncertain. "Under these circumstances," Tappan concluded,
"those whom I represent will wait awhile to see what course is to
be pursued."[16]

Tappan's hesitance in the matter was understandable, but it served
no purpose. Although colonization schemes would continue to gain
respectful attention in the North, and although some blacks were in
fact shipped to free states as servants and laborers, the mass of Southern blacks under federal control remained in the South where, as
Butler insisted, they best served the Union's military needs.[17]

III

As Tappan suspected, Butler's tenure at Fortress Monroe was brief.
In mid-August 1861 he was transferred from eastern Virginia to begin
preparations for the capture of New Orleans. Butler's efforts at Fortress Monroe had not attracted the attention and notoriety that would
later color his career as commander of federal forces in the Department
of the Gulf. Nevertheless, his early decisions in Virginia helped determine the outlines of future government policy toward Southern blacks.
The contraband decision, moreover, gave the general a good name
among abolitionists and Radicals. E. L. Pierce publicly praised the
general, and Lewis Tappan was quick to offer his congratulations.
The long-time political abolitionist, Elizure Wright, likewise thanked
Butler for his "noble stand," believing that the contraband decision
was proof that the Constitution was an antislavery document after
all.[18]

Despite this praise, Butler grew dissatisfied with his initial policy of accepting all fugitives within his lines. Well before his transfer, he admitted that the growing number of contrabands under his control had become a "disaster."[19] The swelling black population, particularly of women and children, far exceeded the number the army could profitably employ. Some system of organization was necessary to usefully employ the able-bodied while supporting the dependent. The task of developing a bureaucratic structure for the administration of contraband affairs fell to General John E. Wool, Butler's successor.

General Wool found the problem of supporting dependent blacks a pressing one and immediately requested instructions from Secretary Cameron considering their care and treatment. Cameron suggested that if contrabands had become a burden at Fortress Monroe they could be put to good use around the federal city. He therefore authorized Wool to send all able-bodied blacks, along with their families, to General G. B. McClellan at Washington to work on the capital's defenses. Wool's concern, however, was not with the able-bodied, whom he managed to employ in various ways, but with the large population of women and children entirely dependent on the government for their subsistence.[20]

Of the more than 800 contrabands reported within federal lines at Fortress Monroe late in July, more than 500 of them were women and children. By March 1862 the total contraband population had grown to approximately 1,500 and the number of women and children totaled about 850. Some of the women and children were used as cooks and servants, but most could not be employed. While Wool occasionally sent consignments of laborers to McClellan for work on the defenses of Washington, the problem of caring for the destitute was not thereby solved. As the winter of 1861-1862 approached, Wool necessarily made plans to employ and support blacks under his command without relying on outside aid.[21]

In the fall of 1861 Wool adopted a wage system which served to rationalize army care of destitute blacks. In October the general ordered all officers and soldiers enjoying the services of black servants to pay monthly wages of at least eight dollars for men and four for women. After deductions for the cost of clothing, the wages went to the quartermaster who managed the funds for the benefit of destitute blacks. In short, those blacks actually employed received no payment at all; their earnings were simply applied to the care of the non-laboring population.[22] In November General Wool applied a wage scale to army laborers. At best, an exceptional first-class hand might receive three dollars per month for his own use. The balance of the laborer's wage, as the servant's, went into the quartermaster's fund for the support of dependent blacks.[23]

General Wool's wage system was little more than an accounting scheme to justify support of dependent blacks. The responsibility of caring for destitute and dependent contrabands was quickly assumed by the scores of Northern missionaries who journeyed South intent upon the improvement of the black man's lot. General Butler had rebuffed efforts to begin missionary work during the summer of 1861,[24] but once General Wool had established his program for the care of dependent blacks, the field was opened to Northern benevolence. The American Missionary Association (AMA) led the field in eastern Virginia. The New England Freedmen's Aid Society also sent representatives, and Pennsylvania Quakers established missions at Williamsburg and Yorktown later in 1862. The early AMA arrivals concentrated their efforts on education, and a permanent school soon functioned near Fortress Monroe.[25]

The work of the AMA, however, was not exclusively educational. Charles B. Wilder, the most influential of the Association's agents at Fortress Monroe, had very little to do with the operation of contraband schools. Wilder arrived in Virginia early in 1862 from Boston as the AMA's superintendent of relief operations at Fortress Monroe. He quickly won favor with General Wool, and in March 1862 received the general's official recognition as superintendent of contrabands in the Hampton area.[26]

Wilder moved to abolish the quartermaster's fund and to secure for the contrabands direct payment of wages. Although Wilder believed that wages should be determined according to individual abilities and services, he suggested that average men without a trade should receive ten dollars per month in addition to rations and medical aid. Skilled men, in Wilder's view, should receive fifteen dollars monthly, while children over eighteen and women should receive five dollars.[27] Wilder's suggestions were close enough to Wool's previous scale to win approval, and the superintendent proceeded to suggest a more ambitious plan for the support of dependent blacks. In April 1862 Wilder urged General Wool to allow blacks not employed by the army to care for themselves, "with what aid we can give them," on abandoned farms near Hampton. Wool agreed and authorized Wilder to assign plots of land to individual blacks.[28]

Early in May 1862 the general dispatched Wilder to Washington to explain to Edwin M. Stanton, the new secretary of war, the purpose of the agricultural program. In his introduction of Wilder to Stanton, General Wool explained that the purpose of his actions since the fall of 1861 had been to develop a system by which the government could employ all the labor it required at a low rate and, at the same time, avoid the cost of caring for the sick and infirm. Superintendent Wilder explained to Stanton the details of what was necessary and presumably emphasized his agricultural plans to render the blacks self-sufficient.[29]

Wilder found Stanton "very cordial," and left Washington with the distinct impression that General Wool's course was fully approved and that "we shall soon see better times for our Col'd friends."[30] Despite his enthusiasm, the times were not auspicious for the development of the agricultural program he proposed. Executive and military attention in eastern Virginia focused almost exclusively during the spring and summer of 1862 on General McClellan's ill-fated peninsular campaign. Advancing cautiously up the Yorktown Peninsula toward Richmond, McClellan floundered before the Confederate capital late in June. When President Lincoln, accompanied by Secretaries Chase and Stanton, visited Fortress Monroe early in May, they came to supervise the destruction of the feared Confederate ironclad, the *Merrimac*, and the capture of Norfolk—not to investigate Superintendent Wilder's plans for the former slaves.

In the midst of the confusion of McClellan's campaign, moreover, Fortress Monroe received a new commander. Major General John A. Dix arrived early in June 1862 to replace Wool, and Wilder once more faced the problem of gaining a commander's confidence. During McClellan's retreat, the new commander had little time to consider contraband policies. By the time McClellan returned with his army

to Washington early in August, an entire season had passed without
the establishment of any permanent program for the care and employment of arriving blacks.[31]

IV

Under the circumstances, the reign of General Dix promised to be
gloomy indeed—the more so since there was nothing in Dix's previous
career to suggest that he might receive Wilder's efforts at Fortress
Monroe sympathetically. As commander of the Department of Pennsylvania with headquarters at Baltimore, Maryland, Dix had repeatedly
identified himself with those who would protect slave property and
the rights of slaveholders. "Our cause," Dix observed to General
McClellan, "is a holy one, and should be kept free from all taint."
The war had nothing to do with blacks, Dix explained, and unless
commanders acted forthrightly to exclude fugitives from their lines,
advancing Union armies would drown in a black tide. Well after the
House of Representatives passed Owen Lovejoy's resolution urging
non-enforcement of the Fugitive Slave Law, General Dix directed a
subordinate at Annapolis to undertake "the most searching inquiries"
to uncover an escaped slave allegedly hiding in his camp. To avoid
similar embarrassments in the future, Dix directed the officer to
exclude blacks from his lines. The general was solicitous as well
toward slaveholders in ostensibly rebellious areas. Shortly before
federal troops invaded Accomac and Northampton counties, comprising Virginia's Eastern Shore, Dix assured local slaveholders that
"special directions have been given not to interfere with the condition
of any person held to domestic service."[32]

Dix was predisposed to oppose emancipationist goals, but conditions in eastern Virginia worked in Superintendent Wilder's favor.
Inexorably, the population of blacks under federal control rose from
approximately 1,500 early in 1862 to nearly 5,000 by the end of the
year. With the fall of Norfolk in May, Union lines extended to include
another 10,000 blacks.[33] There was no longer any doubt, moreover,
that federal officers must accept all fugitives. In March 1862 Congress
adopted an additional article of war which prohibited officers (on pen-
alty of dismissal) from aiding in the capture or return of fugitive
slaves. By mid-July Secretary Stanton successfully engineered the pas-

sage of the second Confiscation Act which declared contraband slaves—those belonging to persons in rebellion—henceforth and forever free. At the same time, Congress authorized President Lincoln to accept blacks in government service, promising those so employed ten dollars a month (three dollars of which might be deducted for clothing) plus rations.[34]

Although Lincoln moved cautiously, his administration clearly shared congressional interest in mobilizing Southern blacks. Following the passage of the second Confiscation Act, Stanton asked the German-born political scientist and encyclopedist, Francis Lieber, to submit an opinion on the proper wartime use of Negro contrabands. The former South Carolina University professor and slaveholder concluded in August 1862 that conditions required a positive and humanitarian employment of blacks as armed menials, and warned that the South would benefit from any delay in their mobilization.[35] Once President Lincoln issued the preliminary Emancipation Proclamation in September, there could no longer be any doubt that government policy required the collection and organization of contraband blacks.

Although the pressure of events soon forced General Dix to follow an emancipation policy at Fortress Monroe, Wilder and the American Missionary Association lost few opportunities to advance their program and solicit the general's favor. George Whipple, corresponding secretary for the AMA shared Wilder's fear that Dix's sympathies would strengthen the hand of "proslavery" officers. While visiting Dix in Virginia during June 1862, Whipple sought official support for agent Wilder and may have repeated Lewis Tappan's suggestion, made the previous year to General Butler, that blacks be sent North. Dix was understandably preoccupied with McClellan's Richmond campaign, and Whipple left for Washington without having effected any visible change.[36]

Once Dix addressed himself to the contraband problem following McClellan's withdrawal in August, his earlier hostility to emancipation was effectively dampened by emerging national policies. Dix could no longer hope to exclude blacks from his lines, but he nonetheless saw them as a great "embarrassment" to his troops. For the time being, the general was willing to leave the balcks under Superintendent Wilder's care. But with Stanton's approval, and perhaps at Whipple's suggestion, Dix asked each of the New England governors to support a policy of removing as many contrabands as possible to the free states, where they could be temporarily cared for until the conclusion of the conflict.[37]

As might have been expected, the response of the New England governors was less than enthusiastic. Only Rhode Island's executive responded positively to Dix's request. Several made no reply at all, and John A. Andrew of Massachusetts, a Radical with abolitionist support, answered with open hostility. There was no need for black labor in the North, Andrew insisted, and to send blacks North would simply render them a race of "homeless wanderers." Contrabands should remain in the South where the government could arm the able-bodied and provide for the dependent. Andrew's response doubtless reflected prevailing Northern opposition to Negro migration, but the Radical governor had also put his finger on the central weakness of any removal scheme. To be sure, Dix was correct in his description of the contrabands' suffering. Disease was indeed rampant, and the general's estimate that from four to six blacks died each day at Fortress Monroe was probably no exaggeration. Superintendent Wilder, in fact, lamented that conditions were so bad that some blacks lost heart and returned to their masters. But the removal of any sizable number would only compound the suffering. And, if the government wished to mobilize blacks for war, removal was simply out of the question.[38]

Despite the efforts of Wilder and the AMA, and notwithstanding the federal government's developing interest in mobilizing Southern blacks, federal policy toward blacks in the Hampton Roads area remained ambiguous. Lincoln's preliminary Emancipation Proclamation served in one sense to culminate the trend toward an emancipationist policy. But in its final form, the proclamation designated four counties in eastern Virginia (in addition to Accomac and Northampton counties on the Eastern Shore) to be loyal, and exempted them from its provisions. General Dix, who was sympathetic to the plight of Unionists in the area, had already moved to restore civil government in Norfolk and promised to protect loyal citizens and all their property. While the freedom of blacks fleeing from the enemy was assured after January 1, 1863 (when the final Emancipation Proclamation was issued), black residents of loyal counties remained legally enslaved. Congress restrained General Dix from seeking out the masters of fugitive slaves, but when loyal masters retained actual possession of their slave property, Dix promised recognition and protection.[39]

These qualifications and ambiguities were real and troublesome to Wilder as he worked to achieve a comprehensive and vigorous government program for contrabands. Despite the limitations, Wilder pressed Dix with remarkable success to enforce the orders issued by his predecessor, General Wool. Although Dix had continued to recognize Wilder as superintendent of contrabands, the recognition did not become official until September 1862 when the commander placed Wilder on the army payroll. In January 1863 Wilder was commissioned captain and assistant quartermaster. Henceforth the former missionary supervised freedmen as an officer of the Union army.[40]

Wilder's fear that General Dix would undo the work of Generals Butler and Wool proved unfounded. But the uncertainty which resulted from McClellan's campaign and the arrival of General Dix prevented the superintendent from carrying out his plan to settle contraband blacks on abandoned farms. By the time Dix officially recognized Wilder's authority, the season for beginning an agricultural program had passed. In fact, little beyond private relief efforts had been made during 1862 to improve the lot of the arriving blacks. In the meanwhile, as Wilder discovered, Union soldiers welcomed any excuse to condone mistreatment of blacks by local whites. If the occupied counties were to be considered loyal, the task of securing the freedmen's liberty would be harder still. Rebels and their sympathizers were becoming increasingly daring, Wilder thought, and unless the president defined matters, the situation would deteriorate further. With the issuance of the final Emancipation Proclamation on January 1, 1863, Lincoln did indeed define matters, but it was hardly as Wilder had hoped. The Tidewater counties of York, Elizabeth City, Norfolk, and Princess Anne were exempted from the terms of the proclamation, and slavery in eastern Virginia continued.

By the end of 1862, then, conditions had not much improved, except that Wilder and the AMA teachers claimed to have the blacks

"well embued with the spirit of liberty and education so as not to
be worth much to slavery."[41] Positive plans would await the spring.
In the meantime, General Dix, rebuffed by the New England governors, took steps to provide for the contrabands during the winter.

V

As General Butler had concluded before him, Dix also believed that
the blacks within his lines were best cared for in the South with whatever combination of organization and aid the federal government and
Northern benevolent agencies could provide. Still anxious to isolate
the blacks from his troops, Dix concentrated arriving fugitives at Newport News. The arrival of a largely Irish regiment to man the Union
batteries at that point, however, shortly necessitated another move,
this time to Craney Island, across Hampton Roads at the mouth of
the Elizabeth River.[42]

Dix had never been anxious to have fugitive blacks within his lines,
but his reluctance was in part the product of very practical considerations. Union troops were at best contemptuous of the black refugees
and were frequently brutal toward them. The exceedingly large proportion of women and children among the contrabands left them particularly vulnerable to every manner of trickery and degradation.
When the commander described the blacks under his charge as an
"embarrassment," he accurately described conditions within his command. On Craney Island, the blacks would be carefully isolated from
the troops, and would be kept busy with whatever labor they could
perform. Most of the dependent blacks north of the James River—with
the exception of those under Wilder's care near Hampton—were collected on the island for the winter of 1862-1863.[43]

If any evidence was needed to justify such isolation, the troops at
Newport News soon provided it. When Dix issued the order for the
transfer to Craney Island, the soldiers took to the countryside, rounding up blacks as if they were so many rabbits. Armed troops hunted
the area, herding captives onto the open decks of a steamer to await
shipment to Craney Island. John Oliver, a black teacher supported
by the AMA, was shocked to see women and children left exposed
on decks and wharves for nearly two days as the hunt continued. Many

of the freedmen were sick and feeble, and the late autumn exposure proved fatal to at least one. Oliver reported that between forty and fifty black men, viewing the army's action as an attempt at re-enslavement, disappeared during the night, "saying good by [sic] union I never will come within your lines again."[44] Too late, Dix directed the commander at Newport News to see that such abuses ceased. "These people are in our care," the general reminded his subordinate, "and we are bound by every principle of humanity to treat them with kindness and protect them."[45]

Dix was hardly a sentimentalist, however. When he learned early in November 1862 that about 150 blacks lived in the area around Newport News as squatters outside government control, he ordered them removed. The blacks had settled on deserted farms, living by what crops they raised "and by stealing." The soldiers at Newport News regularly raided these farms, taking what produce they could. In response, the blacks had managed to arm themselves, although Dix was assured by his officers that the weapons were being collected "as fast as they can be found."[46] As the Union troops collected the contrabands for shipment to Craney Island, the process of disarming the blacks was probably completed.

Despite the brutality of the removal, the new arrangement seemed to please missionaries as well as army men. An AMA teacher, who reported over a thousand contrabands on the island early in December, expected a total population of three or four thousand, and predicted that Craney Island would become "the great field of missionary labor" among the contrabands in eastern Virginia.[47] Orlando Brown, an army surgeon from Massachusetts, supervised the organization and care of the blacks on Craney Island, but the burden of work among the inhabitants was carried on by Lucy and Sarah Chase, missionaries from Worcester, Massachusetts, supported by the Boston Educational Commission of the New England Freedmen's Aid Society. By mid-January 1863 nearly two thousand blacks peopled the island, and their numbers continued to grow. The problems of relief and organization were all but overwhelming. Most of the arrivals lacked adequate clothing and suffered in the damp, cold wind that swept over the exposed island. Missionaries were shocked by the diseases and filth as well as by the degraded condition of the blacks they encountered. Calls went out for coarse, practical clothing, and solemn resolves were made to uplift the race so long degraded by chattel slavery.[48]

The Chase sisters came to Craney Island in December 1862. Like most missionaries, they found the blacks appealingly quaint and picturesque, as well as apallingly degraded and ignorant. The sight of an old, bearded black man sitting before an open fire talking to children evoked a romantic image that seemed to invite the palette and brush of a master artist. But when a shipload of contrabands arrived, the scene took a less touching form. "They come almost wholly destitute of clothing, covered with vermin, and extremely ignorant," Lucy Chase wrote describing the arriving blacks; "they ought to enter freedom through the path of moral restraint."[49] Whether Orlando Brown possessed the Chase sisters' romantic zeal is not certain, but he clearly shared their notion that the blacks needed enlightened guidance to overcome the degrading influences of slavery.

It was a conviction shared by General Dix, Orlando Brown, and the Chase sisters alike that charity was misplaced on a people whose training must henceforth be toward self-reliance. The blacks, it seemed, must be taught to provide for themselves. Therefore, instead of giving clothing away, Lucy Chase proposed that her Worcester supporters send unfinished goods to be cut and sewn by the women on the island. The sisters reported almost a hundred women busy making beds, and since there was no time to be lost in dispelling the black man's ignorance, alphabet cards were attached to the walls. "We consider it feasible to unite study and sewing," reported the energetic Miss Chase, "and keep heads and fingers busy."[50]

Orlando Brown was also eager to have the island community operate vigorously and effectively. The superintendent divided the population into "squads," appointed leaders from among the men, and held them directly responsible for the cleanliness and orderliness of their units. As soon as planting was possible, Brown ordered the predominantly female population to the fields where they labored in traditional gangs directed by the "squad" leaders.[51] Lucy Chase thought Superintendent Brown's emphasis on traditional labor quite wise. "Dr. B. says it is nonsense," observed Miss Chase, "to talk of the negroes as being (now) a superior race, and already fitted for freedom." To extol the blacks in the manner of "ignorant, enthusiastic philanthropists" seemed simply to condone the "barbarious" teachings of slavery. "We are to give them a *chance*!" insisted Miss Chase, "which they have never had."[52]

Orlando Brown, whose attitude toward the freedmen the Chase sisters found so sensible, had come to the Hampton Roads area as a surgeon with the 18th Massachusetts Volunteers. The enormous black population which came under Union control after the fall of Norfolk in May 1862 required care and organization, and the city's commander detailed Brown as superintendent of contrabands. After managing the blacks on Craney Island during the winter, Brown served as superintendent of black refugees for the area south of the James River. With the establishment of the Freedmen's Bureau in March 1865, General O. O. Howard appointed Brown assistant commissioner for the state of Virginia.[53]

Brown's concern for the welfare of the blacks was continuing and genuine, but it would always be a matter of controversy precisely what sort of care and assistance the former slaves required. Some American Missionary Association teachers found Brown overly concerned with rendering his charges self-sufficient. He placed considerations of employment, they thought, before education, and seemed interested in saving money for the government rather than caring for his charges.[54] But Superintendent Brown, as Wilder, had entered a wider field of responsibility than the teachers who criticized him. For good or ill, control over blacks in eastern Virginia became increasingly centralized and was incorporated into the army's command structure. As army officers, Wilder and Brown sought ends different from those of the missionaries. Their authority rested on their ability to serve the army's purposes while providing for the blacks. As the 1863 season began, Wilder's proposals of the previous season began to bear fruit, and General Dix anxiously settled freedmen on abandoned lands, hoping to relieve the government of their support and to isolate them from hostile white troops.

VI

Federal contraband policy and administration developed gradually in Virginia as the usefulness of the blacks and the needs of the Union army became clear. A similar development occurred in the Newbern area of North Carolina which, by mid-July 1863 was joined with the Hampton Roads area as the combined Department of Virginia and North Carolina. In February and March of 1862 federal troops commanded by Brigadier General A. E. Burnside captured Roanoke Island and the town of Newbern. The advancing federals found the blacks "wild with excitement and delight," and a continuous stream of contrabands arrived within Union lines from surrounding plantations.[55]

Although the blacks did their best to make themselves useful to the arriving troops, General Burnside was no more pleased with their presence than were his Virginia counterparts. Newbern seemed "overrun with fugitives," a situation creating a "great source of anxiety" for the commander. The blacks were maddeningly adept at slipping through woods and swamps; Burnside confessed that even "if we were so disposed," it would be impossible to exclude them from his lines. The general therefore employed the black population—which swelled to 7,500 by late summer—as best he could. The bulk of contrabands labored to erect fortifications around Newbern. Burnside set a scale of wages for them which compared roughly with the rate set at Fortress Monroe several months earlier. Common laborers at Newbern received eight dollars per month plus rations and clothing. (Average hands at Fortress Monroe received ten dollars per month, but the cost of clothing was deducted.) The contraband population of about a thousand that remained on Roanoke Island was similarly put to work. These blacks, however, received somewhat higher wages (ten dollars a month for men, four dollars for women and children), and the same issue of rations and clothing. To superintend the growing black population, Burnside appointed Vincent Colyer, a representative of the U. S. Christian Commission, an organization concerned primarily with the moral lives of the soldiers.[56]

Although efforts to organize freedmen in the Department of North Carolina quickly approximated patterns set at Hampton Roads, President Lincoln put a sudden halt to Superintendent Colyer's program. Lincoln, anxious to restore loyal government in the area as quickly as possible, appointed Edward Stanly, a native of Newbern and a strong Unionist, to be war governor of North Carolina. An outspoken anti-abolitionist, Stanly took office on May 26, 1862, and worked vig-

orously to govern the Union-occupied area according to antebellum
state laws. Stanly refused to recognize contrabands as anything other
than fugitive slaves and whenever possible returned blacks to their
masters. Similarly, the war governor closed Colyer's contraband
school and effectively undermined the superintendent's efforts to
organize the blacks as free laborers. After Colyer visited Lincoln early
in June in the company of Senator Charles Sumner to protest the governor's actions, Stanly modified his position and permitted Colyer's
school to reopen. But the enforcement of antebellum slave laws continued, and Colyer returned North in July discouraged. Lincoln's support for Stanly shortly faded under Radical opposition, and when the
Emancipation Proclamation went into effect in January 1863, without
exempting occupied portions of North Carolina, Stanly admitted defeat
and resigned.[57]

Freedmen affairs in the Department of North Carolina were reorganized in the spring of 1863. In May Horace James, a Boston Congregationalist minister and chaplain with a regiment of Massachusetts
volunteers, was detailed as superintendent of contrabands. Chaplain
James viewed the issues of the war as a Radical. Although Union
forces had not "*introduced* the negro into this war," he told the members of his regiment during an Independence Day celebration at Newbern in 1862, "he is in it, and in every part of it, and can no more
be expelled from it than leaven can be removed from the loaf that
has begun to ferment."[58] Although James entered the field as an army
officer, he, as Wilder, corresponded extensively with the AMA,
reporting frequently on his progress and the work of the AMA
teachers. By the middle of July 1863, when the Departments of Virginia and North Carolina were combined, Horace James coordinated
freedmen education, relief, and employment at Newbern in the same
manner as C. B. Wilder and Orlando Brown in Virginia. These three
men administered the government's freedmen policy in Virginia and
North Carolina for the duration of the war.[59]

During 1863 the federal government settled on a war policy involving the mobilization of Southern blacks. The decision came slowly
and, in many quarters, reluctantly. In some respects it was a desperate
decision made by men who had experienced military defeat and feared
for their political futures. The "Irish element," as Secretary of the

Navy Gideon Welles noted in January 1863, grew increasingly dissatisfied with the war. Lamentably, "partyism" seemed stronger than "patriotism" in most Northern states. Thus, while most whites harbored an "unconquerable prejudice" against blacks and found the notion of black soldiers repugnant, Welles confessed that "all our increased military strength now comes from the negroes."[60]

By the end of 1863, the government's policy was clear. "The fortunes of war," Secretary Stanton told Congress in December 1863, burdened the government with the care and support of large numbers of dependent blacks. However bothersome to Union troops, these refugees represented a greater loss to the enemy. The president's Emancipation Proclamation encouraged slave defection, and all fugitives, the able-bodied and the dependent alike, represented a financial loss to the Rebel master.[61] Whatever one's opinion of the black man's status, his wartime usefulness and the necessity of his mobilization could no longer be denied. By such reasoning fugitive slaves became contrabands and finally freedmen, but the condition of their lives and the organization of their labor involved matters which went beyond considerations of military necessity. In approaching these matters, the freedmen superintendents reflected the government's interest in maintaining traditional patterns of social and economic organization. Emancipation would not become synonymous with independence.

2

The Freedom to Labor

★

The efforts of Superintendents C. B. Wilder, Orlando Brown, and Horace James to settle contrabands on abandoned lands did not require radical changes in the antebellum social structure. The superintendents, in fact, shared the prevailing belief in the superiority of the white race. Their programs were not revolutionary, but they did hope to create a class of independent freedmen farmers who, they believed, would constitute enough of a change in Southern society to permit the independence and practical equality of the mass of blacks.

Almost as a matter of necessity, Wilder, Brown, and James developed policies toward the freedmen which combined the missionary's paternal concern with the army's insistence on military priorities. Their own views of the freedmen were neither contemptuous nor particularly enlightened; the climate of opinion in which they worked, however, made even their minimal efforts to aid the freedmen difficult. As the blacks who entered Union lines soon discovered, Northern soldiers generally found a crude amusement in the harassment of contrabands. Typically, a group of soldiers with McClellan's army during the peninsular campaign cornered a black boy, insisting angrily that he was a secessionist. Astonished, the boy denied the charge, but as the soldiers grew more threatening, he gave in, admitting that he must in fact be a Rebel if the Yankee soldiers said he was. A fresh round of harassment naturally followed, ending only when the soldiers tired of their sport.[1] Although Wilder, Brown, and James disliked such crassness and found their efforts in the contrabands' behalf hindered by the hostility of Union troops, they were by no means free themselves of the white man's tendency to see blacks as innately less worthy than himself.

It was on a somewhat more urbane level, then, that Orlando Brown amused himself with what he saw as the simple ignorance of a house servant. To the delight of the white ladies in his parlor, the superintendent questioned his cook and housekeeper one evening on her religious views. "Where is heaven?" Brown asked his servant. "Heaven can be here below sir, as well as above," the woman dutifully replied. "Do you think hair will be straight there?" Brown continued. "Oh, yes sir," was the answer, "hair will be straight there." Lucy Chase, the New England teacher, found the exchange wonderfully entertaining. "Oh how charming Nancy is!" she exclaimed of the servant to her Northern friends; "I really love to be ruled by her."[2] On occasion C. B. Wilder was likewise prone to take advantage of his charges. In July 1862 the superintendent shipped two black men to Boston as substitutes in the draft for his two sons. The blacks were "glad of the chance," he insisted, evidently confident that good works were not incompatible with self-interest.[3] And Horace James, who would later justify the fatal shooting of a freedman on one of the plantations under his control as necessary for labor discipline, thought that his experience among blacks proved that miscegenation debilitated the black race. "Mixture of blood," he declared to a Northern audience, "diminishes vitality and force, and shortens life." He was willing to grant that an infusion of white blood benefited the "cerebral development" of blacks, but what was gained intellectually, he said, "is lost in tendency to scrofula, and other diseases."[4]

Similar attitudes of racial condescension, which doubtless some enlightened individuals of the age managed to overcome, were by no means uncommon in the Northern antislavery community. The American Freedmen's Inquiry Commission (AFIC), composed of the social reformer Robert Dale Owen and two abolitionists (Samuel Gridley Howe and James McKaye), reflected the paternalism and condescension that characterized the Union's best wartime programs involving freedmen. In March 1863 Secretary Stanton asked the AFIC to recommend methods of protecting, improving, and usefully employing those blacks freed by Lincoln's Emancipation Proclamation. The commission members visited Virginia during the spring of 1863 and issued a preliminary report late in June indicating the direction they believed freedmen administration should take.[5]

The commissioners agreed with the policies of Wilder, Brown, and James recommending that blacks generally be paid wages and, when possible, be settled on land that one day they might own. The commissioners also shared the three superintendents' opinion that charity toward a free people was misplaced and recommended that contraband camps serve only as temporary points of collection and distribution. Arriving blacks should be "disposed" of as quickly as possible as army laborers or plantation hands.[6] While charity seemed misplaced, the commission expressed concern that the freedmen receive proper guidance to lead them out of the degraded habits of slavery. It seemed crucially important that the newly freed blacks receive proper guardianship from men of moral worth. The former slave, insisted the AFIC report, "is found quite ready to copy whatever he believes are the rights and obligations of what he looks up to as the superior race." If the example placed before the freedmen was a model one, they would pattern themselves accordingly, even if their new conduct proved "a restraint upon the habits of license belonging to his former condition." The formalization of marriage ties seemed particularly important; in the commissioners' view, black men who refused to accept the responsibility of family life should be denied the joys of cohabitation.[7]

Although Robert Dale Owen privately urged confiscation and redistribution of the largest Southern estates, the commission, in its official reports, avoided discussing economic reforms. At best, the commission proposed that existing programs be continued and that the blacks who settled on abandoned lands should somehow be permitted to purchase homesteads in the future. The blacks would need "temporary aid and counsel," the AFIC conceded, until they became accustomed to their "new sphere of life." But if the government secured the freedmen's civil rights and extended to them the equal protection of the law, they could and should be left to take care of themselves. The activities of the AFIC were largely responsible for the creation of the

Freedmen's Bureau in March 1865, but its reports made clear that
the government's wartime programs designed to organize and protect
the freedmen would not be expanded with the return of peace. Limited
as the efforts of Wilder, Brown, and James were, their programs, and
those of their counterparts elsewhere in the occupied South, represented the zenith of reform.[8]

In the implementation of their agricultural program, Wilder, Brown,
and James no longer responded simply to considerations of military
necessity. Unlike the situation in other areas in the occupied South,
in Virginia and North Carolina the agricultural skills of the blacks
proved of no great value to the federal government. On the South
Carolina Sea Islands, in Louisiana, and along the Mississippi River,
cotton culture promised enormous returns to private investors and to
the government, once the labor of the freedmen was organized to raise
the Southern staple. Such an incentive was absent in Virginia, but
the freedmen superintendents pressed ahead with their efforts to settle
blacks on abandoned lands as self-sufficient and, in some cases, independent farmers.

Although circumstances delayed the settlement of blacks on abandoned lands until the spring of 1863, Wilder suggested such a plan
early in 1862. "I have received 80 to 100 men contrabands," the
superintendent wrote General Wool in April. The men were accompanied by a larger group of women and children who required considerable government support. Would it not be better, Wilder asked,
"to induce as many as possible of all who do not work for the government," to settle on nearby abandoned lands, and "there take care
of themselves with what aid we can give them."[9] Apparently, Secretary Stanton assumed that surplus blacks would be settled in this way
as a matter of course. His assistant secretary of war, who thought
Wilder "will accomplish great good for these people," reported late
in March that, as the army advanced and the land was abandoned
by whites, "the slaves can readily be placed in condition to sustain
themselves without becoming a burthen upon the Government."[10]

Early in 1863 Secretary Stanton appointed Wilder captain and
assistant quartermaster, and empowered him to take possession of
abandoned property in the Hampton Roads area. Blacks capable of
cultivating and managing farms might occupy the land for the season

under whatever terms and conditions Wilder and the commanding general approved.[11] Since the army employed most of the able-bodied men, the contraband farms were operated largely by women and children. But, by promising the blacks one-half of the net proceeds of the crops they raised and by providing the necessary guidance along with whatever teams and implements could be located, Commanding General Dix confidently predicted that all but the very old and the very young would be able to provide for themselves.[12]

During the 1863 season, freedmen occupied about fifty farms, including the property of former President John Tyler and former Virginia Governor Henry A. Wise. Since a number of whites in the area maintained possession of their property and reacted hostilely to government efforts to settle blacks on neighboring lands, the project was not without its hazards. Evidently feeling threatened himself, Wilder denounced these quasi-Unionists as "cowards, assassins, and spies." He attributed the kidnapping and murder of several blacks to this class, and warned Secretary Stanton that successful cultivation of abandoned lands could not be carried on without protection from such "obnoxious traitors."[13] Harassment continued, but Wilder's agricultural plans progressed all the same.

In the midst of the first season of free labor farming, Wilder submitted more detailed plans to facilitate the settlement of blacks on abandoned lands.[14] In August, Simeon S. Jocelyn, one of the founders of the abolitionist American Missionary Association, visited eastern Virginia, and with Wilder toured some of the freedmen farms near Hampton. Jocelyn reported that the blacks gave "every evidence of industry, and interest in the result of their labor." The elderly abolitionist was also convinced that the efforts of Wilder and Brown to place freedmen on abandoned lands, giving them "all the motives of the yeomanry of the North," were of the utmost importance to the final disposition of the former slave.[15]

II

Jocelyn was perhaps overly enthusiastic, but efforts to provide for the blacks had certainly changed since General B. F. Butler first declared three Virginia fugitives contrabands of war in May 1861. Butler returned to Fortress Monroe in November 1863. Now the veteran of administrative battles in Louisiana, Butler insisted upon the careful organization and control of blacks under his command. To insure that Wilder's agricultural efforts did not restrict the army's use of the freedmen, Butler established within his command a central authority for the administration of freedmen affairs.

Butler, who had opposed the recruitment of black troops while commanding at New Orleans, now recognized the enlistment of blacks as the "settled purpose of the Government." To carry out this policy effectively required careful organization. The best wartime use of able-bodied men, in the commander's opinion, was in the army, not on farms. All males from eighteen to forty-five who could pass the surgeon's medical examination were declared eligible for service and were prohibited from other forms of employment. To encourage the cooperation of the blacks, Butler promised a bounty of ten dollars for each recruit and subsistence rations for the families of enlistees. Eligible blacks who did not enlist were considered unemployed, and idleness, as Butler made clear, would not be tolerated.[16]

Although concerned primarily with raising black troops, Butler gave some attention as well to the organization of women and children. "Political freedom rightly defined," proclaimed the general, "is liberty to work." Those who worked should enjoy the fruits of their labor; those who did not should not benefit from the labor of others. Able-bodied blacks who refused to work would therefore be arrested and forced to labor on government fortifications, and army rations would be denied their families. "Negroes have rights so long as they fulfill their duties," continued Butler, and for those who labored dutifully, the general encouraged prompt and full payment. Although Butler's orders permitted higher wages for skilled workers, laborers generally received the same pay as black soldiers.[17]

Because Butler thought the freedmen ignorant and largely helpless, he acknowledged a certain paternal obligation toward them. To care for and protect the freedmen and render them self-supporting, Butler placed their general management in the hands of his aide-de-camp, Lt. Colonel Josiah B. Kinsman. Directly responsible to Kinsman were C. B. Wilder, who supervised freedmen in the occupied territory north of the James River; Orlando Brown, who continued to superintend

Negro affairs south of the James; and Horace James, whose authority in North Carolina received the new commander's sanction.[18] While this new arrangement served Butler's purposes for recruiting black troops, it offered no new departures for the freedmen and noticeably omitted discussion of plans to settle blacks on abandoned lands.

All programs involving freedmen remained subordinate to purely military needs. As Grant pressed his campaign against Richmond, the demand for laborers far outstripped the local supply, despite Butler's careful organization. Grant, believing that about a thousand able-bodied blacks lived around Newbern, requested that Butler have the lot transferred to Virginia for labor on fortifications at City Point. Officers at Roanoke Island and Newbern extravagantly offered blacks sixteen dollars per month plus rations, but the freedmen remained unwilling to move north. "The negroes will not go voluntarily," reported Butler's aide early in September 1864, "so I am obliged to force them." Two hundred blacks were seized and shipped to City Point, and the aide promised another "large lot," although he doubted that it would be possible to fill Grant's quota of one thousand men.[19]

The enormous demand for labor existed despite a steadily rising contraband population. The number of blacks under federal control in Virginia rose from about 15,000 late in 1862 to a reported peak of over 70,000 by the end of the war. Of these, more than half were female, and no more than 10,000 were enlisted in the army. The bulk of the freedmen were thus of little use to the army and were organized to do what work they could by Superintendents Wilder, Brown, and James. Early in 1864 nearly 20,000 blacks were listed as unemployed in the Department of Virginia and North Carolina, about half of them receiving government rations.[20] The growing contraband population, combined with the government's incessant need for manpower, produced a well-developed administrative structure which served the army's purposes. Policies were vigorously pursued by the government when military necessity seemed to require it. But on matters of direct concern to the freedmen—the improvement of living conditions and the initiation of programs for postwar development—action was indeed halting.

III

Despite its modest purposes, Wilder's agricultural program received the enthusiastic support of Massachusetts Radical Francis W. Bird, who visited the Hampton Roads area in 1863. On the two estates Bird visited, including the property of former Governor Henry A. Wise, he found populations of sixty to seventy freedmen, half of whom were capable of field labor. On the Wise farm, thirty-eight field hands had planted three hundred acres and raised over five thousand bushels of corn. Bird also visited a smaller operation directed by a native white overseer. Here four freedmen with their families, provided with government seed, utensils, and teams, raised several hundred bushels of corn and sweet potatoes and marketed about three hundred dollars worth of milk. Bird saw in such figures evidence that blacks would work as free laborers. Near Norfolk, the Massachusetts politician visited one of the farms under Orlando Brown's supervision which seemed to lay the foundations for ''an industrious and self supporting peasantry.'' Brown had settled about thirty freedmen with their families on ten-acre plots surrounding a central farm. The plots would provide the blacks with their subsistence, as Bird described the plan, while leaving the owner of the central farm with an adequate labor supply.[21]

Although Bird hoped that capable freedmen would emerge from the war as owners of plots adequate for their subsistence, in all other respects, the labor systems he described approximated postwar sharecropping and tenant farming arrangements. As the agricultural system operated under the superintendent's direction, freedmen families capable of independent farming were allotted ten-acre plots or small farms which they worked on shares, while the larger number of blacks worked on plantations in traditional field gangs, receiving half of the estate's net produce.[22]

For those who worked the large estates in gangs, the agricultural system functioned primarily as a means of making formerly dependent blacks self-sufficient. In some cases garden plots were allotted, but the substantial labor was done in gangs under the direction of a government-appointed overseer who kept account of the amount of labor done by each hand. Once the government's expenses were paid at the end of the season, half of the net proceeds were divided among the freedmen according to the amount of labor performed. In a good year, some blacks might earn tidy sums, but the aim, as Orlando Brown admitted, was to make "the labor of the negroes support them."[23]

The 1863 season was not an enormous success and the uncertainty of the promised half share created resentment among the freedmen so employed. One of C. B. Wilder's overseers admitted that the blacks under his direction would be better satisfied with wages of from six to eight dollars per month rather than the less tangible half share. "There are a great many," the overseer observed, who believed that "they don't get what they ought to have." If fixed wages were paid, the hands would be sure of getting something. As matters stood, the overseer complained, there was little incentive to work. With a wage system, he concluded, blacks could be dismissed if they did not work.[24]

Despite the season's shortcomings, Wilder made plans to extend and somewhat alter farming operations in his district. Planting was extended beyond the Hampton area to include James City, York, and Warwick counties on the Yorktown Peninsula.[25] During 1864 Wilder supervised operations on eighty-five farms. Forty estates were rented directly to freedmen, either for cash or produce. Another thirteen estates were divided among some thirty blacks who farmed their allotments as sharecroppers. The government's share varied according to the quality of the soil, the value of the property, and the amount of assistance required. Some blacks so employed paid as little as one-fifth of their crop to the government and others paid as much as one-third. The largest number, however, paid a quarter share. In all cases, the government held a lien on the crops to insure the payment of debts. The remaining thirty-two farms controlled by Wilder were evidently operated as freedmen farms, employing dependent blacks under overseers for a half share of the season's profits.[26]

According to C. B. Wilder's summary, the 1864 season, relative to the previous year, was outstandingly successful both for the government and the freedmen. At the end of the season, Wilder reported government profits of over $6,000 with more than $3,000 outstanding. The farms, Wilder claimed, realized combined profits of approximately $20,000. With about 11,000 blacks engaged in various types of farming early in 1865 under the supervision of Wilder and Brown, some freedmen, particularly those who rented their land, might have enjoyed sizable profits. Prosperous as the season was, however, there is evidence to suggest that those blacks with independent status as renters and tenants during the war had been freedmen farmers in antebellum Virginia.

The 1860 census listed nearly 5,500 free Negroes in Princess Anne, Norfolk, and Nansemond counties (Orlando Brown's district), and another 2,000 in Elizabeth City, Warwick, York, and James City counties (under Wilder's direction). Excluding those free blacks living in the towns of Norfolk, Portsmouth, and Hampton, almost 6,000 rural free blacks resided in the occupied counties in 1860. Most of these rural free blacks had worked as farm laborers, but many enjoyed some independence as tenant farmers and a few owned farms. In Nansemond County, where free black farmers fared particularly well in antebellum Virginia, there were eighty-six free Negro farmers in 1860, and fifteen owned farms of one hundred acres or more. In all of the occupied counties, there were thirty-one free blacks who owned farms of this size.[27]

Superintendents Wilder and Brown made a clear effort to distinguish between antebellum slaves and free blacks when they took a census of the freedmen in their districts,[28] and it is possible that they tended to grant former free blacks independent farming status more readily than former slaves. However antebellum free blacks fared under federal authority, those who were capable of renting land for cash during the war clearly came from exceptional prewar circumstances. Moreover, the combined profits for 1864 which Wilder reported indicated that individual profits, particularly for this elite group of renters, could have been quite large.[29]

The agricultural system may have operated effectively for individual blacks during 1864, but it could not accommodate the mass of contrabands. As early as June 1864, Orlando Brown informed Colonel Kinsman that he had occupied "all the land subject to seizure" within the limits of his district, but it came "far short" of the amount required to employ all the blacks under his supervision.[30] The government controlled forty-six plantations in Norfolk and Princess Anne counties early in 1865, and managed to employ almost 3,000 freedmen. Yet, according to a census taken by the freedmen superintendents early in 1864, the two counties under Brown's supervision contained over 13,000 blacks.[31] The situation was little better in the Hampton area. In January 1865 Wilder reported 8,000 freedmen lived on abandoned lands, 5,000 of whom he considered self-supporting. Yet, according to his census of a year earlier, his district contained more than 10,000 blacks.[32]

In spite of all their efforts, Wilder and Brown had failed to place all of the blacks under their care on abandoned lands, and, as the war ended, only a handful enjoyed anything resembling independent status. Moreover, the conditions of war which allowed some blacks to be placed on abandoned lands would not long continue. The end of hostilities brought, for most black farmers, an inexorable process of dispossession.

As early as February 1864, General Butler addressed himself to the problem of the returning Confederate whites who sought to reclaim their property by pledging fealty to the federal government. In a gesture of protection for black farmers, the general ordered that lands occupied by freedmen under contract with the government could be restored to prewar owners only after the season's harvest or following suitable payment for investments and improvements.[33] Dispossession could thereby be delayed, but not prevented. To make matters worse, early in 1865 the Treasury Department proposed to sell several occupied plantations for unpaid taxes. Wilder (who later purchased six plantations near Fortress Monroe) sought to postpone the sale, arguing that to dispossess freedmen who were already self-supporting would simply increase government expenses. Wilder warned Commanding General E. O. C. Ord that if the sale came before the end of 1865, "it will defeat our success and a very large increase of expenditure would necessarily follow."[34]

Combined with the problem of returning landowners and the proposed tax sales was the enormous new influx of blacks following the fall of Richmond early in April 1865. Blacks in the Piedmont area moved in large numbers toward Hampton, Norfolk, and Portsmouth. Their arrival presented Union commanders with precisely the same contraband problem they had earlier faced in 1861 and 1862. The treatment that arriving blacks received in 1865, however, indicated how closely the black man's status was tied to the North's military needs. In 1865 blacks suddenly ceased to be militarily useful. Commanders and freedmen superintendents worked diligently, not to encourage slave defection from the countryside, but to stop the migration from farms to cities.

Major George J. Carney, who replaced Colonel Kinsman late in 1864 as general superintendent of freedmen in the Department of Virginia and North Carolina, vainly sought authority from Commanding General Ord to settle arriving blacks on abandoned lands outside the Tidewater cities. If, as he seemed to realize, the justification of military necessity no longer applied, the argument of expense surely remained persuasive. Carney reported that a large number of blacks were leaving their plantations between Norfolk and Richmond, and were "needlessly over populating" the Tidewater area, "adding to the expense already too large to the U.S. Government." Carney hoped the commander would prohibit blacks from entering the vicinity of Norfolk and Hampton, and would settle the refugees on outlying abandoned property.[35] Although Carney insisted that all the labor necessary would be made available to white farmers, General Ord chose other means to stem the flow of black refugees.

IV

In May 1865 General Ord acted to bring a swift end to government support of freedmen. He realized that the deed must be done quietly, lest the strict measures outrage Northern humanitarian sentiments. "It is not deemed proper to stop the issue of rations suddenly," the general wrote a subordinate, "because it might raise a cry at the North." Instead, freedmen superintendents should be directed to open offices and hire out unemployed blacks as quickly as possible. The women and children, who would be likely to remain dependent on the government, should be gathered in groups and worked as launderers for the general population. "A little hard work and confinement," General Ord reasoned, "will soon induce them to find employment, and the ultra philanthropists will not be shocked."[36]

Edward W. Coffin, Wilder's assistant superintendent of freedmen at Yorktown, was sensitive to General Ord's mood, and reported that all of the able-bodied men in his district were "compelled" to support themselves, and "in no case are rations knowingly issued to such." The superintendent was fearful lest unemployed blacks congregate in the cities or form settlements of their own in the countryside, "living a life of idleness and crime." Every effort was made to bind blacks to white employers, by force "if necessary." It was a matter of maintaining social stability, Coffin thought. "The sooner they are taught that liberty is not idleness and license the better."[37]

Orders requiring the employment of blacks and restricting their movement quickly followed. The commander at Petersburg, Virginia, informed the black population that it was wrong to believe that "with their liberty they acquired individual rights in the property of their former masters." On the contrary, the general insisted, a master had the right to refuse his former slaves anything, and was "no more bound to feed, clothe, or protect them than if he had never been their master." Blacks were prohibited from entering the cities and could remain on the plantations only if they entered into contracts with the white owners. Special employment officers kept lists of unemployed blacks; planters seeking hands were urged to examine the rosters and choose the hands they needed. Freedmen refusing employment when offered would be denied government rations.[38]

In North Carolina, freedmen faced the end of hostilities with even less security. Because federal control of land in the area was severely restricted, agricultural operations were correspondingly limited. Of the more than 17,000 blacks under Union control in the area by the close of the war, not more than 6,000 were employed on farms and plantations on the mainland, and only a handful of these were independent farmers. More than half of the total number of contrabands in the district were unemployed; these blacks were rather rudely provided for in camps located near the fortified towns of Newbern, Beaufort, Plymouth, and Washington. Only on Roanoke Island, where some 3,000 blacks were lodged for safekeeping, could Superintendent James claim any success in guiding the former slaves toward independence and self-sufficiency. On the north end of the island was a rather shabby contraband camp, but on the south end, James settled selected freedmen on twelve-acre plots fronting on a regular pattern of streets and avenues.[39]

The Roanoke Island "colony" enjoyed only a very limited success, and, with the end of the war, federal forces in North Carolina had no use for blacks. Commanding General Schofield therefore recommended to white planters that they hire their former slaves as servants and laborers, and advised the freedmen that when "allowed to do so," they should remain with their former masters and labor faithfully. The general warned that blacks would not "be supported in idleness."[40] Former masters, as Schofield saw matters, continued to bear the responsibility of parents or guardians for the care of dependent blacks. Whites might not "turn away the young or infirm" residing on their land, and in return the government required able-bodied freedmen to remain on the land as laborers.[41]

Despite army efforts to maintain antebellum standards of social stability, the hope of creating an elite class of black farmers was not yet dead. As a "small step" in this direction, General A. H. Terry, commanding the army in Virginia, recommended that the confiscated land held by the Freedmen's Bureau be "broken up into small holdings," and that "the best and most intelligent" of the freedmen be settled on them "upon such terms that with industry and economy they may ultimately become owners of the land."[42] Moreover, Secretary Stanton, reacting to a scheme by white planters to fix the freedmen's wages, collected information concerning landholding, wealth, and loyalty in several Virginia counties. A policy of confiscation seemed imminent.[43]

In the meantime, several of the farms in the Hampton area upon which C. B. Wilder had settled freedmen were sold by the Treasury Department for unpaid taxes. Wilder, in association with several Boston friends, bought six of these estates. The superintendent proposed to resell three of the farms in small plots to the freedmen and operate the others with hired black labor, as had been the practice under government auspices during the war. Since Wilder was superintendent of Negro affairs at the time of the purchases, General Ord charged him with speculating at the expense of his black charges. Wilder was finally dismissed by General Ord, although Adjutant General Lorenzo Thomas, who inquired into the affair at the request of Secretary Stanton, reported that the superintendent's motives seemed honest. Wilder himself insisted that he purchased the plantations only to prevent their control by speculators who would not provide for the blacks settled on them.[44] Wilder's postwar efforts, however, were shortlived. He left Virginia in June 1866 after a brief career with the Freedmen's Bureau.[45]

In North Carolina, Superintendent Horace James made a similar attempt to continue under private control the type of agricultural organization begun during the war.[46] After the formation of the Freedmen's Bureau, James served as superintendent for the Newbern district, and in partnership with Eliphalet Whittlesey, Bureau Commissioner for the state, bought three farms in Pitt County. James left Newbern to manage the estates and patterned their organization after wartime free labor experiments. Both James and Whittlesey, however, were discredited by enemies of the Bureau following the murder in March 1866 of one of James' hands. Reorganization of the Bureau in North Carolina ended James' ventures, and the former chaplain returned to Boston and the ministry.[47]

Despite some hopeful signs, the postwar period witnessed no new effort to confiscate Rebel property and establish blacks as self-supporting farmers. In a small way, the American Missionary Association implemented Wilder's plan to provide some blacks with land. The AMA's corresponding secretary, George Whipple, purchased 175 acres in the Hampton area in May 1867 and for the next four years sold small tracts to over forty freedmen. Largely because of Whipple's efforts, the number of Negro landowners in Elizabeth City County increased sixfold during the 1860s, and totaled 121 by the end of 1870.[48] But most freedmen who had settled on abandoned property during the war were quickly dispossessed. Samuel Chapman Armstrong, founder of Hampton Institute and assistant commissioner of the Freedmen's Bureau for the district including Hampton, Virginia, witnessed the conflicts between the freedmen who had farmed lands under government direction and returning Confederate soldiers who reclaimed their property. "There was irritation," Armstrong admitted blandly, and it took him two years to settle all the claims. In the end, the dispossessed blacks were told to work for the white landowners or face starvation. Once rations were stopped, Armstrong found the freedman's resourcefulness surprising. "The negro in a tight spot," he thought, "is a genius."[49]

The freedmen were indeed in a tight spot, but they did not always accept dispossession without a degree of resistance and a good deal of bitterness. A Quaker teacher at Yorktown observed "great distress" among the people living on a nearby estate used by Superintendent Wilder during the war as a freedmen farm. The land was theirs, the blacks insisted, by virtue of their lifelong labor as slaves. Besides, the Yankee soldiers had told them they could stay there as long as they lived. The residents could not be reasoned away, but they were soon physically removed.[50]

The programs of agrarian reform in Virginia and North Carolina dismantled following the war were not particularly vital, but they had briefly offered a modest alternative to the pattern of restoration for whites and repression for blacks which characterized Reconstruction. The programs begun by Superintendents Wilder and Brown had never seriously challenged official preoccupations with the freedman's military usefulness. At best, the plans advanced by the superintendents envisioned only minor changes in antebellum patterns of labor organization and social control. Reform efforts remained perpetually subordinate to military needs, however, and with the restoration of peace, the need for even very modest reform programs ceased.

3

Reform and Social

Continuity

★

It frustrated C. B. Wilder to see his efforts in Tidewater Virginia ignored by the antislavery press. Wilder's reform programs were tenuous at best and, if any were to survive the war, Radicals and abolitionists would have to lend their enthusiastic support. "If you will take the trouble to inform yourselves of the facts in the case," Wilder wrote the abolitionist *New York Independent* concerning his work at Hampton Roads, "I think you will be fully satisfied." The superintendent called for a full application of the confiscation acts in the occupied counties of Virginia and insisted that hundreds of blacks, employed under his direction during 1863, could purchase homesteads if permitted. "Can you not afford to lend the cause the occasional, momentary use of your pen and press?" asked the neglected superintendent.[1]

The need for reform was clear enough. Abolitionists had long argued that slavery was sin, and it required no great insight to perceive that emancipation might not bring total absolution. Slavery involved specific relationships between master and servant which, unless specifically attacked, would become pillars in a postwar Southern labor system. Although the Union's military needs made emancipation

49

necessary, the federal government throughout the occupied South encouraged social stability and continuity rather than fundamental reform. As always, the impulse for reform would have to come from Radicals and abolitionists. Wilder grew somewhat bitter as he saw reform-minded Northerners concentrate their attention and energy on Port Royal, South Carolina, where federal occupation seemed to portend sweeping change.

The concentration of reform energies at Port Royal was important, but it was also misleading as an indication of federal policy. Elsewhere in the occupied South, programs for the freedmen's advancement were more frankly subordinate to purely military needs and considerations. In some cases, as on Virginia's Eastern Shore, the reform impulse never influenced federal policy. Nevertheless, the Sea Islands seemed uniquely significant to antislavery Northerners. Long famous for its luxury cotton, the Sea Islands area symbolized the heart of the Confederacy. Even more important as a stimulus for reform was the fact that the entire white population had fled the islands in the face of the Union advance.[2] But if Port Royal provided reformers with a fertile field of labor and a focus for their energy, it likewise revealed their inability to improve, in any dramatic and substantial way, the condition and status of Southern blacks. In the end, blacks on the Sea Islands fared no better than the freedmen on Virginia's Eastern Shore, where federal authorities enforced Negro subordination without interference or censure from Radicals and abolitionists.

It was fitting from the antislavery point of view that the slaveholders themselves should clear the path for emancipation in South Carolina. The departure of the white population from the Sea Islands became crucial to the development of federal policy and distinguished the islands from all other areas of federal occupation. After all, the Yankees had not come as liberators, and Commanding General T. W. Sherman had assured the islands' slaveholders in advance that he intended to protect loyal citizens and preserve local institutions. The whites fled all the same, taking with them what they could, but largely failed to dislodge their slave property. As federal troops occupied Beaufort, they found themselves the unwitting possessors of more than 60,000 acres of arable land and about 10,000 slaves. While Union forces elsewhere in the occupied South gradually developed programs to deal with growing contraband populations, the situation at Port Royal demanded immediate action and extensive organization.[3]

Secretary of the Treasury Salmon P. Chase took an immediate interest in the Port Royal situation. In December 1861 he sent his young friend Edward L. Pierce (formerly General B. F. Butler's superintendent of contrabands at Fortress Monroe) to superintend the contrabands on the islands and organize their labor. Pierce eagerly undertook the assignment and soon organized a labor system which, with few changes, existed throughout the war.

Pierce visited the Sea Islands early in 1862 and devised a plan to make the blacks self-supporting and the cotton plantations profitable to the federal government. According to Pierce's scheme, the administration of the various plantations was assigned to superintendents, each having full authority to enforce "a paternal discipline" over the blacks.[4] While at Port Royal, Pierce met Mansfield French, an Ohio evangelist and abolitionist who was then investigating contraband conditions for the American Missionary Association. The two men (both of whom had an interest in the physical and intellectual improvement of the blacks) soon returned North—Pierce to Boston and French to New York—to recruit the superintendents and teachers necessary to accomplish their respective work.

The first plantation superintendents arrived early in March 1862, and began organizing the islands' laborers to plant the new season's cotton crop. Despite Pierce's abolitionist and Radical connections, his agricultural program began with very modest goals. The contrabands were as yet legally slaves, and the superintendents refrained from encouraging them to think of themselves as freedmen. Under Pierce's management, the blacks hopefully would become self-supporting while the islands' cotton crops enriched the federal treasury. Pierce felt confident that the system would also prove the superiority of a free labor system. Under benevolent guidance, the blacks would discredit the Southern claim that their race would labor steadily only under compulsion.

Intent on demonstrating the profitability of free labor, Pierce found it prudent to continue antebellum plantation organization and routine. Somewhat self-consciously, therefore, the plantation superintendents assumed many of the roles of the former overseers. Invariably,

Pierce's superintendents retained the old field gang system as well as the black slave drivers. Similarly, the superintendents restricted the movement of blacks and generally prohibited hands from leaving the plantations without written authority. Although the notion of "free labor" implied wages, the superintendents began their efforts without the money to pay their hands. While they expected, indeed demanded, faithful work from the blacks, in return they promised simply good care and education.[5]

The hands found little cause for jubilation in the new Yankee labor system. Indeed, when the accustomed rations of clothing, tobacco, molasses, and salt were not forthcoming in the new season, the blacks were quick to grumble. More worrisome for the superintendents was the reluctance of many blacks to continue planting the traditional staple. Most of the hands willingly cultivated crops of corn and potatoes, but worked the cotton crops grudgingly. As a result, the nearly 4,000 hands working under Pierce's system planted almost 6,500 acres of corn and more than 1,000 acres of potatoes, but only 3,000 acres of cotton. By antebellum standards, productivity was low indeed, and the superintendents proved willing to use harsh means to improve discipline. Edward Philbrick, who later purchased a number of cotton plantations in the Port Royal area, superintended a large tract on St. Helena Island and faced open rebellion on at least one occasion. Two of Philbrick's men simply refused to work the time required in the cotton fields, and threatened to take what food they wanted if their rations were stopped. Philbrick managed to subdue the unruly hands, but the danger of violence was ever present. Some of the Yankee superintendents carried pistols at their sides to maintain order and enforce obedience.[6]

II

It quickly became clear that the system of free labor that Pierce and his superintendents hoped to develop in the Sea Islands did not require basic changes in existing patterns of land use and labor organization. Pierce and his colleagues were cautious and considered their first task to be the moral and intellectual improvement of the downtrodden slave. But war rendered the missionaries' efforts tenuous, and the army's growing interest in the military usefulness of blacks positively discouraged benevolent reforms. With his belief that slavery and martial law were "incompatible" in a free country, Commanding General David Hunter declared all blacks within his command "forever free" and ordered the mobilization of the able-bodied men as soldiers.[7] Hunter's order had the ring of truth for Radicals and abolitionists, but the general shortly confused matters by forcibly impressing blacks. Pierce complained to Secretary Chase that such violent measures only increased the hostility of the blacks, "who do not yet understand us."[8] Hunter compromised somewhat and returned black foremen and plowmen to the plantations, but Pierce insisted that his labor force had been crippled and could barely cultivate crops of corn and potatoes to prevent starvation or dependence on government rations.

Hunter's orders were premature, and President Lincoln shortly modified them. But the commander was not mistaken in thinking that government plans justified a policy of mobilizing Southern blacks. Lincoln's rebuke was mild and reassuring. It carried with it none of the curtness that characterized a similar exchange with General John C. Fremont the previous August. Indeed, emancipation as a military necessity was becoming federal policy.

The concept of military necessity required army control of freedom. In the spring of 1862, Secretary Stanton moved to end the conflicts between army officers and Treasury agents in the Sea Islands by reorganizing plantation administration under army control. Late in April, Stanton directed Brigadier General Rufus Saxton, formerly at Port Royal as chief quartermaster under General T. W. Sherman, to take full charge of abandoned plantations and the blacks. Stanton authorized the general to make whatever rules and regulations seemed necessary for the successful cultivation of the land and the organization of laborers. It was "expressly understood," moreover, that Saxton was subordinate only to Commanding General Hunter.[9] Saxton offered Pierce a position on his staff, and Secretary Chase urged his agent to work with the general. But Pierce chose to withdraw, leaving the field to Saxton and the army. Finding the existing powers of the plantation superintendents incompatible with his authority, Saxton regrouped the plantations into districts and appointed general superintendents to each. In all other respects, however, the free labor system remained unchanged, and the 1862 season was remarkable neither for its productivity nor its profitability.[10]

The season's poor cotton crop did not speak well for the efficiency of a free labor system, but the wages received by the blacks hardly provided a powerful incentive for faithful labor. Although the plantation superintendents worked their hands from March 1862, the first funds for wages did not arrive until late April, when Pierce received $5,000 to pay almost 4,000 hands. For the entire period from February 1862 to January 1863, hands received combined wages of $34,527.21, or average yearly wages of about nine dollars.[11] Once General Saxton began paying army laborers at the rate of five dollars per month for common laborers and eight dollars for skilled hands, the superintendents experienced increasing difficulty keeping blacks on the plantations.[12]

Edward Philbrick, a plantation superintendent who took pride in his business-like approach to cotton planting and freedmen's affairs, was the first to alter the labor system in the face of lagging production and labor unrest. Philbrick had experienced a good deal of trouble on his plantations, and, in an attempt to improve morale, he abandoned the old gang system during the 1862 season, replacing it with a less rigid division of labor based on incentive. To each family, Philbrick assigned a garden plot, to be worked whenever and however the hands wished. From these plots blacks were expected to provide their own subsistence. In addition, Philbrick assigned specific sections of cotton land, varying in size according to the wishes of the hands. Wages were paid for planting, hoeing, and picking.

Although General Saxton retained the gang system throughout the 1862 season on other plantations, planting operations generally were reorganized according to Philbrick's incentive plan early in 1863. Thereafter, all blacks provided their own subsistence from their garden plots, and the government assessed a corn tax to provide fodder for plantation animals. Blacks who chose to support themselves as fishermen or truck gardeners, instead of working in the cotton fields, paid two dollars each month for their houses and gardens. Ordinary field hands received houses and plots free of charge, and earned a basic rate of 25 cents per day for labor in the fields and 2.5 cents per pound for picking.[13]

The plantation superintendents frankly hoped that the new labor system would create a black peasantry. Eventually blacks would become the owners of their garden plots. With the hands thus assured of an independent source of subsistence, and the planters well supplied with wage laborers, one superintendent predicted enthusiastically: "We shall have as happy and contented a peasantry as the most ardent abolitionist could desire." Although missionaries and superintendents alike agreed that the islands' blacks should become a free peasantry, the degree of independence they should enjoy involved questions which generated considerable disagreement. The Direct Tax Law, passed by Congress in June 1862, made possible the sale of abandoned plantations and provided the instrument for the creation of a black peasantry. But the Direct Tax Commission, appointed by President Lincoln to carry out the law, soon became embroiled in the conflict over means.[14]

III

On the basis of their conviction that the islands' blacks should become a free peasantry, the tax commissioners conceived a plan for the sale of abandoned lands which envisioned a mixed settlement of white landowners and black laborers, the latter with freeholdings ranging from five to twenty acres. To provide for the blacks, 16,629 acres of more than 60,000 acres open for sale were reserved for the freedmen and for "charitable purposes" at a preferred rate of $1.25 per acre.

Although the provision for "charitable purposes" necessarily reduced the amount of land open to individual blacks, the commission's plan could have provided most blacks with modest landholdings. With an expanded black population of 15,000, the reserved acreage could have provided 200 heads of families (or 1,000 blacks, based on an average of five persons per family) with twenty-acre farms and five-acre plots for most of the remaining 2,800 families.

The government approved a more radical policy in December 1863, permitting preemption of up to forty acres on all the land owned by the government, but soon reverted to the original tax commission plan. Men like Edward Philbrick, who had a direct interest in the continuation of the plantation system, argued that the preemption policy would destroy the islands' economy and ruin the blacks as free laborers. The government and those with substantial interests in the Sea Islands were willing to see the blacks own plots of land, but remained opposed to any plan which would destroy the plantation economy.[15]

Modest as the tax commission's plan was, it allowed some blacks to become small landowners in the Sea Islands. Those who profited most from the tax sales, however, were not the former slaves, but Northern entrepreneurs like Edward Philbrick and his Boston partners who, by purchase and lease, gained control of one-third of St. Helena Island.[16] Philbrick, who had been the first to abandon the old gang system, believed that good business principles required free labor. Similarly, the well-being of the freedmen required good business principles. But while it would certainly have been no service to the freedmen to develop programs which ran counter to prevailing economic conditions, it was clear that Philbrick's reforms were of little profit to the blacks.

Philbrick began his private planting operations in the spring of 1863 and paid his hands at the government rate of 25 cents per day. Assuming that the freedmen worked six days each week, the hands earned basic monthly wages of about $6.50. Taking the largest plantation as an example, and referring to the first nine months of operation, Philbrick reported to the New England Freedmen's Aid Society average monthly wages of $6.64 per hand. But wages were considerably lower on the smaller estates. During 1863 Philbrick paid his 500 hands combined wages of only $20,000, or average monthly wages of $4.40 for the nine-month season. Moreover, since hands went unpaid during slack months, real monthly earnings, for a twelve-month period, must have averaged about $3.30, or half of the theoretical wage. Early in 1864, Philbrick raised his rate of pay to 55 cents per day, or about $14.00 monthly, but lost time probably continued to depress real wages.[17]

Philbrick's wages, and those paid by government superintendents on the Sea Islands, compared poorly with government rates for field hands elsewhere in the occupied South.[18] Moreover, since Philbrick netted $81,000 for the 1863 season, his wages were artificially low. Although Mansfield French of the American Missionary Association and other missionaries complained of the low wages, Philbrick insisted that higher pay would "diminish" industry rather than stimulate it, by making it too easy for the blacks "to supply their simple wants."[19]

From Philbrick's point of view, it was no small matter that, in the midst of civil war, men who shared his paternalistic sentiments toward blacks were able to protect some freedmen from the ravages that awaited an unarmed, unorganized, plain folk. Indeed, whenever these paternalistic designs conflicted with the army's military needs, the freedmen generally suffered. But at times, the logic of military necessity transcended brutality and pointed to innovations the social significance of which went well beyond paternalistic care and missionary programs of relief and education. Thus, the most thoroughgoing program for blacks in South Carolina came not from Radicals or self-proclaimed friends of the freedmen, but from William Tecumseh Sherman, a battlefield general with an ill-concealed distaste for blacks and for those laboring among them.

In the wake of Sherman's march to the sea—which ended victoriously with the capture of Savannah, Georgia, on Christmas Eve, 1864—thousands of black refugees crowded into the coastal areas of South Carolina and Georgia. In a sweeping measure, designed at once to free the army from the inconveniences and cost of caring for destitute blacks and to secure the coastal area from enemy harassment, Sherman issued orders in mid-January 1865 reserving the entire coast from Charleston to the St. James River in Florida, and thirty miles inland, for the exclusive settlement of blacks. Able-bodied men would continue to be organized as soldiers, but any three "respectable Negroes, heads of families," who desired to settle on the land reserved for their use, would be permitted to select an area and divide the land among themselves in farms not to exceed forty acres of arable land. Sherman left the settlement of the blacks to General Saxton, and by mid-1865, 40,000 freedmen occupied individual farms.[20]

Sherman's plan was radical, but it relied for its justification on the military needs of the federal government. With the war's conclusion, the plan no longer seemed practical, and without legal title to their land the freedmen were quickly dispossessed. Sherman himself had no interest in the postwar status of the freedmen, and did not view dispossession as defeat. Similarly, although the Yankee missionaries and plantation superintendents at Port Royal actively sought to influence the freedmen's future, few among them hoped to liberate the blacks from traditional plantation labor.[21] Reform-minded Northerners

of various persuasions expended a good deal of energy in South
Carolina during the war. But once the conflict ended, the objects of
their concern were neither more independent nor less impoverished
than freedmen who had not enjoyed the Yankee reformers' wartime
guidance and care.

IV

Though the results were minimal, the intensity of reform efforts
at Port Royal was exceptional. Elsewhere in the occupied South, reformers were overwhelmed as much by the bewildering dimensions
of the contraband problem as by the predominantly military concerns
of the federal government. In areas nominally loyal to the federal government, reform efforts were sometimes wholly absent. Such was the
case on Virginia's Eastern Shore where federal authorities protected
planter interests without interference from reform-minded whites.
Nevertheless, by the end of the war, blacks on the Eastern Shore could
not be clearly distinguished, in terms of their condition and status,
from freedmen on the Sea Islands.

At the outset, the federal government pursued remarkably similar
policies in the Sea Islands and on the Eastern Shore. Union armies
invaded both areas in November 1861 and carefully assured local
whites that slavery would not be disturbed. In neither case did the
Union army expect to achieve a major military victory. The counties
of Accomac and Northampton, comprising Virginia's Eastern Shore,
were occupied primarily to secure the adjoining Maryland counties
(which contained most of that loyal state's slaves) from secessionist
influences. Conditions at Port Royal soon encouraged certain reform
efforts, but federal policy on the Eastern Shore remained steadfastly
conciliatory.[22] Shortly before the invasion, General John A. Dix proclaimed that "special directions" had been given federal officers "not
to interfere with the condition of any persons held to domestic service." To insure the execution of this policy, Dix instructed his
officers not to admit blacks within Union camps.[23] Unlike their fellow
slaveholders at Port Royal, moreover, the white residents of the Eastern Shore remained at their homes and the occupying troops, advancing without opposition, did not disturb them.

Although the Eastern Shore counties were technically a part of the Confederacy, the federal government chose to treat them as a loyal area. Lincoln exempted Accomac and Northampton counties from his Emancipation Proclamation, and it was not until October 1864 that any systematic attempt was made to supervise the treatment and employment of blacks on the shore.[24]

Until the last months of the sectional conflict, war and emancipation did not disrupt the antebellum relationship of master and slave on the Eastern Shore. In February 1864 a Union officer reported that some blacks on the shore worked for wages, while others labored without pay for their old masters.[25] But a number of blacks, antebellum free Negroes, had earned wages for some time. The 1860 census reported almost 4,400 free blacks in Accomac and Northampton counties, and a slave population of about 8,400. Most free black farmers were employed as tenants, but three blacks owned respectable farms of one hundred acres or more.[26] When Colonel Frank J. White, the new superintendent of labor, arrived on the Eastern Shore in October 1864, former slaves and free blacks alike experienced at first hand the most coercive effects of federal authority.[27]

Colonel White had no patience with paternalistic schemes to assist blacks. Instead, he enforced a contract labor system first developed by his commander, General B. F. Butler, in Louisiana. The colonel disliked missionary types who lived among the blacks to teach them by "contact and example." Such "enthusiasts" seemed to lack the "hard, practical sense" essential to the proper supervision of black laborers. Nor did White find the efforts of C. B. Wilder and Orlando Brown in Tidewater Virginia particularly worthwhile. It seemed to him "communistic" to settle blacks on government farms. Separate black communities, he insisted, would simply increase the "distrust and hostility" of native whites. A contract labor system, which was acceptable to whites, would serve to smooth the way for a postwar adjustment of the South's labor system.[28]

Although the Eastern Shore had been spared the most disruptive influences of the war, the presence of occupying troops noticeably unsettled the blacks. Planters complained to Colonel White that the former slaves, as well as the free blacks, refused to work and insisted on "living in idleness," existing largely by raiding white plantations.[29] The colonel promised to restore order and supply planters with "all the labor they may require," providing they in turn would apply to army agents for laborers and sign contracts with the blacks they wished to employ.[30]

Although repressive in its effect, there was nothing devious or indirect about Colonel White's labor system. The colonel directed his provost marshals to take a census of the black population indicating those who were without steady employment or those who failed to work faithfully. Planters in need of hands were directed to review the provost marshals' lists of "idle" blacks, and laborers were required to enter into contracts with planters offering work. The colonel prohibited "bad or cruel" punishment, but also warned blacks that "insolence, insubordination or improper conduct" constituted contract violations punishable by the military authorities.[31]

Since the colonel's system required the enforced subordination of blacks to white employers, the relatively large number of rural free Negroes presented special difficulties. In an effort to control tenantry and the degree of independence it implied, Colonel White directed that planters renting houses or farms to blacks must post bond with the provost marshals and report "any continued idleness or improper conduct upon the part of the tenant." Moreover, the colonel strictly limited the number of blacks permitted to employ themselves in a skilled trade to one-tenth of the working force in each district. Colonel White permitted skilled blacks to work "at such times and places as they chose," only after the laborers had obtained a certificate of good character from four "responsible citizens."[32]

Colonel White's system was intended primarily to supply white planters with labor and suppress "idleness" among blacks. Even so, it did not altogether ignore the needs of the freedmen. For those who led "regular [,] honest and industrious" lives, White promised government assistance in sickness or unavoidable destitution. For those incapable of regular labor, the colonel established a government farm, providing subsistence and requiring light work or none at all from the residents. But Colonel White carefully kept the number of dependent blacks small, preferring, for example, to provide occasional rations to women whose wages were insufficient to raise their children rather than complete government support.[33]

As far as Colonel White was concerned, his labor system promoted prosperity among the blacks. Some freedmen rented farms, he reported, and all enjoyed comfortable homes and "good wages." Woodcutters, the colonel claimed, earned from twenty to thirty dollars a month. Oystermen averaged $1.50 per day, and mechanics earned a "comfortable subsistence." Male farm hands, the colonel continued, averaged twelve dollars a month, with board and clothing.[34]

The wages White claimed for farm laborers in his district compared favorably with rates reported elsewhere in the occupied South.[35] They were perhaps higher than antebellum rates for free Negroes.[36] But extant contracts negotiated under White's direction indicate that actual wage levels were considerably lower than those reported by the colonel.[37] While White claimed that male field hands received an average wage of $12.00 per month, existing records indicate an average wage of $5.80, less than half that sum. White's statement regarding female field hands appears closer to the truth. The colonel claimed average female wages of $3.00 per month, and extant records indicate average wages of just below $2.50. Yet, thirty-one of the fifty-two females whose records remain were employed as domestic servants and their average monthly wages were just over one dollar. Moreover, nearly half of the domestic servants received no payment beyond room and board. If existing contracts are representative, Colonel White's system was a parody of free labor.[38]

Clearly, white planters on the Eastern Shore had little complaint with the government's labor system. Since most blacks were forced to accept contracts as farm laborers, there was no need to pay attractive wages despite a labor shortage. Although the black population as a whole did not rebel against the coercive federal system, at least some openly resisted it.[39] Colonel White reported that Griffin Collins, a former free Negro whom White described as "industrious and well to do," had begun organizing blacks in opposition to the labor system. Collins, the colonel complained, publicly damned the labor system and announced that he, for one, would not obey the colonel's orders. He advised his fellow freedmen to do likewise. "He refused to do anything," White reported, "which would in any way recognize my authority . . . and defied me to enforce my orders."[40] Griffin Collins, evidently related to John and John T. Collins, the only blacks in

Northampton County who owned farms of one hundred acres or more, had enjoyed an exceptional antebellum status. Colonel White's coercive methods clearly angered the former free Negro and he threatened to address a written complaint to Secretary of War Stanton. The federal authorities, however, had little patience with his impudence, and Colonel White shortly received directions to send "the Black man Collins" to Norfolk for military trial.[41]

The high percentage of free Negroes in Accomac and Northampton counties, and the conciliatory federal policy toward local whites on Virginia's Eastern Shore sharply distinguished the area from the South Carolina Sea Islands. Yet, in the end, the condition of the freedmen in both areas remained substantially the same. Programs involving blacks varied less dramatically throughout the South, and federal policy toward freedmen in occupied areas was by no means uniform. But labor programs in these two areas made one point clear. The traditional patterns of social and economic organization that characterized the slave system would not automatically wither away with the abolition of that peculiar system. Likewise, substantial reforms would require more than the evangelical zeal and benevolent paternalism of the Port Royal missionaries.

PART II

LOUISIANA

4

The Origin of the Contract
Labor System

★

The details of federal policy varied from one area of Union occupation to another. Likewise, the energies of Northern reformers were unevenly applied among the blacks under Union control. But federal policy toward Southern blacks followed a fundamentally logical progression. The key to this progression was military necessity—the exigencies of a widening war effort.

Union armies in the East had gained no more than a foothold in Virginia and the Carolinas. But in the West, federal troops soon penetrated the South's "black belt" region with its fertile soil, extensive plantations, and enormous slave population. In the fall of 1861, as federal forces occupied Virginia's Eastern Shore and the South Carolina Sea Islands, General B. F. Butler and Admiral David G. Farragut began operations against New Orleans. During the winter, General U. S. Grant moved against the Confederate defenses in Tennessee. By June 1862 Union troops held New Orleans and Memphis, and, with expanding federal control of the Mississippi Valley, swelling numbers of western contrabands soon dwarfed the black populations under Union control in the East.[1] General Butler, who occupied New Orleans on April 29, 1862, quickly realized that conditions in his military department required a policy towards blacks considerably different from those policies already adopted at Fortress Monroe and Port Royal.

In the East, with the exception of Virginia's Eastern Shore, blacks were either abandoned or owned by masters openly in rebellion. Under those circumstances, federal authorities had regarded slaves as contrabands of war. Unlike Fortress Monroe and Port Royal, New Orleans and the surrounding Department of the Gulf was more than a foothold in Rebel territory. Here federal control extended over a large area which submitted to its rule. Arguments of military necessity did not apply in the absence of war, and the contract labor system, which federal authorities first imposed upon blacks in Louisiana, spread through the entire Mississippi Valley after the fall of Vicksburg. Although Radicals and abolitionists looked more favorably upon the labor programs inaugurated in the East, the organization and employment of the enormous western contraband population more accurately predicted the postwar status of Southern blacks. With the final collapse of the Confederacy, the new Freedmen's Bureau completed the task of contractually binding freedmen throughout the South to plantation labor.

Benjamin Butler found New Orleans to be "a city of the first class," surrounded by rich and fertile land. For the most part, its inhabitants followed their usual professions, and far from being in a state of rebellion, they endeavored "in good faith to live quietly under the laws of the Union."[2] From the outset, Butler undertook to reassure uneasy whites. "All persons well-disposed toward the Government," he promised, "will receive the safeguard and protection of the armies." More to the point, he vowed that "all rights of property of whatever kind will be held inviolate," subject only to the "laws of the federal union."[3] Butler's troops came not to free slaves, it was clear, but to restore Louisiana to the Union. The commander dealt sternly with opposition, but he was not one to see the war as a battle against slavery. Nothing, from his point of view, could be gained in Louisiana by the disruption of existing labor arrangements.

Under Butler's administration, fugitive slaves were frequently returned to their masters. The *Daily Picayune* reported at the end of

May that Butler "has ordered the return of quite a number of slaves . . . to their owners and their homes." Reportedly, six Negroes were taken "in irons" to an owner across Lake Pontchartrain. Predictably, the *Picayune* was "glad to hear of this very proper action" on the part of the commanding general.[4] At the same time, Butler quieted the fears of the French consul, who warned of imminent Negro insurrection threatening the lives and property of the Department's French citizens. Butler thought it natural to find an "imitative race" emulating the rebelliousness of its superiors, but he promised full protection against disorder.[5]

Anxious to placate local whites when possible, Butler reversed his Fortress Monroe contraband policy. In the Department of the Gulf, he employed those blacks he found useful and excluded the rest, "leaving them subject to the ordinary laws of the community." But the problem was not so easily solved. Fugitives already within Union lines, and those entering in spite of Butler's efforts, added to the already heavy burden of public relief in New Orleans. Moreover, since Butler assumed that the first blacks to flee their masters were generally of the worst sort, he was troubled lest his exclusion of new arrivals reward "the adventurers, the shiftless, and wicked to the exclusion of the good and quiet." The *Daily Picayune* shared the general's low opinion of runaways and suggested that Butler not only discourage contrabands but actively exclude them from federal camps.[6] The contraband policy developed at Fortress Monroe did not seem to apply in New Orleans. Butler requested new instructions from the secretary of war.[7]

Mindful of President Lincoln's cautiousness on the slave issue, the War Department preferred to evolve policies involving Negroes slowly and quietly. Stanton urged commanders to use their discretion and avoid controversy. Thus, while Butler's course of action at New Orleans was determined to some extent by the government's desire to restore loyal rule to Louisiana, the way was left open for mildly emancipationist policies provided they progressed discreetly. Justifications for such policies were well established by the spring of 1862. Butler's own contraband policy, sanctioned by the War Department at Fortress Monroe early in 1861, had involved *de facto* emancipation.

Moreover, in March 1862 Congress had prohibited Union officers from enforcing the Fugitive Slave Law.

Nevertheless, Butler chose to assist civil authorities in Louisiana in the protection of slave property. Because successful occupation seemed to require the goodwill of slaveholders, Butler reversed his Fortress Monroe policy and used the Union army to maintain slavery.[8]

II

Butler's defense of slavery in Louisiana reflected the uncertainty of Lincoln's administration concerning the future of slavery. But it was characteristic of Butler's temperamental shortcomings as a commander that he permitted the contraband issue to become embroiled in a personal feud. As a result, conditions which otherwise might have clarified federal policy toward the slaves of loyal masters became confused in a struggle between Butler and a subordinate commander.

General John W. Phelps, commanding federal forces four miles above New Orleans at Camp Parapet, permitted fugitive slaves to enter his lines and steadfastly refused to surrender blacks to their masters. Phelps' conflict with Butler began in May 1862, shortly after the occupation of New Orleans when a slaveowner approached Butler seeking the return of a bondsman hiding within Phelps' lines. Butler approached Phelps politely, expecting his subordinate to eagerly follow the commander's practices in such cases. "If I have any use for the services of such a boy," Butler wrote, "I employ him without any scruple; if I have not I do not harbor him." But Phelps had no intention of returning the slave to his master, and the next day, when a similar situation arose, Butler's tone grew impatient.

Two men, described by Butler as "gentlemen and planters," requested the return from Camp Parapet of several slaves belonging to them. Their labor, the planters insisted, was needed to repair levees above the city. "This," Butler warned Phelps, "is outside of the question of returning negroes." He believed Phelps would not hesitate to send his own soldiers to repair the levees, "let alone . . . workmen who are accustomed to this service."[9]

But Butler and the planters who applied to him for assistance were interested in more than the maintenance of levees. They sought methods of maintaining slave discipline under federal occupation. The chief officer of the civil police in the parish surrounding Camp Parapet thus reminded Butler that General Phelps presented a clear challenge to plantation order. He insisted that Phelps' actions demoralized the slaves and openly contradicted Butler's own proclamation to the people of Louisiana. The police chief suggested that the congressional nullification of the Fugitive Slave Law—upon which Phelps based his actions—could be circumvented by directing federal officers not to allow blacks within their lines and by allowing "Police officers in the Parish to arrest and return all runaways to their owners or deliver them into jail." Except that Butler insisted on keeping all useful blacks, he had already adopted such a policy. The difficulty remained that Phelps refused to follow it.[10]

Phelps' policies were an embarrassment to Butler. He directed Phelps to report in detail the number of blacks within his lines. Phelps willingly admitted that he harbored over forty Negroes who were unemployed and that he permitted such persons to come and go, but, he added defiantly, "The old system of Labor seems breaking up—so much so as hardly to be worth the while to try and save it." Butler, in return, directed Phelps to exclude "all unemployed persons" from his lines.[11]

Phelps did not change his policy, and, as Butler doubtless knew, his obstinance was not simply the product of misunderstanding or negligence. An aide-de-camp sent by Butler to bring order to the plantations around Carrollton and Kenner reported that no progress could be made until General Phelps changed his policies. The soldiers from Camp Parapet, reported the aide, were allowed "to range the country, insult the Planters and entice negroes away from their plantations." When news of slave punishments on neighboring plantations reached Phelps' camp, squads of soldiers set off "to liberate them," with orders to bring them to Camp Parapet for protection. One slave, confined in stocks for burning a barn and engaging in "riotous conduct," was freed by Phelps' men and taken to the camp. Likewise, Phelps reportedly directed the release of three slaves locked in an outbuilding overnight, "notwithstanding the presence of the owners, who protested against the act as one contrary to all orders."[12]

Phelps and his men liberated over a hundred slaves in this manner during the first month of occupation. Butler's aide concluded that while such acts were permitted no slaves in the area would work. Blacks had only to go to Phelps' camp to be free and were consequently "very insolent to their masters." Butler tried once more to change Phelps' course. Another aide visited the camp with Butler's injunction to make a "thorough examination," and see that "order is fully enforced."[13] Phelps remained adamant, however, and by mid-June close to three hundred fugitives had found refuge at Camp Parapet. Reportedly, Phelps assured his charges that "the next news from Washington will free *all* the 'contrabands'."[14] In the end, the antagonists referred their dispute to Secretary Stanton and President Lincoln.

Butler, who had nothing to gain by burdening his superiors with local matters, referred the dispute to Washington at Phelps' insistence. Convinced that the policy Butler carried out in the name of the federal government was at once inhuman and injudicious, Phelps composed a lengthy brief for emancipation. He was confronted, he said, by a large number of blacks forced from their homes by cruel masters and dependent on the army for subsistence. Despite the clearest evidence of need, Phelps found himself unable to aid them under existing policies. It was time that temporizing policies gave way to principled programs. The South, he insisted, had long used "revolutionary" means to maintain slavery. It was time the North used similar means to abolish it.[15]

Butler added his own assessment of the situation to Phelps' letter. Far from turning their hands out, Butler stated, planters were in fact relieved of their slaves by Phelps' soldiers. A planter who had been characterized by Phelps as a heartless Confederate sympathizer seemed to Butler a loyal and "humane" man. If Phelps sought to create a "test case," Butler wished him well, "for the difference of our action upon this subject is a source of trouble." While Butler professed to respect his subordinate's skill, and the "honest sincerity" of his opinion, he felt assured that if his own course was sanctioned, the services of General Phelps "are worse than useless here."[16]

Hardly pleased with such bickering, Secretary Stanton replied that the president would review the matter at his earliest convenience. In the meantime, Stanton urged Butler to exercise his "accustomed skill and discretion," and avoid an open break with Phelps. "Your cordial commendation of his skill," Stanton added dryly, "makes the department very unwilling to forego the aid of his services." Lincoln proved no more willing to remove Butler's adversary. Speaking for the president early in July 1862, Stanton reminded Butler that, as a matter of law, army officers could not return slaves to their masters, and, as a matter of "common humanity, they must not be permitted to suffer." These directions, the secretary added quickly, were not meant to set "any general rule in respect to slavery," but applied only to the case at hand.[17]

In terms of policy, the dispute settled little. Butler, however, thought the decision represented a victory for Phelps and feared for the worst. "The Government have [sic] sustained Phelps about the Negroes," he wrote his wife, "and we shall have a negro insurrection here I fancy. If something is not done soon, God help us all." The news that Phelps was training blacks as soldiers—using sticks in place of guns—did nothing to quiet the commander's fears. On July 30, 1862, Phelps formally requested arms for his men. Butler thought him mad: "Phelps has gone crazy." "He is as mad as a March Hare on the 'nigger question.' " Instead of issuing weapons, Butler directed Phelps to employ the Negroes as laborers. Phelps submitted his resignation, finding it impossible to serve under Butler "without doing violence to my convictions of right and public necessity."[18]

The affair with Phelps illustrated the shallowness of Butler's reputation as a Radical. Treasury Secretary Salmon P. Chase, a Radical with deep antislavery convictions, consistently urged Butler to develop an emancipation policy in Louisiana. Just as consistently, Butler refused. Butler promised Chase in July that he would continue to "treat the negro with as much tenderness as possible," but he insisted that emancipation was entirely out of the question. After Butler's feud with Phelps had ended, Chase again urged the commander to follow the example of General David Hunter in South Carolina and order emancipation in the Department of the Gulf. Finally, after the issuance of the preliminary Emancipation Proclamation in September, Chase hoped that Butler would "anticipate a little the operation of the Proclamation in New Orleans and Louisiana." Chase reminded Butler that according to the second Confiscation Act, the slaves "in any city occupied by our troops and previously occupied by rebels" were declared free. This was the situation in New Orleans, and it seemed clear that "the presumption of freedom" should extend to all blacks, except where proof of a slaveholder's "continuous loyalty" existed.[19] But Butler remained adamant. During the summer of 1862 President Lincoln seemed closer than Butler to accepting an emancipation program.[20]

With the struggle against immediate emancipation temporarily won, Butler developed a labor system for Louisiana that was designed to restore a measure of order to the disrupted plantation economy. Early in November, he appointed a Sequestration Commission to rule on the loyalty of individual planters and to administer the oath of allegiance. Loyal persons would be allowed to manage their property, while abandoned and confiscated estates would be worked for the benefit of the government, presumably by renting or leasing them to loyal parties.[21]

The organization of Negro labor proved more complex. Thousands of blacks, claiming to be emancipated, had already left plantations for New Orleans and other cities. Planters demanded their return and urged Butler to assist them. "Crops of sugar," lamented Butler, "are left standing to waste which would make millions of dollars." Since Congress prohibited the army from enforcing the Fugitive Slave Law, Butler looked elsewhere for the legal justification to enforce labor discipline and return blacks to the plantations. "While we have no right to return them to their masters, as such," he reasoned, "it is our duty to take care of them, and that care includes employment." The United States itself, Butler decided, would employ the slaves in loyal parishes, and would work them "as they have heretofore been employed and as nearly as may be under the charge of the loyal Planters and Overseers." The army would also provide guards for plantations to maintain order and prevent crime.[22]

The contract labor system provided Butler with the legal means of enforcing plantation discipline. If federal troops could not enforce the Fugitive Slave Law, they could hold blacks to their contracts. Butler bound blacks to ten hours of labor daily for twenty-six days each month (twenty in December), and prohibited planters from inflicting "cruel or corporal punishment." But hands guilty of insubordination, refusal to work, "or other crime or offense," would be arrested by district provost marshals and suitably punished, preferably with "imprisonment in darkness on bread and water."[23]

Although Butler's wages were lowered in a few months, able-bodied male hands were promised ten dollars per month, three dollars of which might be deducted for clothing supplied by the employer. Wages for children and women were negotiable, but planters were directed in all cases to furnish "suitable and proper" food for hands and their dependents, and care in case of sickness. The labor system had not long to prove itself, but Butler quickly claimed success. On one estate where the slaves had been returned as wage laborers, production reportedly increased. "With the same negroes and the same machinery," reported Butler, "free labor" managed to produce a hogshead and a half more sugar per day than slave labor. This, Butler thought, proved the incentive power of wages. It also indicated Butler's determination to maintain existing plantation organization. The Union army in Louisiana offered no sanctuary to slaves.[24]

III

Butler's regime in Louisiana raised as many problems as it solved, and in December 1862 he was replaced as commander by General Nathaniel P. Banks. However, Butler's removal was by no means a repudiation of existing policies toward blacks. Although Butler later won favor among Radicals and joined with them to criticize the labor system administered by General Banks, differences between the two commanders were temperamental rather than substantive.[25] Where Butler confronted opposition directly and seemed to welcome controversy, Banks withdrew from open conflict and developed accommodating policies. Neither man was likely to develop singlehandedly a policy of emancipation. Banks proved more effective in restoring civil government to Louisiana, but equally unwilling to disrupt existing patterns of labor organization.[26]

Shortly after assuming command at New Orleans, and following Butler's example, Banks issued a statement "to the people of Louisiana," offering sympathetic treatment to loyal citizens. The army, he promised, would not encourage or assist Negroes to desert their masters. At the same time, he pointed out, officers were prohibited by Congress from using force to compel the return of fugitive slaves. Since slavery was best protected by a government of laws, Banks urged loyalty and a speedy return to constitutional government.[27]

Banks' manner was openly conciliatory. He freed over a hundred political prisoners, reopened churches (closed by Butler for refusing to pray for President Lincoln), and returned a great deal of confiscated property. Although he warned the city's residents that any "disturbance of the public peace will be punished with the sharpest severity known to military law," it was clear that the tone of federal occupation would be lenient. Banks wrote his wife in January 1863 that the city's streets were "filled with women and children who seem cheerful and confident." Such tranquility pleased the new commander. As Chaplain George H. Hepworth, Banks' aide-de-camp, observed, Butler had unwisely "stroked the cat from tail to head." It was Banks' policy "to stroke her from head to tail, and see if she would not hide her claws, and commence to purr."[28]

The matter of Negro labor, however, required vigorous action. Butler's policy of excluding most blacks from Union lines neither removed the lure of freedom which the army represented nor restored order to the plantations. Banks, therefore, took command of a department burdened with black refugees in the cities and disrupted plantations in the parishes. Matters were further complicated by the issuance of the Emancipation Proclamation on January 1, 1863. In theory, Negroes in disloyal parishes were forever free, while those in loyal areas—including New Orleans and its surrounding parishes—would be regarded as slaves.

In fact, plantation labor, whether loyal or not, was disrupted everywhere under Union control. There were between 70,000 and 100,000 homeless and unemployed blacks within Union lines in Louisiana by January 1863, and, although they considered themselves freedmen, they remained, in law, slaves. The Emancipation Proclamation did not disturb slavery in the loyal parishes, but federal officers were prohibited by Congress from enforcing those state laws which would maintain slavery. "The masters," as Banks observed, "had rights in law, acknowledged by the courts of the State, which they could not execute. The negroes enjoyed a freedom which they could not justify in law, except as a consequence of the war.''[29] Slavery in the Department of the Gulf had been effectively nullified and plantation order had collapsed, but the status of blacks remained uncertain. With thousands of black refugees in New Orleans, and smaller groups elsewhere along the Mississippi, it was simply impossible to distinguish between freedman and slave. There was some fear, moreover, that the blacks, with the assistance of Negro troops, might "attempt to anticipate for themselves" the benefits they expected to receive from the president's proclamation. Banks quickly outlined a detailed plan for the organization of black labor.[30]

Like Butler, the new commander sought to maintain order without violating either the terms of the president's proclamation or the laws of Congress. Even in parishes where slavery continued to exist, Congress forbade the use of force to return fugitives. The problem of vagrancy, as it was termed, was no less pressing in disloyal parishes where blacks were technically free. Banks therefore adopted his predecessor's contract labor system. Negroes who left their "employers," directed Banks, would be "compelled to support themselves," by labor on levees and other public works. Furthermore, "vagrancy and crime" would be "suppressed by enforced and constant occupation and employment." For those remaining on plantations, Banks believed that "labor is entitled to some equitable proportion of the crops it produces." The Sequestration Commission was directed to confer with planters "and other interested parties" in order to establish a system of labor which would "secure the objects both of capital and labor." Banks reassured loyal planters that once they accepted the commission's terms, the army would enforce "conditions of continuous and faithful service, respectful deportment, correct discipline, and perfect subordination on the part of the negroes."[31]

In February 1863 the Sequestration Commission announced the terms of its labor system. At the heart of the plan was Butler's labor contract. Negroes, at the commission's direction, would be "induced" to return to the plantations "where they belong." When hands remained on a plantation or returned to it, the commission considered them to have "acquiesced" to the contract, the terms of which would then be legally binding. As suggested in Banks' order, the alternative to acquiescence was forced labor on public works. Contracts obligated hands to one year of "diligent and faithful" labor and "subordinate deportment." In return for the services of laborers, employers were bound to provide food, clothing, proper treatment, and either one-twentieth of the year's crop or a fixed monthly wage. Skilled hands (mechanics, sugar makers, drivers, and the like) would receive three dollars monthly or three shares each of the portion of the crop set aside for labor. Able-bodied male field hands would receive two dollars monthly or two shares, and women, whether field hands or house servants, were promised one dollar or one share.[32]

To supervise the collection and employment of vagrant blacks, Banks chose George H. Hanks, formerly superintendent of Negro labor under General Phelps at Camp Parapet. Abandoned and confiscated plantations, either leased or rented to loyal parties, were administered by Samuel W. Cozzens, a captain in the Quartermaster Department. But the enforcement of labor contracts was the responsibility of district provost marshals. It was their duty to promote the successful cultivation of plantations. Banks did not expect them to negotiate "individual contracts" with each hand. "The fact that they return or remain is to be taken as proof of their assent." Sensitive to the possibility that some officers might find the job of returning blacks to their masters repugnant, Banks argued that those who "advise and assist" the return of hands should feel proud to have secured for Negroes the advantages promised by the labor system.[33]

Most observers did indeed view the new system optimistically. General Banks himself thought it "the best act of my life," and believed it would "solve all troubles . . . about slavery" within three months. The wisdom of the plan, as the general saw it, was that it protected capital while ameliorating the conditions of labor. He hoped it would please Conservatives and Radicals alike. A wealthy business friend wrote the general that his policy provided the "only solution" to the Negro question: "something like a serfdom, carrying out the principles of our vagrant laws, that oblige every man to work for his support." At the same time, the Reverend Edwin M. Wheelock, in charge of Negro education under Superintendent Hanks, believed the plan the "best thing possible." And Chaplain George H. Hepworth, who interested himself in the labor system as Banks' aide-de-camp, found the central idea "just and humane" since it removed destitute freedmen from the city. Captain Cozzens also concurred, claiming that the system "most positively" demonstrated that "free labor" was at once more beneficial to the Negro and more economical to the planter than slavery. Even Salmon P. Chase's Treasury agent in New Orleans informed the secretary that Banks' plan was "working well, and the planters express much satisfaction."[34]

Local whites were generally pleased with the new labor system. Since the blacks required the paternal care of the planters to survive, the *Daily Picayune* thought Banks' orders wise and humane. "Common sense, duty and patriotism alike" seemed to demand such a course.[35] Likewise, the New Orleans creole newspaper, *L'Union*, which included the New Orleans free blacks among its readers, shortly gave the labor system its blessings. Wherever the system of free labor had seriously begun, the editor insisted, it had worked well, proving daily that slave labor was not only odious in itself, but contrary to the interests of the planters.[36]

Had the blacks labored faithfully as quasi-slaves, Banks might well have achieved the universal accord he sought. Plantation hands, however, proved unwilling to submit to the discipline of their masters and overseers. Laborers continued to leave plantations for the city while strikes and outright rebellions stopped work on many plantations. Banks therefore adopted increasingly restrictive measures to enforce the employment of blacks. Anxious to have all employed, the general authorized Superintendent Hanks to establish several government-operated "home farms" to provide work for superannuated Negroes as well as "vagrants." "Let there be no delay," urged Banks. "Put all the negroes to work."[37]

IV

As it became clear that Banks' system would not become moderate with time, opposition to it grew. Northern abolitionists soon attacked the plan as oppressive. "This scheme," reported the New England Freedmen's Aid Society, "if not justly to be called a reenactment of slavery," could hardly be confused with "a system of free labor." As the society noted, Banks insisted that his system was the best possible under the circumstances, and his superintendents were in the habit of commending blacks for bearing up well under adverse conditions. But, the society concluded, Banks clearly regarded "a *freed* man as a very different thing from a *free* man."[38] James McKaye, a member of the American Freedmen's Inquiry Commission, gave General Banks and his system the benefit of the doubt and even described Superintendent Hanks as a "true-hearted and faithful" servant to the "colored people." McKaye was confident, he wrote General Banks, that the commission's report would "serve to vindicate" him from the misunderstandings that existed in the North regarding the labor system. But while McKaye thought Banks' intentions were good, he acknowledged that provost marshals became tools of the planters in the continued oppression of blacks. At best, McKaye thought, Banks' system could be justified only as a temporary measure; the task of liberating blacks from the conditions of slavery remained.[39] As the abolitionist and former slave Frederick Douglass remarked, Banks' labor system defeated "the beneficent intentions of the government" toward the freedmen, if indeed such intentions existed.[40]

The official trend toward emancipation did nothing to reverse Banks' restrictive policies. Indeed, Banks' system enjoyed President Lincoln's full support. Lincoln hoped that, as Louisiana loyalists reconstructed their state for readmission to the Union, they would adopt Banks' labor system. "After all," wrote the president, "the power, or element of 'contract' may be sufficient for this probationary period; and, by its simplicity, and feasibility, may be the better." But the official abolition of slavery, Lincoln insisted, was basic to Northern and congressional acceptance of the emerging Louisiana free state.[41] Banks was sensitive to this mood and carefully removed obvious irritants to emancipationist sentiment.

Noting numerous advertisements in New Orleans in December 1863 "relating to the sale of slaves," Banks argued pragmatically that the events of the past year made the continuance of "such business" impossible. Therefore, beginning on January 1, 1864, all "public notices of this kind" would be removed from the city's signboards.[42] Later in the month, Banks officially suspended the slavery provisions of the antebellum state constitution. The way was thus cleared for the organization of the Louisiana free state constitutional convention, and on September 5, 1864, slavery was formally abolished with the adoption of the new state constitution.

The status of the new freedmen was another matter, and Banks evidently concurred in the state attorney general's decision that emancipation gave blacks the status of white aliens.[43] Nor did the general's new labor regulations of February 3, 1864, relieve the freedmen of the restrictions which bound them to the land as obedient hands. Slavery was abolished, but Banks worked to maintain its social controls and economic organization.

Banks said that his new regulations were based "upon the assumption that labor is a public duty, and idleness and vagrancy a crime." No class of persons was exempt from this universal rule, enforced in enlightened communities "by the severest penalties." Discipline was especially necessary in agricultural communities, and whatever else might change, agricultural labor was not "relieved from the necessity of toil, which is the condition of existence with all the children of God." The abolition of slavery permitted blacks to choose employers. But once the choice was made, and the choice *had* to be made, a contract was thereby formed and hands would be bound to its faithful fulfillment until released by the government. Plantations needed the labor of blacks, and hands were prohibited from leaving their jobs without permission from the district provost marshal.[44]

Banks ordered hands to labor ten hours a day in summer and nine in winter. Although "perfect subordination" was no longer stipulated, freedmen were held to "respectful, honest, faithful labor." Moreover, "indolence, insolence, disobedience," as well as crime, were cause for forfeiture of pay and other punishments permitted by army regulations. Wages were increased somewhat from the maximum of three dollars per month set by the Sequestration Commission, but remained below those originally offered by Butler. First-class hands would now receive eight dollars. Rates of six, five, and three dollars per month were set for less productive hands.[45] An incentive wage of an additional two dollars monthly was permitted for "engineers and foremen" whose faithful service justified it. Wages would be deducted, however, if hands refused to work, were disobedient, or even sick. "When sickness is feigned," the general warned, rations would be withheld as well. Planters could deduct as much as three dollars a month for clothing, but deductions for food and other goods were prohibited.

Banks urged planters to meet the current needs of freedmen by providing food and other goods as payment for extra work, and by permitting the cultivation of a portion of their land on shares. Planters were required, however, to provide garden plots of up to one acre per family for the exclusive use of the freedmen. With the laborers' subsistence presumably secured,[46] Banks urged planters to withhold wages until the end of the season, if they could do so without creating general discontent among their hands.[47]

As before, Banks allowed planters to pay their hands a proportionate share of the crop rather than wages. Under the new regulations, one-fourteenth of the year's net proceeds constituted labor's share. The commander clearly hoped that this latter arrangement would find wide acceptance. From such a beginning, planters might gradually increase the garden plots assigned to freedmen, "until faithful hands can be allowed to cultivate extensive tracts," returning a portion of their crops to the landlord as rent. Banks believed that by progressing from a sharecropping to a tenant farming arrangement, the independent industry of the laborers would be encouraged, and "all the advantages which capital derives from labor" would be strengthened.[48]

Banks reminded skeptical planters that the federal government's interest in a prosperous plantation economy was the only consideration entitling them to favor. Such clemency was "majestic and wise," but not unlimited. Lands not cultivated would be temporarily forfeited to parties willing to manage them. Amnesty granted in the past, moreover, was conditional on future loyalty and faithful adherence to the labor regulations. The general forbade flogging and other cruel punishments. Laboring families were not to be divided, and planters were held responsible for the care of former slaves unable to work due to age or infirmity.

Humanitarian concern for the freedmen was not entirely absent from General Banks' orders, although labor restrictions were clearly dominant. The general promised to establish schools in each district under the administration of Chaplain Wheelock, and a "free labor bank" to protect the freedmen's anticipated savings.[49] However, Banks' modest humanitarian goals had little chance of success, embedded as they were in a system designed to promote plantation productivity and labor discipline. Moreover, those charged with the administration of the labor system proved to be easy prey for planters willing to pay for favors. Provost marshals frequently acted as agents for planters and both Chaplain Wheelock and Superintendent Hanks soon faced charges of fraud.

Wheelock, arrested late in December 1863 for approving irregular payrolls, insisted that he was the innocent victim of enemies hoping to discredit his work. Nothing came of the incident and Wheelock continued, apparently with dedication, to direct freedmen education under Banks and later with the Freedmen's Bureau. Hanks, however, was relieved of duty early in August 1864 and was found guilty of "fraudulently . . . accepting money by way of gratification, and in consideration of the services of certain negro laborers under his charge." He was dismissed from the service in April 1865.[50] Hanks was replaced in August 1864 by Thomas W. Conway, formerly inspector of vagrants under Hanks in New Orleans. A diligent, if not an enlightened man, Conway worked faithfully to keep all blacks employed, and served as superintendent of the Bureau of Free Labor until May 1865 when he became assistant commissioner of the Freedmen's Bureau for the state of Louisiana.[51]

Conway returned honesty to the management of freedmen affairs, but basic policies remained unchanged. The government compelled freedmen to honor the imposed provisions of their labor contracts. Those seeking escape from plantation toil were arrested as vagrants and were returned to plantations, placed on public works, or sent to government home farms. Conway carefully kept the alternatives to plantation labor as unattractive as possible. On the home farms, he noted, "labor is forced." He sought to impress his charges with the fact "that work could in no case be avoided." If blacks became burdens to the government, for whatever reasons, "they must work as hard as if they were employed by contract on the plantation of any private citizen." And, if they labored on home farms, they would receive no pay.

The federal government would not offer blacks respite from plantation labor. Conway believed that this determination was "instrumental in decreasing the number of vagrants" in the department. Although most of the home farm inmates were women, children, the old, and the disabled, Conway nonetheless took pride in his ability to make the farms self-supporting. "It has been determined," he reported, "not to allow the work of caring for the freedmen of the Department to be of any expense whatever to the United States." The home farms, as far as he could see, were "most successful."[52]

Federal labor policies in Louisiana left little room for reform. The war and the abolition of slavery necessarily disrupted the plantation system and weakened antebellum social controls, but the positive actions of the federal authorities successfully minimized the dislocations of war. And the planter, as Chaplain Hepworth noted in regard to Banks' labor policy, "was touched very tenderly, if he was touched at all."[53]

5

A Pattern of Repression

★

Nowhere in the South did army commanders or government officials seek to liberate blacks from antebellum conditions of subordination and dependence. Nevertheless, the institution of slavery could not withstand the pressures of Union occupation. To the extent that Northern armies warred with slaveholders, the success of Union arms benefited Southern blacks. The very existence of slavery was at issue in the war, and the interests of the federal forces in Louisiana, as in the rest of the occupied South, were by no means identical with those of the planters. There was even a degree of benevolent concern expressed for the freedmen's welfare in the federal labor program. The labor system served in part to protect blacks from the ravages of war and the worst abuses of slavery. Ideally, federal officers worked to restore social order *and* insure the humane and just treatment of blacks.

Moreover, the army in Louisiana did not leave all plantations in the hands of their antebellum owners. Abandoned and confiscated lands were leased or worked directly for the benefit of the government. Captain Samuel W. Cozzens supervised these estates for the Quartermaster Department and as an assistant to the Treasury Department agent at New Orleans. By May 1863 Cozzens reported fifty-seven plantations under his charge. Some were leased for one-half of the net profits; others, like the ''Star'' plantation in Plaquemines Parish,

were leased for a yearly rent of one thousand dollars. Thirty-seven
plantations, however, were worked directly for the benefit of the government. On these lands, the government assumed the role of planter.
The places were managed by overseers paid salaries of eight hundred
to one thousand dollars yearly by the government. Superintendent of
Labor Hanks used more than twenty of these plantations as sources
of employment for vagrant blacks under his care. On some
government-operated farms, Cozzens expected little profit and worked
them simply to employ blacks. On others, crops of sugar cane, corn,
and cotton promised handsome profits for the government.

In the spring of 1863 Cozzens reported that about 1,700 hands under
his supervision cultivated approximately 7,500 acres, mostly in cane
and corn. The number of plantations under the control of Superintendent Hanks grew by late summer to thirty-three. Although many of
the farms on the west bank of the Mississippi were disrupted by guerrillas, Hanks claimed to have over 12,000 blacks employed profitably
for the government.[1] Moreover, Hanks and his successor, T. W. Conway, continued to operate the three "home farms" for the employment of superannuated and recalcitrant blacks.[2]

On the home farms, army superintendents worked those who, for
reasons of age, health, or obstinance, were not wanted on plantations
or in the army. These farms, in effect, functioned as forced labor
camps to discourage idleness and vagrancy in the black population.
But they also provided for the basic needs of a class which otherwise
would have suffered greatly from the effects of war. Since Banks
believed in the "necessity of toil," it was indeed unwise, as Superintendent Conway observed, to leave even the aged and infirm "in
idleness."[3] Home farms were established at Donaldsonville, Baton
Rouge, and in St. Charles Parish. By February 1865 the army supervised the labor of 1,416 such "dependents."[4]

About 15,000 blacks labored on plantations and the home farms
in Louisiana directly for the benefit of the federal government. But
more than two-thirds of the blacks under federal control in the Department of the Gulf worked for private planters under General Banks'
regulations. Superintendent Conway reported in the fall of 1864 that
his office recorded contracts involving approximately 35,000 hands,
employed on over 1,000 large plantations. He estimated that another

15,000 blacks worked for small creole farmers but were not registered. In addition to plantation hands, an estimated 30,000 blacks lived in the city of New Orleans, including about 10,500 antebellum free Negroes. Since blacks in the city were subject to the vagrancy provisions of General Banks' orders and were, from time to time, arrested and sent to labor on plantations, the government labor system in Louisiana included about 95,000 blacks.[5]

Control and protection of this black population went hand in hand. Federal forces were at once the agency of social change and the enforcers of social order. While officers sought to maintain the social controls and economic organization of slavery, they adopted stern measures as well to assist and protect blacks. Neither Butler nor Banks hesitated to punish whites when they openly and brutally defied strictures against corporal punishment. Butler fined a New Orleans man five hundred dollars for whipping a slave girl, and Banks' provost marshal general ordered the arrest of several St. Charles men for murder when a slave they severely whipped died of his wounds.[6]

When the threat to blacks came from guerrillas, the federal response was equally firm, if not always effective. Guerrilla attacks concentrated on government-operated plantations west of the Mississippi, and although General Banks thought it inexpedient as a rule to arm hands, Superintendent Hanks instructed plantation laborers in exposed areas near Donaldsonville in the use of weapons. During an attack in June 1863, they reportedly fought bravely, sustaining "their share of the casualties." One hand killed a Confederate major, much to Hanks' satisfaction. Elsewhere blacks were generally defenseless and guerrillas were able, from time to time, to disrupt government plantations. Hanks, however, did his best to provide for his charges. When raids threatened, hands received two days' rations and passes to the nearest fortified position.[7]

II

General Banks' interest in protecting laborers from conspicuous abuse increased as the Louisiana free state movement progressed. The general did not want the return to civil government to be hindered by disclosures of Negro degradation or suffering. The moral life of blacks thus attracted fresh concern. Provost Marshal General James

Bowen, displaying sudden concern in the matter, informed his subordinates that the absence of marriage vows reduced Negroes to "a state of concubinage, destructive to their prosperity and moral elevation." District provost marshals were therefore directed to perform the necessary ceremony, without charge, for as many couples as they could find.[8]

In the matter of employment and wages, the government took steps to ensure laborers of the rather meager benefits of the labor system. As the labor system expanded, reports of mistreatment were not uncommon. Black soldiers at Brashear City, for example, complained that their wives and children suffered at the hands of planters and overseers. Employers frequently charged hands for food and medicine, deducted wages during bad weather, and refused to care for the sick. Children too young to labor were often not fed, and despite directions to the contrary, hands were sometimes dismissed after harvest. Planters also sold goods to their employees at inflated prices, keeping many of them constantly in debt.[9]

As the 1864 season drew to a close, Banks himself moved to prevent planters from openly defrauding their hands. He directed planters to pay their employees entirely in U.S. currency to be counted out in the presence of the district provost marshal or his representative. Employers charging hands more than 10 percent above the net cost of goods would be guilty of fraud "and punished accordingly."[10]

Banks feared that unenlightened planters might discredit his efforts to return Louisiana to civil government. To dispel any doubts about his own sincerity, the commander directed an aide to tour plantations in the department, inspect conditions, and make the government's policy toward the former slaves absolutely clear. The success of civil government required equitable relations between planter and hands. The general therefore wished to know to what extent the former masters had changed their methods of punishment. "Particularly," said Banks, "I desire to know if the negro laborer is treated as a man." It was equally important from Banks' point of view that planters understand perfectly "that the negro children must be educated." If planters obstinately refused to cooperate with the government, they would not be permitted to employ blacks.[11]

Following the adoption of the free state constitution in September

1864, and after the removal of the corrupt George H. Hanks, Superintendent T. W. Conway took a number of steps to force the compliance of planters to the government's labor regulations. Aware that "many outrages" were committed against blacks by employers, Conway promised to punish all offenders.[12] To prevent planters from selling their crops and leaving the department before paying wages, Conway requested and received authority to prevent sales and thus force planters to pay their hands or lose their profits. Banks authorized Conway to seize property, produce, or funds in cases where employers made no provision for paying their hands. By February 1865 Conway reported twelve such seizures, ranging in value from $457 to $5,000, and totaling over $22,000.[13]

Reviewing his efforts in behalf of the freedmen during 1864, Conway exulted in what he saw as the progressive demise of the antebellum planter aristocracy. "What was reaped from the French Revolution," he wrote, "is being realized by Louisiana as the most sweeping result of the war." Another year like the last would "hardly leave any of the old planters on their feet." But if the changes Conway found so appealing constituted a revolution of sorts, it did nothing to improve the status of blacks. Conway himself admitted that hands were frequently treated more justly by "old planters" than by newly arrived lessees; certainly planters professed a deeper understanding of their former bondsmen. Whether from planter or lessee, however, the very abuses Conway sought to correct continued. In March 1865 the provost marshal in Iberville Parish pronounced his district virtually ungovernable. He had immediate control over but a portion of the parish and found it "impossible to accomplish the settlement with the 'Planters' and their 'Laborers' for the past year." Without an armed escort to accompany him, the provost marshal could not venture beyond five miles from his post.[14]

At best, government protection for plantation hands was limited. Federal control was never absolute and regulations protecting free labor necessarily relied on the cooperation and goodwill of planters for their execution. Blacks, it was originally believed, would work faithfully under government protection so long as they were not whipped or otherwise made to suffer. The cooperation of planters, on the other hand, was always considered more elusive. An informant at Donaldsonville assured General Banks that smaller farmers, who owned but a few slaves, would "promptly" accept the government labor system. Although planters were generally opposed to any modification in the slave system, Banks was told, their obstinacy could be overcome with patience. If planters were handled with sensitivity, the local Unionist concluded, the plantation economy could be successfully restored.[15]

In fact, however, Negroes, planters, and the plantation economy proved far more difficult to regulate than Banks was led to believe. Despite the general's best efforts, the state's sugar industry declined steadily until the end of the war, falling from a yearly production of more than 450,000 hogsheads in 1861, before the invasion, to 10,000 hogsheads in 1864. Cotton culture probably fared somewhat better in Louisiana because its cultivation was less intensive. But the decline of the sugar industry reflected the disruptive influence of federal occupation.[16]

III

Whether it wanted to or not, the Union army undermined slavery and the plantation economy. Although blacks were not suddenly liberated from traditional restrictions, they took every advantage of the confusion which occupation produced.[17] Plantation discipline often broke down and thousands of hands left their work for the cities. Donaldsonville, for example, was described in March 1863 as "nothing more or less than a general rendezvous for all the negroes of the country." Banks' Unionist informant in that city urged the reestablishment of the civil police. If chosen from among Union men, they would act in concert with army officers, and "but few negroes would be left wandering idly about." As matters stood, blacks openly "strolled about" Donaldsonville making nuisances of themselves to the whites.[18]

Federal forces could act with considerable effect in the cities, but since their control of the countryside was extremely limited, the army necessarily relied on planters to maintain order. Although the labor regulations promised to protect the rights of laborers, the government's desire for order and plantation productivity tended to serve the needs of the planters. This community of interests did not endear planters to their conquerors. An overseer on a small plantation within federal lines described to his employer the degenerating conditions he faced, and blamed the Yankees. Work had ceased, he explained, after the departure of four of the best hands. Three of them continued "wandering about the premises," giving some hope of returning to their labors, but the fourth had hired himself to a nearby detachment of soldiers as a cook. "I am convinced," said the overseer, that "he was induced to it by the soldiers." The planter promptly protested the injustice to General Banks.[19] Even Captain Cozzens, Banks' superintendent of leased and government-operated plantations, complained that the interference of army officers, including provost marshals, "only breeds discontent among the hands and engenders in them a refractory spirit," which was becoming "exceedingly difficult to control."[20]

Shortage of labor as well as lack of discipline affected plantations throughout the department. In June 1863 the approaching harvest seemed threatened by a lack of labor. The provost marshal in Assumption Parish reported that the number of hands remaining was barely sufficient for the harvest. Planters in the area insisted that they could not afford to lose a single additional hand. In St. James Parish between a quarter and a third of all hands had run off. "It is the general opinion of the planters," reported the provost marshal, "that the negroes will not do a fair day's work unless they are compelled to do so." The provost marshal was willing to try to compel faithful labor, but a diligent search of the parish uncovered only thirty unemployed blacks, several of whom had been arrested for burglary and larceny. Twenty were put on the public works, seventeen returned to plantations, and the remaining three enlisted as Union soldiers in the Corps d'Afrique.

St. Charles Parish reported a similar labor shortage. There were not enough hands, the provost marshal thought, to cultivate or gather the crops standing, and it was impossible to enforce continuous labor. The Negroes recognized no authority, he charged, and considered their time their own, "working when and as long as they pleased, and leaving plantations at their own discretion." The problem was "their idea of liberty" which left them willing to work "only so short a time as possible."[21]

Planters were quick to lay the blame for this state of affairs on

Union occupation. But if the army was one source of the problem it was also the only force capable of restoring order and discipline. Planters therefore offered advice as well as protest. A group of planters from loyal parishes expressed a major concern when they petitioned General Banks to resume police patrols. They understood that the laws of Congress forbade army officers from forcibly returning slaves to their owners, but expressed confidence that the prohibition did not extend to civil authorities. "Should the constitutional right of bearing arms be restored to loyal citizens," they suggested, ". . . the slaves could . . . be made to return and labor steadily."[22]

Planters nearer New Orleans were no more satisfied with federal protection than those in the outlying parishes. One New Orleans area planter complained that although he signed the government's agreement, he nonetheless lost three good hands to the army.[23] Planters meeting at St. Charles expressed alarm over the erosion of "police regulations," although they were confident that the contract system was well-intended and that General Banks would "do everything in his power" to protect their interests.[24] To the south of the city, the Sparks estate (later used as a government home farm) was wholly destitute of hands. Rather than work under Banks' regulations, the blacks reportedly threw down their tools, swore they would "rather die" than accept the proposed terms, and "left in a body."[25]

Underlying planter opposition to Banks' labor system was the conviction that federal persuasion and the promise of wages could never replace coercion as the foundation of plantation discipline. An Assumption Parish planter facing conditions approaching rebellion received the district provost marshal's suggestion of paternal persuasion with disbelief. He was willing to grant the "irony" of paying blacks, but thought it absurd to think they would continue to labor faithfully without coercion. The cultivation, and particularly the harvest, of sugar cane, he argued, required the organization, regimentation, and exact discipline of an army. And what army did not regulate itself with coercion? The planter concluded that the current "unrestricted communication" among blacks, "the demoralized state of their minds, and their contempt for the authority of those over them, clearly point out to those familiar with the negro character, what is in store." Black insurrection seemed imminent.[26]

Most planters welcomed Banks' orders regarding the arrest and forced employment of Negro vagrants. But it was widely argued that "some *coercion* is absolutely necessary" to maintain order on plantations and prevent hands from becoming more "demoralized and irreclaimable than they now are." If the government was willing to force the labor of blacks upon public works, asked one planter, why would it not force their labor on plantations? If planters were to care for dependent Negroes, the government must force the return of the able-bodied. Once Banks returned power to the civil police, a "great portion of these troubles would cease."[27]

As one provost marshal observed, the planters believed that unless they could continue as before with unlimited control of their hands, they would be ruined and Louisiana would become a wilderness. "They complain," reported the provost marshal, "not because of insubordination" on the part of laborers, "but because they can not be allowed to inflict corporal punishment, and . . . make the slave *fear* them."[28]

IV

With few exceptions, planters acquiesced, albeit reluctantly, in the necessity of accepting the government's labor regulations. If they had to pay wages and submit to army supervision in order to maintain a labor force, they were usually willing to do so. At Banks' direction, Chaplains Hepworth and Wheelock toured the plantations at the opening of the 1863 season and presented a pleasant report of operations. Everywhere, the majority of planters appeared willing to accept the terms of the labor system and the hands were reportedly "docile, industrious, and quiet." Hepworth and Wheelock took every opportunity to speak with the blacks, "learn their grievances, if any existed, and counsel patience, civility and industry."

Where the labor system was not accepted, and where the planters were still "wedded to the 'Ancient Regime,' " laborers were found to be "ill-fed, ill-used, miserable and discontented, seizing every chance to run away."[29] The threat of arrest was the only effective means of coercion the planters had left.[30] However repugnant in theory, then, planters accepted the idea of labor contracts. Thus, an Assumption Parish planter who had "purposely" avoided entering into a contract with his former slaves succumbed in the spring of 1865. "It was very distasteful to me," he confided in his diary, "but I could do no better."[31]

The planters' constant protests and suggestions nonetheless had an effect. Banks addressed one meeting of planters in February and reportedly promised the gathering that he would do all in his power to "increase the happiness and prosperity of his fellow-citizens in Louisiana."[32] District provost marshals openly discussed conditions with planters and acted on their complaints. Major H. M. Porter, provost marshal at Donaldsonville, worked particularly closely with Ascension Parish planters. The planters held a meeting in his office in March 1863 "for the purpose of organizing a Police" for the parish, to maintain "order and discipline among the Negroes." The planters sensibly elected Major Porter chairman of the gathering before adopting several resolutions to be presented to Provost Marshal General Bowen in New Orleans. General Bowen, they found, was "entirely content with the resolutions," and was willing "to aid the Planters in the most efficient manner possible."[33]

The provost marshal at Jefferson Parish, John W. Ela, likewise met with planters late in May 1863 to discuss the labor system. The planters, he found, were willing to accept the notion of "free labor" if the Negroes were forcibly "required to work diligently and faithfully." As matters stood, planters had little control over their hands, many of them working very little or not at all. "They want a military guard of one or two men stationed on every plantation," reported Ela. The soldiers could then "*compel* the negroes to work." Although Ela thought the planters did not sufficiently appreciate the changed status of labor, he felt confident that hands in his district were "well contented," and "generally, well treated."[34]

The desire of the various provost marshals for order tended to serve the interests of the planters, but on certain occasions, Union officers went out of their way to assist antebellum masters. General Banks himself directed the arrest of "a Contraband named 'Tony' " who was to be returned to his mistress.[35] Similarly, the provost marshal at Carrollton received instructions to "render all the assistance necessary" in the return of several fugitive slaves.[36]

On occasion, provost marshals adopted the brutal methods of slavery to enforce discipline among hands. When the Negro "Gabel" requested permission from Captain Silas W. Sawyer, provost marshal in St. Bernard Parish, to join the Corps d'Afrique, he was turned away roughly and ordered back to his plantation. Afraid to return to his former master, Gabel hid in the woods and tried to make his way to New Orleans. After being caught by Union pickets, the man was returned to Sawyer, who beat him and returned him under guard to his employer. Apparently with Sawyer's acquiescence, Gabel suffered eighteen hours in stocks followed by six hours of "trussing" and exposure to mosquitos. After another six hours in stocks, the would-be Union soldier received twenty-five lashes and was made to beg the pardon of his former master.[37]

When properly used, the provost marshal's power of arrest was the key to federal control of blacks in Louisiana. The provost marshals obtained for the army the black soldiers and laborers it needed, excluded "vagrant" blacks from the cities, and kept plantation hands on the land. As the pattern and purpose of Negro arrests became clear, few could doubt that the federal government intended to restrict the mobility of blacks and maintain their subordination to loyal whites.

Shortly after General Banks issued his order regulating labor in January 1863, Provost Marshal General Bowen directed his officers to employ "all vagrant negroes" in their districts, organizing them in gangs to repair levees, roads, "and other public works." Provost marshals were to "exact" from the able-bodied "a full day's work every day except Sunday." Blacks who persisted in their indolence would be compelled to work "by such slight punishment as may be effective."[38] Needed repairs would thus be made and idle blacks controlled. The emphasis was on control.

Arrests of black "vagrants" in New Orleans were widespread in the first months of 1863. Indeed, provost guards were overzealous, and some whites protested the harassment of their servants sent on legitimate errands. All blacks were suspect, and the papers of free blacks went entirely unheeded.[39] "Idle" blacks were arrested and turned over to Superintendent Hanks to be returned to masters in the city, distributed to plantations, or put on public works.[40] In a less intensive fashion, the same policy was carried out by provost marshals in the parishes.

In areas where there were civil police, the pattern of arrests was especially repressive. Superintendent Hanks visited plantations in St. Bernard Parish in April 1863 and found that many hands had been arrested by civil police without military authorization, "subjected to the lash" and thus forced to submit to plantation employment. On one plantation, the superintendent found twenty adults and a number of children who had been brought to the place against their will. Hanks had an argument with the overseer on the estate, but later accepted a dinner invitation from the offending planter. Aware of the "extreme sensitiveness" of the planters on such subjects, Hanks was careful to perform his "unpleasant duty" with "extreme courtesy." The superintendent returned to New Orleans impressed with plantation hospitality and satisfied that the arrested blacks were in good hands.[41]

In areas with labor surpluses, efforts were made to transport blacks to locations with labor shortages. The provost marshal in St. Mary's Parish, "after diligent search," arrested every Negro he could find not employed by whites. Fifteen "vagrants and hangers on" were seized and shipped to Superintendent Hanks in New Orleans. Hanks welcomed the consignment and hoped more could be located. "If you have any more vagrants on hand," wrote the superintendent hopefully, "I would be obliged to you if you would send them here, as there is a great demand for laborers."[42] The needs of planters, as well as the army, were well served by such means. In September 1864 General Banks authorized Superintendent Conway to regulate labor transfers throughout the department. Lest planters take advantage of the system to unload superannuated hands, Conway announced he would accept blacks as "surplus" only when assured of their employment elsewhere.[43]

V

While the labor system in the Department of the Gulf did not function for the private benefit of the planters, its features went a long way toward maintaining the type of order they desired. Certainly Banks and his officers had no theories about plantation operations which differed from those held by planters. The government organized work on estates directly under its control with as much concern for discipline and regimentation as any antebellum planter. Indeed, when private interests found themselves unable to govern their hands, Superintendent of Plantations Cozzens assumed control and operated the property with his own regulations. Cozzens occupied a plantation in St. Charles Parish because the hands "refused to work for the owner." The place was becoming "a resort for runaway negroes," and jeopardized discipline on surrounding estates. Cozzens believed that with proper treatment, food, and clothing, most hands would willingly, even eagerly, work for the government. Still, he was no more willing to trust the management of leased and government-operated plantations to such incentives than were private planters. Laborers under government control were subject to severe restrictions, indicating the limits of the notion of "free labor" as it applied to blacks in Louisiana.[44]

In addition to Banks' labor regulations, Cozzens issued detailed instructions to govern hands on leased and government-operated plantations. Cozzens appointed inspectors to report any "derelections of duty" by the hands or lessees, and proceeded to outline the duties of labor. Hands would rise each morning to the sound of the plantation bell and report to the field within thirty minutes. Tardiness exceeding two hours was punishable by loss of a half day's pay. Without shortening the nine to ten hours of faithful labor required by General Banks, Cozzens allowed his hands two hours in the afternoon for dinner. The workday thus extended for twelve hours in summer, eleven in winter. After nine o'clock in the evening, moreover, hands were prohibited from roaming about "at will." Blacks who broke this curfew were fined a half day's wage.

Hands caught leaving the plantation without authorization risked losing a full day's pay. To limit the chance of escape, Cozzens forbade blacks to ride horses or mules. He likewise hoped to increase the difficulty of stealing by prohibiting blacks from owning "any horse, mule, hog, pigs, or cattle." Those fortunate enough to have such property were forced to sell it. In perhaps his most revealing decision, Cozzens ordered blacks not to grow cotton or sugar cane on their own garden plots, allotted them according to Banks' order. The cultivation of cash crops, it was clear, was the exclusive function of the plantation. The independent efforts of blacks were limited to crops of fodder and vegetables for their own consumption.[45]

Despite such detailed restrictions, blacks on plantations under Cozzens' supervision often misbehaved. Where "persuasion," in the form of wage deductions failed, Cozzens was willing to employ more severe measures. "In a few instances," he reported, "when negroes were obstinate and refused to work . . . I have been obliged to resort to the stocks." He found punishments of this type to be generally effective, "not only upon the offenders but upon the others around them." Successful cultivation, Cozzens found, required the "perfect obedience" of hands. Wherever this was lacking, "all attempts at cultivation will prove a failure."[46]

Cozzens' methods served to protect some of the traditional controls over blacks which the war endangered, but the presence of federal troops nevertheless disrupted the plantation system. Some planters abandoned their land and laborers to escape the occupying forces. Slaves throughout the department were quick to make the most of the confusion and flocked to Union-occupied posts and towns. The army's policy toward blacks and plantations was, by and large, practical rather than cynical. Federal officers naturally viewed idle hands and vacant plantations with dismay. Like countless Union officers throughout the South, a commander in Lafourche Parish found thousands of hands "ready to work . . . if properly organized," and large plantations lying in waste.[47] The labor systems set forth by Generals Butler and Banks were designed to supply the needed organization. They were not designed specifically to repress blacks or to profit planters; only to maintain order and restore prosperity.

Had it been possible to do so, federal forces in Louisiana would have avoided collaboration with planters and slaveholders. In the midst of volatile national politics, the safest position was one of impartiality and military aloofness. However, once the decision was made to permit planters to employ their former slaves, a series of restrictive measures became unavoidable. Repression of blacks became essential to maintain the plantation system. Attempts to keep the system without its controls would necessarily end in chaos. "What shall I do?" asked the provost marshal at Donaldsonville concerning blacks who refused to return to their owners. "Are planters to be supported in punishing Negroes upon their plantations?"[48] Under the circumstances, the answer could not be as straightforward. Commanders could not sanction brutality, but they would not permit idleness.

General James S. Wadsworth, who investigated the treatment of Negroes throughout the Mississippi Valley for the War Department in the fall of 1863, found General Banks' restrictions on laborers repugnant. Wadsworth protested to Provost Marshal General Bowen against the policy of forcing hands to remain on plantations. When civil government was restored, Wadsworth argued, slaveholders would be "but half converted, at the best," and blacks would be treated "not as freedmen, but as serfs." It was one thing, of course, to oppose a particular policy and quite another to develop alternative programs. Wadsworth had no program to suggest.[49]

Between the planters' insistence on traditional controls and the army's need for order, there were, in fact, few alternatives. The provost marshal at Kenner, just north of New Orleans, indicated the conditions under which Union officers operated when he felt the need to *defend* himself to his commander against charges from planters that he was too lenient with blacks. "There are not any Negroes lying around," he insisted. Although blacks had applied to him for permission to work for themselves, he had "invariably sent them back to their Plantations."[50]

The actual enforcement of Banks' labor system was never an easy matter and frequently required harsh measures. Frustrated by "indolence and insolence" among laborers, one provost marshal feared that planters would submit to imposition from their hands rather than bring charges against them. Conditions were unstable indeed when a Union officer felt compelled to warn planters that insolence on the part of a few hands "has a very bad effect upon the other laborers."[51] It was hardly a reflection of social stability, moreover, when the provost marshal at St. Charles Parish requested a mounted patrol of at least five men to regulate the labor of blacks.[52]

As planters liked to put it, federal occupation "demoralized" the slaves. Certainly it changed their disposition. Although federal forces in Louisiana sought to substitute antebellum controls with military force, they faced an impossible task. Force alone could not exact "honest and faithful labor" from the black population. The resistance of blacks to continued restriction was widespread in the department and frequently bordered on open rebellion. But the fact that the Union army tried to maintain plantation discipline prevented the wholesale dispossession of whites. The Civil War, as Superintendent Conway observed, worked the financial ruin of many native planters, but it destroyed neither the plantation system nor the continuity of white control.

6

Resistance and Rebellion

★

In the spring of 1863, Union commanders in the South received a series of curious letters from a correspondent in Washington, D. C. On the first of August, the generals were told, blacks throughout the South would launch a systematic rebellion designed to cripple the Confederacy from within and hasten the collapse of slavery. Commanders would do well to assist the insurrectionists by sending trusted contrabands to the interior "with instructions to communicate the plan and the time to as many intelligent slaves as possible." The plot—if it existed—was never carried out. Perhaps it was nothing more than the fantasy of one wistful revolutionary. Southerners, however, reacted with alarm. Confederate President Jefferson Davis received a captured copy of the document and issued "a warning" to his generals in the field. Talk of slave insurrection during the Civil War was a serious matter.[1]

Although the promised uprising did not occur, the incident illustrated the uncertainty with which whites considered the capacities and inclinations of blacks. Neither abolitionists nor slaveholders could effectively analyze the slave personality. Thus, while slaveholders expressed confidence in the docility and faithfulness of their slaves, they took stern measures to suppress potential insurrections. Likewise, the American Freedmen's Inquiry Commission, in its evaluation of the effects of war and emancipation, betrayed an inconsistency charac-

teristic of abolitionist and Radical judgments of the black man's mood.
Blacks were able and willing to bear arms for the Union cause,
reported the commissioners, but their fighting spirit sprang from noble
and entirely commendable yearnings for freedom, not from desires
for revenge. Fears of servile insurrection, therefore, were entirely
unfounded. The commission found the former slave patient, obedient,
and God-fearing; white men would do well to emulate his humility
and Christian forbearance.[2] Nevertheless, Union officials took extraordinary steps during the war to suppress disorders among blacks
and to maintain plantation discipline.[3]

Even in periods of relative sectional harmony, the slave system had
not been placid. Antebellum slaveholders experienced a number of
organized slave rebellions, and it was reasonable to expect that civil
war would increase the dangers of insurrection. Confederates accordingly strengthened and expanded slave patrols, while Unionists
adopted programs to suppress "idleness," "vagrancy," and "crime"
among blacks within their lines. Northern and Southern whites may
well have exaggerated the threat of Negro insurrection, but their fears
were not groundless.[4] The Civil War produced a discernible restlessness among blacks throughout the South, and in areas under Union
control, the freedmen's uneasiness could not be contained wholly
within systems of "free labor." Restlessness produced resistance to
Union controls and at times open rebellion.

Opposition among blacks to federal labor programs emerged most
strikingly in the Department of the Gulf where the contract labor system tied hands to the plantations and enforced their subordination to
local whites. In one respect, it is true, the system benefited laborers.
With all of its restrictions and controls, blacks remained relatively safe
and secure, and the scenes of suffering and death that characterized
contraband conditions in Virginia and the Mississippi Valley were
largely absent in Louisiana. Following the early days of occupation,
seldom more than one thousand contrabands, most of them unfit for
regular employment, required care on government home farms.
Federal labor controls prevented a good deal of dislocation and hardship, but they also produced widespread unrest.

Opposition to the contract labor system appeared first in New
Orleans where an antebellum black population of approximately

10,500 free Negroes and 13,000 slaves swelled during the war to about 30,000 by September 1864.[5] At the outset of Union occupation, the city offered a haven for slaves in the surrounding parishes, and for some time thereafter the status of blacks in New Orleans remained uncertain. Indeed, General Butler found that any move toward emancipation would contribute to the instability of the occupied city. "Accumulated hate has been piled up here between master and servant, until it is fearful," Butler explained, and "a single whistle from me" could bring death to whites throughout the city. In fact, Butler warned, "an insurrection is only prevented by our *Bayonetts*."[6]

II

General Banks continued and expanded Butler's contract labor system, and assumed a frankly conciliatory attitude toward local whites. Shortly after taking command in 1863, Banks ordered all blacks in New Orleans off the streets by eight o'clock in the evening. White citizens, who had complained of pilfering and rowdiness, greeted the curfew warmly.[7] But once the army made it a practice to arrest "vagrant" blacks throughout the city, free Negroes discovered that Yankee soldiers were either not willing or not able to distinguish free men from slaves. One outraged free Negro complained to General Banks that, although federal authorities apparently wanted to return slaves to their owners, "any person may be arrested in the same manner."[8] Literate blacks repeatedly petitioned General Banks for the release of arrested husbands, wives, and children, or for the return of relatives sent to labor on outlying plantations.[9] Despite such protests, restrictions and controls became increasingly systematic. In March 1864 Superintendent Hanks was directed to arrest and employ "all colored persons of either sex who are unemployed, or who have no visible means of support." Although Hanks sought to reassure the "well meaning and industrious Colored Persons" of the city that the object of the order was "one of benevolence and mercy," the intention of the regulations was clear. Whites were directed to issue a "certificate of employment" to servants they found useful and to report "superfluous or insubordinate" blacks to Superintendent Hanks for arrest and re-employment.[10]

When Union forces began enlisting black soldiers in earnest, arbi-

trary arrests increased once more. In July 1863 an officer in charge
of Negro recruitment ordered squads of black enlisted men to "patrol
the city and bring in all able-bodied men of color who have no apparent business." Such a recruitment system, as Superintendent Hanks
complained, encouraged abuses.[11] By April 1864 Superintendent of
Vagrants Thomas W. Conway reported that continued impressment
and arbitrary arrests had created a state of "extreme uneasiness and
excitement" among the city's black population. The often brutal practice of impressment was particularly unsettling. Black men, as Conway pointed out, were willing to die for the government, if necessary,
but deeply resented the abuses they suffered.[12] A group of free
Negroes in Baton Rouge protested that they were "hunted up" in the
streets and "forced into the service" in the same arbitrary manner
as arriving contrabands. "Now we claim to be freemen," they protested. "We were born free, have lived free, and wish to be treated
as freemen." These men were willing to serve the Union cause, but
wished to be drafted in an orderly fashion like whites.[13]

In his own efforts to rid New Orleans of vagrants, Superintendent
Hanks was more careful than most officers to distinguish slaves from
antebellum free blacks. His success in rounding up unemployed members of the former class was attributed in part to the cooperation of
several "discreet colored auxilliaries," which apparently informed the
superintendent of the whereabouts of undesirable vagrants. At the
same time, provost guards received instructions not to arrest free
blacks or Negro servants employed by whites. In any case, persons
who were "well dressed," and had the appearance of being able to
support themselves, were not to be molested. Nevertheless, New
Orleans free blacks were repeatedly victims of impressment and arbitrary arrest. Not surprisingly, they remained hostile to General Banks'
labor policies and provided articulate leadership for the city's Negroes.[14]

The free Negro elite openly opposed Banks' labor regulations and
agitated for the practical emancipation of plantation hands. The federal
labor system seemed to leave the institution of slavery essentially unal-
tered. Official emancipation, the free blacks believed, produced only
"mock-freedmen." Every restriction against freedom of contract and
travel received their condemnation as did the continued existence of

Conway's Bureau of Free Labor, which by March 1865 was denounced as "inconsistent with freedom." A mass meeting of the "Colored Citizens of New Orleans" demanded the creation of a "tribunal of arbitrators," composed partly of freedmen, to review and adjust the actions of provost marshals throughout the department and thus protect black laborers as well as city residents from unjust contracts and arbitrary arrest.[15]

What influence, if any, this articulate protest had on the mass of black laborers in the parishes is difficult to determine. Superintendent Conway, who was the target of some of the protest, thought the New Orleans free blacks excited the "ignorant Freedmen, giving them an idea that they are oppressed," and thus created discontent with the government's regulations.[16] Unrest in the parishes, however, seems to have run considerably deeper than the conventional political protest in the city.

Unlike New Orleans free Negroes, plantation hands were not agitated by the loss of traditional privileges. Federal forces worked to maintain the continuity of plantation life. General Banks' superintendent for confiscated plantations discovered quite early, in fact, that if expected allowances of food, clothing, and tobacco were not forthcoming, there was little hope of inducing hands to labor. Before work could begin, Superintendent Samuel W. Cozzens therefore felt "obliged" to provide hands with the goods, particularly tobacco, which they expected. The superintendent also found it expedient to favor industrious hands with weekly rations of coffee. Successful plantation management required that Yankees be at least as indulgent toward labor as the antebellum masters.[17]

But if plantation hands found themselves no worse off as a result of federal occupation, their condition was generally no better. Superintendent Conway acknowledged that planters tried every means to continue "their old habits regarding the slaves." At the same time, the unsettled conditions resulting from the war made it "next to impossible" to administer effectively "any general system of protection for the laborers." There was, then, little to stop planters from treating their hands as slaves. Conway acknowledged this, but was nonetheless convinced that the evils resulting from the injustice and heartlessness of some employers were not as dangerous as the fate awaiting a population of idle blacks. Better that they labor essentially as slaves than not labor at all.[18]

Although Conway's control over planters was far from absolute, he assumed that hands were generally content and "socially, and morally" improved. Most planters, he thought, followed the regulations, and he expected laborers to end the season with average savings of fifty dollars. But if hands actually enjoyed such earnings, Conway made no mention of it in his later reports. Rather, what Conway described as "average" earnings represented a theoretical maximum. He was well aware that the wages stipulated in Banks' orders struck outsiders as pitifully low, and in an effort to dampen criticism in the North, he suggested that blacks could earn profits, in addition to their wages, from crops grown on their one-acre plots. "First-class hands receive one acre of ground," announced Conway, "which will produce one bale of cotton, worth at present more than $400. There are many who will derive this addition to their stipulated pay."[19]

This pleasant description of affairs was entirely disingenuous. The one-acre plots assigned to heads of families were specifically designed as vegetable gardens; some blacks had been strictly prohibited from raising anything else. The fact was that the very best a first-class male hand could earn under Banks' system in 1864 was five dollars per month after authorized deductions were made for clothing. If the man had only himself to support, consumed nothing (like soap and tobacco) on credit, and lost no more than two months due to sickness, bad weather, and slack seasons, he might end the year with fifty dollars. It seems more likely, however, that the mass of blacks fared no better than those near Brashear City who remained perpetually in debt to their former masters once deductions were made for time lost and goods purchased on credit.[20]

Wages were largely illusory, but for blacks the continuity of social controls, rather than the absence of pay, was perhaps the best measure of the white man's intentions. General Banks' labor regulations virtually prohibited individual travel without written permission from a white employer or provost marshal. Unauthorized movement in cities or parishes was considered vagrancy, and offenders were subject to arrest and forced labor. The justifications for such restrictions, of course, were never stated in antebellum terms (the danger of com-

municable diseases, many officers said, made such controls necessary), and enforcement was not absolute.[21]

But large-scale movements as well as mass meetings of blacks were
strictly controlled. When blacks at Donaldsonville advanced plans for
celebrating the Fourth of July in 1864 together with neighboring plantation hands, their efforts were promptly halted by Superintendent
Hanks. "The colored population can take part in the celebration of
the 4th of July," he directed, "but in no extraordinary numbers."
In any case, plantation hands were not to enter the city.[22] Likewise,
although the black residents of Thibodaux were allowed to hold a New
Year's Eve ball, their revelries were strictly regulated. A provost
guard was assigned to "enforce order and protect the colored people
in their enjoyments," and the festivities abruptly ended at midnight
at the soldiers' direction.[23]

Most provost marshals shared local prejudices against blacks and
enforced standards of racial subordination. Time and again the provost
marshal in Ascension Parish heard and sustained charges against
blacks who, by any objective standard, were guilty only of self-
defense. In one case, the Union officer sentenced a female plantation
hand to thirty days in prison for "insolence and disobedience of
orders." The woman had offended her mistress by refusing to accept
a weekly ration of meat, claiming it was not sufficient. The planter
and his overseer later entered the woman's cabin, disarmed her of
a knife, and while restraining her husband at gun point, administered,
by the planter's own account, about forty or fifty blows with a stick.
"This woman," the planter charged before the provost marshal,
"cursed us all the time, using very insolent language."[24]

Not only did provost marshals work closely with planters to enforce
General Banks' labor regulations, they also supported native whites
and civil police in the punishment of unruly hands. Resistance to the
authority of Southern whites therefore required resistance to the Northern army as well. In St. James Parish, for example, the provost
marshal authorized a local sheriff to arrest two plantation hands for
insulting their master. When the arrests were made, a hand called
"Jasmin" demanded the release of the prisoners. The sheriff
threatened to shoot anyone who interfered, but Jasmin drew a pistol
of his own and swore to shoot back. The sheriff withdrew empty-

handed, but the provost marshal later arrested all three offenders and sentenced Jasmin to thirty days in jail.[25]

In exceptional cases, when Union authority was also challenged, federal forces acted to protect blacks by punishing offending whites. But, for the most part, federal authorities intervened only to enforce obedience and discipline among blacks. Moreover, with the adoption of the Louisiana free state constitution early in September 1864, blacks had to rely on the civil courts for justice. Superintendent Conway shared General Banks' conviction that this development insured equal justice for blacks. "With the new Constitution as their foundation," he exulted, "they can demand protection and justice in any court in the Department." Blacks could testify and bring suit like any white man, and Conway thought the need for federal protection in judicial matters had thereby ended.[26]

III

The continuity of treatment and conditions which blacks experienced after the official demise of slavery produced widespread frustration, protest, and rebellion. The contradiction between theoretical freedom and practical slavery was felt most powerfully by black soldiers. As elsewhere in the South under federal occupation, able-bodied black men in Louisiana were impressed into the army. As elsewhere, this arbitrary measure produced opposition and resentment. But unlike black soldiers in other areas of federal occupation, those in Louisiana contributed directly to conditions of unrest on the plantations.

Despite the belief of Northern emancipationists that Negro recruitment involved a tacit recognition of the freedman's manhood, black soldiers were seldom treated differently from laborers on plantations. The problem, from the point of view of federal officers, was to achieve a balanced, and total, use of manpower. The individual needs and aspirations of black men found no place in such calculations. When impressment threatened the plantation labor supply, for example, General Banks intervened and ordered a number of men who had been "arrested . . . for the Corps d'Afrique" released and returned to employers.[27] Recruitment continued, although presumably with greater concern for the planters' needs for labor. One recruiter was told that orders against "impressment" should not be regarded as absolute, although violent and rude measures should be avoided, and that the number of hands taken from plantations should be carefully tallied to distribute the burden of conscription equitably among the planters. The recruiter was ordered to St. Bernard Parish to procure "forthwith" one hundred "able bodied volunteers."[28]

The need for laborers and soldiers, as well as the fear of disorders, insured a continuous and thorough search for idle blacks. Negroes arrested by provost marshals for minor offenses were surrendered to recruiters on demand. When General Banks learned that some twelve thousand black men were thought to be hiding in swamps behind Algiers, Kenner, Carrollton, and New Orleans, he ordered a sweep of the areas by federal troops and the enlistment of all captured blacks.[29]

It could be argued that military discipline held white men as well as black in involuntary servitude. However, General Banks never allowed this sort of equality to obscure his very practical purposes. To distinguish black regiments from white fighting men, Banks reversed Butler's policy of commissioning free Negroes as officers. Black soldiers as well as black laborers were held subordinate to whites, and were, of course, prohibited from leaving their camps except with passes or in the company of officers. The men were prevented from visiting their families on plantations or in the cities, and but few passes were issued to relatives wishing to visit soldiers.[30]

Banks, always apologetic about the existence of Negro troops, used them significantly in battle only once—during the battle for Port Hudson in May 1863. On this occasion, the black soldiers distinguished themselves, and Banks himself attributed the final success of the campaign in large measure to their efforts. But with this exception, black troops in Louisiana were confined to labor details and garrison duty.[31] In part Banks restricted the activity of black troops because the hostility of white soldiers seemed to require it. But the fear of black insurrection, led by black soldiers, was always close to the surface. Although Northern emancipationists insisted that black soldiers would submit to the laws of civilized warfare, unsettled conditions in the Department of the Gulf kept whites uneasy.

General Butler had earlier betrayed his nervousness on insurrection, although he professed to believe that properly organized Negro regiments were the best protection against it. If blacks were armed and given officers of their own race, Butler claimed, there was little chance of revolt. "Do you suppose," he asked, "if the French General at St. Domingo had given Toussaint a captaincy, there would have been any trouble?" Butler therefore commissioned as officers in his Corps d'Afrique mulattoes who had led the New Orleans free Negro militia before the war. They were well qualified, Butler thought, and in every way gentlemen. But he remained skeptical of their worth in combat. Why, he asked one of these officers, "if you are really in earnest, and willing to fight for your rights, why have you not risen, and, aided by the United States, got your liberty?" With considerable hesitation the officer responded: "To which of the commanders of the United States army should we apply for assistance, in case we make an insurrection?"[32]

The exchange struck Butler as humorous once he left Louisiana, but both his question and the officer's response reflected a mutual distrust and even hostility. If Negroes would indeed make good soldiers, Butler had asked in essence, why did they not fight their oppressors? Butler's successor was even more distrustful of black troops. General Banks quickly rid the Corps d'Afrique of its Negro officers, replacing them with poorly qualified whites.[33] Butler's query seemed to have another meaning for Banks. Negro soldiers, as Banks discovered at Port Hudson, would indeed fight. What, then, would prevent them from leading an insurrection? In any case, the federal army stood as a bulwark against servile rebellion.

Banks gave a hint of the type of response he was prepared to make in the case of insurrection during a brief mutiny of black troops at Fort Jackson. The rebellion occurred primarily because Banks had permitted his subordinates to transfer their most incompetent officers to the black regiments. Banks himself admitted that the men commanding black troops were generally poor officers. As a result, soldiers were often brutally treated and, at Fort Jackson, were provoked to rebellion.[34]

Stationed at Fort Jackson, the 4th Regiment, Corps d'Afrique, was commanded by Colonel Charles R. Drew, a man quick to strike his black soldiers for minor offenses. The regiment's lieutenant colonel, Augustus C. Benedict, was even more harsh and less tactful. On

December 9, 1863, Benedict publicly whipped a soldier for a minor infraction. Colonel Drew witnessed the episode but chose to say nothing. Within minutes at least half of the garrison of black troops were firing their weapons in the air and threatening to settle the matter with Benedict once and for all. Through persuasion and, doubtless, threats, Colonel Drew managed to quiet the enraged troops; by evening the fort was once more calm and orderly.[35]

The mutiny, as it developed, was hardly a major threat to the security of the department. But reports of the rebellion created panic among officers in New Orleans. Banks' chief of staff, Brigadier General Charles P. Stone (who thought Negro troops worthless and who was responsible for their continual assignment to fatigue duties) ordered the provost marshal general to place his guard under arms and to increase patrols of New Orleans that night. "There is a serious revolt among the colored troops," Stone informed General Bowen. "Give no reasons to *anyone* for your additional patrols."[36] Banks himself was quite alarmed. As he explained later, it was impossible to get accurate information during the night. But if the blacks were earnestly in rebellion, the commander was prepared to crush them. A regiment of white troops moved to the vicinity of the fort during the evening and a battery of artillery arrived in position the next morning. In addition, Banks requested gunboats from the navy. Nothing happened that night, Banks later reported, to "impair . . . confidence in the efficiency and reliability of black troops." But at the time, the commander displayed very little confidence indeed.[37]

The Fort Jackson mutiny made two things clear: the treatment of black soldiers in the department was often extremely brutal, and commanding officers had some reason to fear Negro insurrection. The experience of the mutiny changed nothing, however. Lieutenant Colonel Benedict was arrested, but Colonel Drew, who was equally responsible, was promoted to command the 76th U.S. Colored Troops, which included the old 4th Regiment, Corps d'Afrique.[38] Negro troops remained restless, and their uneasiness was not confined to Fort Jackson.

Black soldiers were agitated not only by the treatment they received from federal officers, but by the misuse of their wives and families, who were either held by contract on plantations or left vulnerable to arrest as vagrants. Well before the trouble at Fort Jackson, Colonel Drew reported that many of the men in his regiment were anxious for the safety of their wives and children. Nearly every day the wife of some soldier in Drew's regiment was "spirited away" from New Orleans and sent to labor on a plantation.[39] Similarly, a company commander complained to the provost marshal in Brashear City about the treatment of the wife of one of his men. While employed on a plantation leased by Captain Cozzens, the woman fell sick, and the manager refused to furnish her with rations or medicine. "The woman has been for weeks subsisting upon what she could beg from others," an investigator reported; but no action on the matter was recorded.[40]

The army's paramount concern was to maintain order and prevent vagrancy. Mistreatment of blacks did not seem a pressing issue, and it stimulated little action. Faced with official intransigence and hostility, black soldiers began liberating their families with the timely assistance of a few whites. On one occasion, a squad of black soldiers, accompanied by a Connecticut private, removed fourteen hands from a plantation in St. Charles Parish, placing them on a government farm near Camp Parapet. The provost marshal, who wanted the blacks returned to the plantations, reported that such incidents were altogether too frequent.[41]

In St. Barnard Parish, a number of black soldiers carrying passes as "recruiters" went from plantation to plantation removing carts and animals, as well as women and children, and threatening whites who interfered. "A band of negroes thus assembled to the number of seventy five," reported the provost marshal. They went "singing, shouting and marauding through the Parish disturbing the peace." The next day another group of black soldiers appeared at the home of a planter, loaded their muskets, and "demanded some colored women whom they called their wives."[42] Four black "recruiters" were arrested in Plaquemines Parish after they had stopped work on several plantations, "placing guards over the owners and threatening to shoot any damned white man who interfered."[43]

Such attempts at liberation were only temporarily effective. The army permitted no alternative to plantation labor for the mass of blacks. Moreover, while service in the army contributed to the black man's sense of dignity and his impatience with continued restrictions, the organization of blacks as troops placed controls over them which served to prevent widespread upheaval. Unrest among black troops found release in isolated incidents, but powerful forces held them in check. Outraged at his treatment by white officers, one black soldier warned that a man could not serve two masters. Both the Rebel master and the Union master, he thought, wanted the black man's services: the one to grow his crops, the other to fight his battles. "Black soldiers and white officers," he promised, "will not play togeather [*sic*] much longer."[44] But the power of white officers remained firm, and under the circumstances, the army proved a more effective agency of control than the traditional plantation system.

IV

As their hostility to white officers indicated, blacks measured their freedom not in abstract terms of slavery and emancipation, but by their independence from white domination. Although isolated on their plantations, laborers experienced the same sense of unrest that affected Negro troops. Slavery was never a tranquil institution, but Union occupation brought a noticeable increase in the unruliness of blacks in Louisiana. Stealing became widespread, and whites sought protection against Negro vagrants, laborers, and soldiers alike. Loyal citizens in Jefferson Parish, living near Camp Parapet, complained of harassment from black soldiers. A group of whites captured two offenders digging potatoes one evening, but found themselves quickly threatened by a party of twenty-five black soldiers approaching with fixed bayonets and threatening to fire if the prisoners were not released. White soldiers were thereafter detailed to protect the residents. The department quartermaster was similarly troubled by a "gang" of thirty vagrant blacks in the same area who habitually made off with government cattle and sheep. The mayor and city council of nearby Carrollton appealed to the provost marshal for protection from marauders whose nightly "depredations," they claimed, continued to grow in "boldness and audacity."[45] Whether vagrant, soldier, or field hand, blacks sensed the increased vulnerability of whites and acted accordingly.

Black soldiers, visiting plantations and defying white authority, provided one source of disruption and disorder.[46] More frequently, idleness and thievery increased to the point of chaos. Superintendent Conway was willing to give "due allowance" to the ignorance of the blacks and the effects of the "diabolical system from which they have emerged." But when disorders became serious, even rebellious, he felt compelled to put the blame in some cases squarely on the Negroes. "There are often times serious troubles," he admitted, "growing out of the perversity and wickedness of some of the Freedmen themselves." He found them frequently "insubordinate, vicious, and obstinate in their disposition to do wrong." In the face of such rebelliousness, the enforcement of General Banks' orders was no easy matter.[47]

The most frequent act of rebellion was simply refusal to work. When there were but a few hands involved, the disrupters were promptly arrested by the provost marshal and forced to work either on home farms or public works. Superintendent Hanks received a number of hands from Jefferson Parish who had refused to work and had caused "a good deal of trouble" by defying all authority. The provost marshal was anxious to be rid of the troublemakers, and directed his soldiers to take whatever action seemed necessary to protect the families of planters, restore order, and gather the season's crops.[48]

Occasionally, striking hands voiced specific grievances. Thus, laborers on a St. Bernard Parish plantation, led by a "preacher" who was employed on the place as a blacksmith, refused to continue to work and demanded their full pay as well as passes to go to New Orleans when they wished. By the time the provost marshal heard of the affair, the blacks were on the road to the city. He arrested the lot, but found them unalterably opposed to returning to work.[49] Hands on a plantation near Carrollton were no less adamant. They refused to continue to work, and, backing up their arguments with arms, demanded free papers from their master. The planter managed to escape from the place, and returned shortly with the civil police and a detachment of provost guards. The blacks were rapidly disarmed, and, with the protection of Union troops, the planter was able to flog several of the leaders.[50]

Provost marshals were quick to aid embattled planters, but the threat of punishment no longer had the desired effect on unruly hands. A planter near New Orleans reported that, despite the presence of a provost guard, almost half of his labor force steadfastly refused to work. The men, in this case, would no longer allow their wives to labor in the field. The army guard proved ineffectual, and at one point was seized by the hands who "disarmed him and handled him rudely."[51]

Where order dissolved, whites and blacks grew increasingly violent. One overseer, attempting to maintain discipline, suddenly found himself threatened by a number of his hands. "Some of them," he wrote the provost marshal, "wish to hang me other wished [*sic*] to cut me to pieces." The rebels left the plantation without doing harm, but returned several weeks later demanding passes permitting them to travel. The overseer refused, ordered them off the place, and threatened to shoot any who remained. The blacks had weapons of their own, however, and a gun battle ensued. The overseer fired several shotgun blasts at quivering corn stalks and dodged several returning volleys, but apparently no one was injured.[52]

V

The intensity and purpose of rebelliousness varied greatly from plantation to plantation. In some cases, unrest developed from a limited reaction to specific injustices; in other cases, blacks revolted against all forms of white authority. On a Plaquemines Parish plantation, where hands rebelled against their overseer late in April 1864, discontent could be traced to specific causes. Hands from the same plantation complained to the provost marshal in nearby Jefferson Parish that they had never received their share of the previous season's crops. The provost marshal was sympathetic but was unable to accomplish anything for them. He ended his efforts by referring the matter to his superior, hoping that justice might be done, "as I found them a most obedient and faithful set."

However, nothing was done, and, with little hope of receiving anything for their labor during the current season, the hands refused to work. The provost marshal for Plaquemines Parish, who said the hands "could not—or would not" give any reason for their action, immediately sent a civil police officer to restore order. But when the policeman attempted to arrest several blacks he considered ringleaders, "he was beset upon by at least twenty—with hoes, shovels and hatchets," and shortly felt "obliged to leave." The provost marshal himself then visited the place and found it in a "riotous and subordinate state," although after threatening harsh punishment, he succeeded in restoring order.[53] Had these laborers been justly treated from the start, their rebellion might have been avoided. But in other cases, rebellions were general, having as their purpose not the righting of particular wrongs, but the destruction of white authority.

With the advance of federal troops along the Bayou Teche early in 1863, plantation hands deserted in droves to federal lines. Some attached themselves to the Union troops, but others reportedly banded together, "resolved upon taking the lives of their Masters and their families and appropriating and destroying property as their impulse may lead."[54] Where they were present, federal troops assisted in restoring order. Thus, a company of Massachusetts troops garrisoned the town of St. Martinsville in April 1863 to protect its residents from a mounted band of blacks. When the insurrectionists showed themselves near the town, local whites joined with the New England soldiers to attack them. In the ensuing battle, two or three of the blacks were killed and several others wounded. Their leader, a creole named Theodule Melancon, was taken into custody by the federal soldiers, but five of his black followers were left to the mercy of the townspeople. All were promptly hanged from a nearby bridge as a grim warning to potentially rebellious blacks.

The insurrection near St. Martinsville had reportedly been organized by Melancon and some "straggling soldiers" (evidently deserters from black regiments) "for the purpose of pillaging the country, killing the men, and children, and ravishing the women." Similar outbreaks were reported elsewhere in the area. The frightened white population along the Teche was willing to take the federal oath of allegiance, "or do almost anything if they can be protected." Whenever possible, federal forces were willing to offer such protection.[55]

Despite overt repression, however, Union occupation stimulated rather than deterred black uprisings, even in areas where federal control was well organized. Hands on a St. Barnard Parish plantation, for example, armed themselves with lead-headed clubs, drove off the overseers, proclaimed themselves self-governing, and elected two "colonels" to lead them. Similarly, hands on two estates in adjoining

Plaquemines Parish armed themselves with clubs and cane knives to drive off their white employers and overseers. On all three places, provost guards quickly restored order, although some of the rebels escaped to the woods. In each case, guards remained on the plantations to prevent further uprisings.[56]

Runaway slaves and plantation disorders were by no means foreign to the antebellum South, but they became almost commonplace in Louisiana during the Civil War. The threat of Negro insurrection was real, and it was a measure of the success of federal labor policies that these scattered rebellions were contained. For blacks, who sought on all levels to rid themselves of antebellum controls and white authority, the repressive role of the federal government was bitterly effective. Neither General Butler nor General Banks could completely maintain antebellum standards of organization and control. It was well within their power, however, to prevent blacks from dispossessing white planters.

PART III

THE MISSISSIPPI VALLEY

7

Mobilization for War

★

1

On Independence Day 1863, the Confederate garrison at Vicksburg surrendered to Union forces and the entire Mississippi Valley, with a black population estimated to exceed 700,000, fell to Northern control. By the summer of 1863, the federal government had settled on a policy toward Southern blacks. Labor programs already underway at Hampton Roads, Port Royal, and New Orleans revealed the developing logic of Northern war aims. John Brown's army would not revolutionize the South. But as the North's war aims widened to include the mobilization of freedmen, the institution of slavery necessarily collapsed. In the Mississippi Valley after the siege of Vicksburg, blacks no longer seemed simply an embarrassment or an encumbrance to Northern troops. Union officers actively collected, organized, and employed contrabands in a manner designed to strengthen the Union cause with both men and money. Army officers from Memphis to Natchez enlisted or impressed able-bodied black men as soldiers. And, with General Banks' contract labor system as a foundation, federal authorities in the Mississippi Valley mobilized cotton lands and contrabands to serve the Union war effort. Under Yankee control, Southern plantations and Southern blacks swelled Northern coffers and hastened the collapse of the Confederacy.

The mobilization of land and labor in the Mississippi Valley came not out of moral concern for the freedmen, but as a matter of military

119

necessity. Before the siege of Vicksburg, the administration of contraband affairs in the Mississippi Valley had developed according to
a familiar pattern. During 1862, as Northern armies drove through
Confederate defenses on the Tennessee and Mississippi rivers and
occupied portions of western Tennessee, Arkansas, and northern Mississippi, thousands of contrabands had escaped to Union lines. General
H. W. Halleck vainly directed western commanders to exclude
unnecessary blacks, but as a practical matter it soon became impossible to ignore or reject the flood of fugitive slaves. When, in September
1862, the preliminary Emancipation Proclamation promised freedom
to blacks throughout Mississippi and northern Louisiana, some form
of care and organization of contrabands seemed necessary. In
November, General U. S. Grant appointed Chaplain John Eaton, of
the 27th Ohio Volunteers, superintendent of contrabands for the Mississippi Valley.

As Grant pressed his operations against Vicksburg in the spring of
1863, and as the area under Union control expanded, the problem
of providing for contrabands grew increasingly complex. Every excur-
sion and raid into the interior produced more fugitives, and the movement of Union troops made it difficult for the army to protect and
support large numbers of freedmen. Few contrabands could be effectively employed by the army. The commanders, despairing under the
growing burden, looked elsewhere for means of supporting surplus
blacks. General Stephen A. Hurlbut at Memphis reported that conditions in that city were beyond his control. He was charged, he wrote
President Lincoln in March, with the subsistence of about 5,000 contrabands, mostly women and children. He issued them government
rations on his own authority, although they were in addition to the
Negroes actually employed by his forces and therefore "a weight and
incumbrance." More distressing was the large number of blacks
(Hurlbut estimated them to exceed 2,000 in Memphis alone) who
existed wholly outside military control. Living without government
support, they "crowded into all vacant sheds" and lived "by begging
or vice." In the general's view they could look forward to nothing
but "disease and death." Hurlbut noted that there were several nearby
farms and plantations whose owners required only sufficient labor to
become prosperous once more. The season was right, the owners will-

ing, and a supply of labor available, the general despaired, but he lacked the authority "to bring them together."[1]

Conditions in the contraband camps everywhere along the Mississippi River were shocking and none who visited them could doubt the wisdom of Hurlbut's suggestion to remove the blacks to plantations. Maria R. Mann, niece of the educator Horace Mann, labored among contrabands at Helena, Arkansas, and looked favorably on any scheme to settle the blacks on plantations. "Anything," she thought, was better than the idleness and squalor that characterized the camps. The physical condition of the contrabands, if nothing else, demanded immediate attention. Within one month at Helena more than half of the blacks died, although their places were quickly filled by arriving fugitives.

While treating sick and dying contrabands in the Sanitary Commission Hospital at Helena, Maria Mann witnessed terrifying scenes of suffering and death. Countless contrabands who had lived for months exposed to the elements without proper food or clothing came to the hospital covered with swellings and open sores. Diarrhea consumed scores of feeble blacks, and all were "eaten up with vermin." The dead were too numerous for Christian burial, and corpses were piled into carts together with the carcasses of army horses and mules for burial in common pits. The horrors of camp life demoralized the blacks, Miss Mann reported. Some died, others returned to their masters, but worst of all, thought Miss Mann, the women were frequently reduced to prostitution by the want of food and clothing. Maria Mann welcomed the opportunity to turn her back on "this Sodom" and settle the blacks on abandoned plantations.[2]

Superintendent Eaton was hardly pleased with the conditions in the contraband camps under his supervision, and he too encouraged the return of blacks to the land. Eaton agreed with General Hurlbut that loyal planters still in possession of their land should be allowed to hire Negroes under contracts enforced by the government, but he also hoped that the government would establish model plantations within which "capable" blacks would be allowed to farm small plots independently. Eaton submitted his ideas to Secretary of War Stanton in March 1863, but received no reply.[3] Although his ideas lacked official sanction, Eaton hoped to launch his agricultural program with private means. The government's failure to act on the matter was lamentable, Eaton wrote the abolitionist Levi Coffin, but "we need not falter at their fault." If the federal government would not lead the way, the field was nonetheless open to "friends of the cause." "We shall look for implements and seeds at once," Eaton wrote Coffin hopefully.[4]

II

While Superintendent Eaton made private plans, military needs encouraged the federal government to act officially. Several days after the Emancipation Proclamation went into effect on January 1, 1863, President Lincoln met with Secretary Stanton and Secretary of the Navy Gideon Welles to discuss the organization of blacks in the Mississippi Valley. The president was now anxious to raise black troops, although he expressed concern that freedmen caught bearing arms might be executed by the Confederates. Lincoln therefore suggested that Stanton organize black soldiers to garrison posts along the river where they were not likely to fall into Rebel hands. The president urged both secretaries, moreover, to develop plans for the profitable employment of all contrabands.[5] Late in March, Secretary Stanton directed his adjutant general, Lorenzo Thomas, to visit the Mississippi Valley and adopt a program enabling blacks "to support themselves," and "to furnish useful service" to the Union cause as soldiers and laborers.[6] General Thomas embarked upon his task with bureaucratic vigor and soon outlined a program designed to restore the prosperity of the plantation economy, protect the Mississippi River from guerrillas, and return the freedmen to the land as wage laborers.

"In the last few days," Thomas wrote Stanton from Cairo, Illinois, on April 11, 1863, "I have thought much of the best manner in which to take charge of, and usefully employ, these descendants of Ham, for their own good and for the benefit of the government." It would not do, he thought, to collect them in large camps, as was then the practice, employing those needed and sustaining the rest on government rations. Nor should the government seek to move them to the free or border states. In the free states, blacks would arouse the hatred of native whites, and in border areas they would be liable to kidnapping and re-enslavement to the benefit of the Confederacy. General Thomas, looking toward their ultimate colonization outside the United States, concluded that for the time being they must remain in the South, behind government lines and be "put in positions to make their own living." The army should employ all able-bodied men as laborers and teamsters or conscript them as soldiers. Those unfit for service, along with the women and children, should be placed on abandoned plantations "to till the ground."[7]

Such a program, Thomas thought, would add considerably to the Union's military effort. Negro regiments could protect the plantations and perform garrison duties, thereby freeing white troops for field service. More significantly, black soldiers could operate effectively against Confederate guerrillas, particularly, thought Thomas, along the Mississippi, "as the Negroes, being acquainted with the peculiar country lining its banks, would know where to act effectively." Thus, the contraband problem would be solved and the North strengthened militarily at the same time.

Thomas worked out the details of his plan with General Grant. Since the west bank of the Mississippi protected the Union's line of supply from Memphis to Grant's base at Providence, Louisiana, above Vicksburg, the two generals decided to settle the west bank as much as possible with a loyal population. To begin with, contraband laborers and captured supplies would be transferred to the west bank to strengthen loyal planters, "thereby weakening the enemy" on both sides of the river.

As Grant launched his Vicksburg campaign, contrabands in the Mississippi Valley became a part of the Union's military strategy. On April 10, 1863, at Milliken's Bend, Louisiana, above Vicksburg, General Thomas, with the authority of Secretary Stanton, put his agricultural plan into effect. The task of securing a loyal population along the Mississippi's west bank went to three commissioners, who were appointed to superintend the leasing of abandoned and confiscated plantations to persons of "proper" character and qualification. The commissioners would also enforce the "mutual obligations" between employer and employee. Lessees, in turn, could draw what labor they required from the army contraband camps, posting bond with the commissioners for their employment and good treatment until February 1, 1864, at which time contracts would be renegotiated. If the commissioners were unable to locate sufficient lessees of proper character and qualification, they were directed to appoint superintendents who would direct the labor of the blacks on government-operated farms. In any case, self-sufficiency and total employment was the goal, and superintendents were cautioned to keep contrabands from becoming burdens upon the government.

At the same time, Thomas established a scale of wages for freedmen employed on leased estates. Males over fifteen years old were to receive $7.00 a month, while females of the same age would receive $5.00. Children between twelve and fifteen were scheduled to receive half the wage assigned to adults of their sex (that is, $3.50 for boys, $2.50 for girls). Children under twelve, by Thomas' orders, would not be employed in the field.[8]

The success of Grant's operations against Vicksburg opened an even wider field to Thomas' program. Hundreds of plantations and thousands of black laborers came under Union control. Superintendent Eaton visited Grant during the siege of Vicksburg in June and reported that about 8,000 contrabands required immediate care.[9] With the fall of Vicksburg and the subsequent capture of Natchez, a vast number of blacks fell into Union hands. Thousands collected at various points along the river seeking federal protection; by November they were said to number about 20,000.[10]

In August, Grant ordered the extension of Thomas' agricultural plan to the Vicksburg and Natchez districts. He instructed the provost marshal at each military post to see that all blacks were "employed by some white person," or sent to the camps provided for contrabands. Thomas arrived in Vicksburg a few days later to raise Negro troops, but he also proposed measures for women, children, the aged, and the infirm. He considered it "expedient" that all such persons remain on the plantations where they formerly had been slaves, provided such places were within Union lines. Future lessees of abandoned property, moreover, would be "permitted to employ these females and children in any capacity most suited to their ability."[11]

The fall of Vicksburg increased President Lincoln's interest in the general mobilization of blacks. He was anxious, he told Secretary Stanton, that a "renewed and vigorous effort be made to raise colored forces along the shores of the Mississippi." Lorenzo Thomas, Lincoln thought, was doing a fine job. "The evidence is nearly conclusive," he told Stanton, "that Gen. Thomas is one of the best, if not the very best, instrument for this service."[12] Stanton, however, found Thomas personally detestable and had sent the aging general west in part to get him out of the War Department. Stanton, then, had reason to distrust Thomas' contraband program, but he did nothing to weaken the adjutant general's authority in matters relating to freedmen. Aware of Lincoln's interest in the total employment of blacks, and evidently pleased to have Thomas out of Washington, Stanton left the contrabands to the care of his adjutant general.[13]

Aware of the latitude allowed him in matters relating to blacks, and anxious to restore idle cotton lands to productivity, General Thomas took steps to return blacks unfit for military service to the plantations as laborers. The contraband camps, he reminded Superintendent Eaton in October, were only for temporary use and should serve as depots supplying labor to the army and the plantations, not as permanent black settlements. "With this object in view," Thomas ordered the superintendents of all such camps to furnish the hands, "male, female, and children," that were called for by loyal planters and Northern lessees.[14]

To ensure that the contraband camps facilitated both the recruitment of black troops and the cultivation of plantations, General Thomas shortly organized two special regiments of "Louisiana Volunteers," composed of blacks considered unfit for field service but capable of garrison duty. Thomas acknowledged Superintendent Eaton's responsibility for the "general guardianship" of the entire contraband population and appointed the former chaplain as colonel of the first of these special regiments. Colonel Eaton thereafter registered arriving blacks and supplied the necessary plantation labor. Eaton's former assistant, Samuel Thomas, became colonel of the second special regiment and assumed responsibility for the Vicksburg and Natchez districts. The several contraband camp superintendents became officers in the new regiments and henceforward acted as agents for the freedmen, negotiating all contracts between employer and employee. Eaton and Samuel Thomas continued to administer the contraband camps, which were to be maintained as long as points of collection and distribution seemed necessary. In addition, Eaton received authority from General Thomas to occupy certain plantations to be worked by the "infirm, vagrant or idle,'' in the manner of the "home farms" in Louisiana. Under the new plan of organization, then, blacks would be collected at contraband camps from Memphis to Natchez to be employed by the army, private planters, or on Eaton's home farms.[15]

Vulnerable to guerrilla attacks, the Mississippi Valley in 1863 was a dangerous place for Northern men to settle as loyal producers of cotton. To encourage Northern lessees, General Thomas' leasing program purposely offered an attractive opportunity to daring speculators. One lessee calculated the cost of growing cotton under wartime conditions at eight cents a pound. Since he expected that the crop could be sold on an inflated market at fifty cents a pound, the prospects for realizing a large return on the funds invested were, he admitted, "alluring in the extreme."[16] General Thomas' labor system was attractive to the lessees, but it soon drew criticism from a variety of sources.

III

Army men and civilian missionaries who claimed to be concerned about the freedman's welfare were particularly critical of Thomas' failure to adequately protect blacks from oppressive employers. It soon became apparent, for example, that Thomas' choice of commissioners for leased plantations left something to be desired. The original three appointees—George B. Field, Lark S. Livermore, and Abraham E. Strickle—were apparently honest, capable men. Of the three, however, only Field continued at his post for any length of time. Strickle, a former captain in the Commissary and Subsistence Department at Cincinnati, contracted typhoid fever at Vicksburg and died early in March. Livermore, chaplain with the 16th Wisconsin Volunteers, returned to his former duties under John Eaton as superintendent of contrabands at Providence, Louisiana. General Thomas hastily appointed two replacements, both of whom were lessees. Only Commissioner Field, apparently a civilian, was not financially involved in the plantation system, although one critic insisted that he had relatives who were lessees "and next year he intends going into it largely himself."[17]

If the principles of the leasing commissioners were questioned, those of the majority of lessees were generally damned. A lessee in the Natchez area described his colleagues as "unprincipled men" who undertook the enterprise solely for speculative profit. They were as brutal with their laborers as the worst slaveholders, he thought, and it was common practice to swindle the freedmen of their wages. One enterprising lessee who obtained a profit of eighty thousand dollars "never paid his negroes a penny."[18]

Representatives of freedmen aid societies were also shocked to discover what sort of men employed the former slaves. Samuel R. Shipley, representing the Friends' Association of Philadelphia, visited the Mississippi Valley during the fall of 1863. He noted unhappily that lessees often were dishonest and that in some cases they were local whites who had been overseers before the war.[19] James E. Yeatman of the Western Sanitary Commission (which extended its efforts to contraband relief after the fall of Vicksburg) concluded that most of the lessees were "only adventurers, camp followers, and 'army sharks.' " Their only interest, thought Yeatman, was in profit, and they cared little whether they made it "out of the blood of those they employed or from the soil."[20]

The promise of wages proved to be the cruelest deception for the contrabands. The scale set by General Thomas struck Shipley as unreasonably low for the type of field labor required. With cotton prices what they were, he thought the lessees could afford wages approaching thirty-five dollars a month, five times the sum stipulated by Thomas.[21] Low as the scale was, hands who were not simply defrauded rarely received the full rate. For one thing, as Yeatman discovered, two dollars a head was generally deducted for yearly medical attendance which, he found, was never given. The cost of clothing, as authorized by General Thomas's orders, was deducted from the workers' pay. Moreover, Yeatman claimed that hands were paid, not by the month, but by the number of days actually worked. Thus, excluding Sundays, the daily wage for a man was roughly twenty-seven cents. If the planter furnished but ten days of work in a month, the hand could earn only $2.70. And, since General Thomas' orders did not state otherwise, hands received no pay until the end of the season at which time deductions for food, clothing, and sick time were made. With such a system, it was not difficult for lessees to avoid the payment of wages altogether.[22]

Criticism of General Thomas' system came from army men as well. General David Hunter, whose efforts to raise black troops at Port Royal in 1862 marked him as a Radical, offered a stinging indictment of the leasing system and of government policy toward blacks generally. From the time that General Halleck had been permitted, "unrebuked," to exclude blacks from federal lines, "the whole course of the Government has been one of iniquity toward the negro." Hunter thought that the leasing system was the latest in a long series of injustices. Not only were two of the leasing commissioners lessees, Hunter charged, but they were also the "meanest sort" of Rebels, entirely proslavery in inclination and altogether unfit to administer Negro affairs. As the result of government policies, blacks were forced to work for little more than subsistence while lessees enjoyed enormous profits.[23]

Rear Admiral David D. Porter, commander of the Mississippi Squadron, likewise saw the lessees as "greedy adventurers" interested simply in raising a single profitable crop. They therefore treated their hands brutally and "chastise[d] them worse than their former masters did." To make matters worse, the leased plantations were exposed to guerrilla attack. Plantations were frequently burned, blacks killed, and the country lining the Mississippi, instead of being secured, was left in a state of desolation. Porter believed that the plantations could be successfully run only by their original owners. Although Rebels at heart, he thought their economic interests would render them sufficiently loyal. While they would balk at paying their former slaves wages, the admiral believed they would welcome a sharecropping arrangement "allowing their Negroes a certain percentage of all they raised."[24]

General John P. Hawkins, commander of the First Division, U.S. Colored Troops, opposed any sort of contract labor system. There should be no labor contracts, he thought, that bound black people to a year's or even a month's labor. "It is strength contracting with weakness," he insisted, "and results in oppression." Black labor should be as free as Northern white labor: employers free to dismiss at any time and employees free to quit. "In fact," Hawkins concluded, "I want no law for the negro as if he were a child and had to be taught everything for under this guise of protection we rob him of every right."[25]

Despite General Hawkins' remarks, most criticism of the existing system focused on its callousness rather than on its paternalism. Anti-slavery men, in fact, urged the government to protect the interests of the freedmen as a father would protect his innocent and defenseless children. "It is the duty of the Government," wrote Yeatman, "to exercize a wholesome guardianship over these new-born children of freedom; to guide, direct and protect them at least in their infancy, and to see that injustice and inhumanity are not practiced upon them—to make them realize that they are freedmen."[26] Impressed with Yeatman's findings, the abolitionist *New York Independent* took it for granted that "the present system will be abandoned," and that another would be created, headed by men who understood that they were "charged with the welfare of a liberated race."[27]

IV

As criticism of General Thomas' leasing system mounted, Secretary Stanton, who genuinely despised his adjutant general, appointed Brigadier General James S. Wadsworth to investigate conditions in the contraband camps and on the leased plantations. A Free Soil Democrat and Stanton's political friend, Wadsworth reported that it seemed to be the tendency in the Mississippi Valley and in Louisiana "to establish a system of serfdom." However, for the time being, he thought General Thomas' system to be generally sound. The "docility" of the people made it necessary for the government to make the first financial arrangements, no matter how that might violate notions of freedom of contract. "The difficulty," said Wadsworth, "was not that these people were getting too little, but that you could not get them on to the plantations from the contraband depots." The future demand for black labor, moreover, required that lessees enjoy "great profits" at the outset of their rather dangerous undertaking.[28]

Despite his fear that blacks might become "serfs," Wadsworth did not argue with the fundamental purpose of Thomas' program, which, as he saw it, was to regenerate the debased "African Race"; restore occupied territory to productivity; and, by introducing Northern men

and methods, "make the people of the South homogeneous with those
of the North." He agreed with General Thomas that, despite the
efforts of philanthropists and the army, the contraband camps were
sites of "great suffering." He therefore urged the removal of the
people to plantations where they would find "comfortable houses, gardens and employment." This was as far as Wadsworth believed emancipation would go. The blacks should not expect confiscated lands
to be redistributed among them. On the contrary, such property should
be sold to Northern men who would "carry out the same system that
Southern men are now carrying out, under our system, that is, they
will employ these people." As a "practical measure," Wadsworth
did not think reconstruction in the South would go further than that.[29]

In order to render the leasing system more effective, however,
Wadsworth suggested several changes. He thought it essential that
some black men be spared military service for employment by lessees.
"A small number of able-bodied men," he explained, "are still necessarily employed on the Plantations." Moreover, despite his own belief
that widespread redistribution of lands among blacks would not occur,
he reported that "it is by many deemed probable" that a considerable
portion of the "African population" of the South would eventually
become "Peasant Cultivators" of small plots between ten and fifty
acres in size. He acknowledged that the area's cotton culture made
such small holdings practical (although hardly efficient), since a family could raise its own food in addition to several bales of cotton for
market. Despite his interest in revitalizing the plantation system with
Northern men and methods, Wadsworth recommended that the War
Department provide blacks with land "to a modest extent."[30]

James Yeatman argued for more sweeping changes in the leasing
system and convincingly presented his proposals for reform to Secretary of the Treasury Salmon P. Chase late in 1863. Returning from
a tour of the Mississippi Valley, Yeatman was shocked at the "injustice with which the freedmen are treated, the continuing of them
in a state of involuntary servitude, worse than that from which they
have escaped. . . ." Yeatman blamed General Thomas rather than
Colonel Eaton for this state of affairs. Yeatman found Eaton to be
a devoted man who shared the concern that the freedmen receive "the

rewards of their labor and the enjoyment of their rights." Yeatman was willing to excuse the leasing system as perhaps the best that could be devised on the spot, but he remained convinced that the experience of one season pointed clearly to the need for reform.[31]

The injustices of Thomas' system began with the lessees who with few exceptions, according to Yeatman, exploited their hands brutally. The grotesqueness of the situation was heightened for Yeatman when he reflected that most of those employed on the plantations were women, children, and the aged. Those who were too young, ill, or infirm to profit lessees were supposedly sent to government "infirmary farms" supervised by Colonel Eaton. But Yeatman discovered that contrabands requiring medical attention were often hired to lessees who left them "greatly neglected and poorly provided for."

The result of such harsh treatment, reported Yeatman, was the general demoralization of the contrabands who in freedom not only found their physical condition worse, but discovered as well that their Northern liberators treated them every bit as slaves. "The poor negroes are everywhere greatly depressed at their condition," reported Yeatman. "They do not realize that they are free men."[32]

Yeatman shared the interest of Generals Thomas and Wadsworth in encouraging the settlement of Northern men on confiscated and abandoned plantations. But he believed that small farmers should be given preference over the large, speculative lessees who rushed to take advantage of Thomas' plan. A larger loyal population would thus settle along the river and protect it from guerrillas. In addition, Yeatman was convinced that small farmers would take better care of a few hands "morally, physically and mentally" than speculators who hired a hundred or more. The injection into the Mississippi Valley of virtuous, small, Midwestern farmers would reconstruct the South and bind the nation together. At the same time black farmers who were able to stock and plant the land should be encouraged to lease their own farms. Yeatman had visited several black lessees who had been aided in their undertakings by Commissioner Field, and found them all doing well.[33]

Yeatman's criticisms were significant, for he successfully, if temporarily, replaced Thomas' program with a Treasury Department plan designed largely by himself. But if Yeatman was critical of the callousness of Thomas' system, he did not challenge its basic premise. While he approved of Commissioner Field's policy of leasing small plots to a few blacks whose training as slaves had qualified them to manage farms and employ hands, and while he looked hopefully to the displacement of the larger plantations by Midwestern-style farms, Yeatman expressed no interest in widespread confiscation and redistribution of lands among blacks.

He was interested, rather, in proving that blacks, whose labor was vital to the Union cause, would work as well in freedom as they had as slaves. "Coercion," Yeatman declared, "is not essential to make the negro work." Contrabands had been freed in the Mississippi Valley "and still they steadily went forward with their work, some of them accomplishing fully as much as under the eye of a master and the lash of the overseer."[34] Like most men of his day concerned with freedmen affairs, Yeatman did not seek to overturn the South's plantation system, but to demonstrate that chattel slavery was morally wrong and economically unnecessary as well.

As the object of growing criticism, General Thomas did not remain silent. He readily acknowledged that all was not running smoothly, but he was convinced that the fault lay outside his system. The blacks were indeed demoralized, but this resulted from a change in their habits "from daily work to comparative idleness," and from being necessarily collected together in large camps. The general sought to get them out of the camps and back to their accustomed chores. The planters, he assured Stanton, were willing to hire the blacks and to adopt "any policy the Government may dictate." Moreover, there were inherent hazards in any leasing program. The movement of troops necessarily left certain plantations exposed to enemy attack. Thus, while Grant concentrated his forces against Vicksburg, Rebels attacked Milliken's Bend, Louisiana, scattering and driving off the "negroes and stock" of several plantations. It was some time before the lessees were able to collect their hands and convince them to begin work again. If the plantation policy was to be successful, Thomas insisted that the government had to encourage lessees to face such personal and financial risks.[35]

The development of a system to mobilize land and labor in the agriculturally rich Mississippi Valley involved policies which necessarily limited the effects of emancipation. The decision to use black laborers and the plantation system as Union weapons of war precluded fundamental reforms. However well-intentioned, Yeatman's reforms would be of little practical consequence.

8

A Question of Authority

and Reform

★

I

The program adopted by the federal government to mobilize contraband labor and abandoned lands in the Mississippi Valley raised for the first time the question of administrative authority in matters relating to blacks. Army officers throughout the South had assumed responsibility for Negro affairs as a matter of military necessity. But Treasury Secretary Salmon P. Chase also claimed some authority in the development of labor programs. For several months during the winter of 1861-1862, Treasury Agent Edward L. Pierce had administered Negro affairs at Port Royal. General Rufus Saxton took over full control of the islands' labor system early in 1862, but he was careful to cooperate with Treasury agents in matters relating to land divisions and sales. There was a mutual respect between Saxton and Chase. Chase approved of Saxton's labor programs and supported them.

But Chase viewed the situation in the Mississippi Valley with outrage and alarm. Not only did Thomas' system shock those, including Chase, who considered themselves friends of the freedmen, but the army-appointed leasing commissioners carried out functions which were properly the responsibility of Treasury agents. In March 1863

Congress had placed the administration of abandoned and confiscated property with the Treasury Department. Thomas' leasing system therefore usurped Treasury authority. When James Yeatman of the Western Sanitary Commission presented his criticisms of the system to Chase, the secretary listened approvingly. Yeatman hoped to circumvent General Thomas and his program by establishing, under Treasury Department authority, a system which would protect the rights of the contrabands as free laborers. Secretary Chase concurred and laid plans to assume control of Negro affairs in the Mississippi Valley under the broad wartime powers of the Treasury Department.

At the outset of the war, the Commercial Intercourse Act of July 1861 had given the Treasury Department extensive powers to regulate trade in disloyal sections of the country. Special agencies of the Treasury Department were created to correspond roughly with the various military departments. These agencies were administered by special agents, appointed by Secretary Chase, who acted in lieu of customs officers in the regulation of trade to and from rebellious states.[1] Matters were complicated, however, by the fact that the power to seize property lay effectively with the army. The first Confiscation Act of August 1861 provided for the forfeiture of property (including slaves) used in the aid of the Rebellion. The power of the federal government, through its armed forces, to seize Rebel property was increased a year later by the second Confiscation Act, which declared the slaves of traitors free, forbade the return of fugitive slaves by the army, and provided for the forfeiture of property belonging to leading Confederate officers and officials (although such forfeiture—at President Lincoln's insistence—would not continue beyond the "natural life" of the offender). As a result of these acts, generals in the field enjoyed wide *de facto* powers (confiscation could be accomplished legally only by court action) to occupy Rebel property for military purposes.[2] It was in this context that Adjutant General Thomas had formulated his leasing program early in 1863.

In March 1863, however, Congress specifically authorized the Treasury Department to administer all captured and abandoned property. Property of Rebels absent in the service of the Confederacy was legally considered "abandoned," and although no attempt was made to confiscate such property, it was given over to the Treasury Department to be administered for the benefit of the federal government.[3]

If the conflict of authority which these laws created was not clear to Congress, it must have been apparent to Secretaries Stanton and Chase, once General Thomas instituted his leasing program in the Mississippi Valley. For whatever reasons, however, neither Stanton nor Chase immediately interfered with Thomas' plans. Perhaps they realized that centralized military control of contrabands and abandoned lands was necessary until the conclusion of operations against Vicksburg. At any rate, by October 1863, William P. Mellen, Treasury agent for the Mississippi Valley, received instructions from Chase to assume control from the army of abandoned lands and plantations not required for military purposes. Stanton had issued similar orders to army officers a week earlier.[4]

General Thomas greeted the transfer of authority with foreboding. He was concerned that the new arrangement might jeopardize his entire program. News of the transfer reached Thomas as he and General James S. Wadsworth toured the Mississippi Valley inspecting Negro troops, contraband camps, and leased plantations. Wadsworth, who unlike Lorenzo Thomas enjoyed the confidence of Secretary Stanton, assured the adjutant general that his leasing program would continue unchanged. On returning to Washington, Wadsworth promised to "satisfy Mr. Chase that you are right," and if the Treasury agents in fact took control of the plantations, they would adopt Thomas' system.[5]

Wadsworth did, indeed, satisfy Chase. The secretary wrote to Mellen in December that he agreed fully with Wadsworth's report and that the plantations should be leased according to Thomas' plan. Stanton, said Chase, had not yet decided upon a permanent policy. Until a final plan was devised, the plantations should be leased in the manner begun by Thomas. Chase agreed with Wadsworth that the principal objective was to get the Negroes out of the contraband camps "and restored to their accustomed employments under the free labor system" as quickly as possible. The secretary also expressed confidence in Commissioner Field and thought he deserved great credit "for his consideration of the colored people," and for leasing, when he could, directly to them.[6] Yet, after meeting with James E. Yeatman a few days later, Chase revised his assessment of Thomas' program and launched an attempt to gain control of Negro affairs in the Mississippi Valley.

Yeatman had accompanied his report to the Western Sanitary Commission on the condition of the freedmen with *Suggestions of a Plan of Organization for Free Labor, and the Leasing of Plantations*. Representing the commission, he presented his entire program to Chase in December 1863. A strong and long-standing antislavery man, Chase was known to favor the emancipation policies of the Lincoln administration. Chase received Yeatman warmly and examined his proposals with care in the company of Thomas D. Eliot, Radical congressman from Massachusetts and author of the recently introduced Freedmen's Bureau bill. Chase approved the general outline of Yeatman's plan and asked that he meet with Agent Mellen to work out the details. Chase wired Mellen to wait for Yeatman in Cincinnati before proceeding down the river to take control of abandoned plantations.[7]

II

Chase was greatly impressed with Yeatman's criticisms and proposals. He wrote Mellen that he read with interest much of what Yeatman had written on the matter and that he had "conversed with him quite freely on the whole subject." While Chase did not commit himself to Yeatman's proposals in every detail, he commended the entire report to Mellen's consideration, confident that the agent would adopt that which he found "expedient and practicable." Chase had urged Yeatman to take personal supervision of the leasing system, but Yeatman had declined, insisting that his field of labor lay outside of the government.[8]

Chase had learned enough from Yeatman concerning the operation of Thomas' system to revoke his earlier instructions to Mellen. Aware that two of the three commissioners appointed by Thomas to lease plantations were themselves lessees, Chase directed Mellen to make sure that such men were not appointed to administer the Treasury Department program. Chase thought Treasury agents should be sincerely interested in the "elevation of the freedmen," and in improving their living conditions. As a first step in dismantling the army's program, Chase directed Mellen to consider as void all leases negotiated by Thomas after October 9, 1863, the date Secretary Stanton transferred abandoned lands to the Treasury Department.

Although Chase left the details of the new leasing arrangements to the consideration of Mellen and Yeatman, he advised his agent of the general principles he wished to see followed. The interests of the laborers, Chase believed, should be considered basic to any leasing arrangements. Lessees should be bound to prompt weekly or monthly payments, and the wages themselves should be sufficiently high to "induce the laborers to desire the employment." Moreover, the practice of assigning freedmen to labor on particular plantations, with little or no regard to their own interests, should be discontinued.

Whenever possible, Chase recommended that plantations should be leased to associations or partnerships of the laborers themselves. Likewise, he believed that when portions of plantations could be leased to one or several Negroes, "there should not only be no hesitation but great readiness" to make such arrangements. "Few things," the secretary believed, "will more contribute to the improvement of the condition of the freedmen and to the productiveness of the country than their occupation of the soil as managers under leases made directly to them." Anxious to see such land reform, Chase authorized Mellen to begin making plans for the division of certain plantations. Landlords, Chase wrote, should be encouraged to sell small parcels of land—forty, eighty, or a hundred and twenty acres—to freedmen who could raise the necessary capital for payments. To encourage such benevolent desires among Southern planters, Chase proposed to suspend the provisions of the confiscation acts in cases where planters thus provided for their former slaves. Although he could not yet speak for the president on the matter, he was confident that Lincoln would approve such a measure. In the meantime, Chase believed Mellen's authority was sufficient to begin surveying boundaries for such subdivisions.[9]

After meeting in Cincinnati, Mellen and Yeatman proceeded to Memphis where they worked out the details of a new leasing arrangement with the advice of certain "practical men"—presumably lessees or potential lessees. Yeatman conceded that the regulations were not perfect, but he believed them to be an "advance in the right direction" since the "rights of the freedmen" were considered along with those of the lessees. The intent had been "to do justice to them both."[10] While certain concessions were made to the planters, Yeatman's original proposals were adopted with few changes.[11]

In the new program, home farms replaced contraband camps as labor depots and homes for those unfit for plantation labor. Here, under the direction of Treasury superintendents, contrabands would be collected, classified, and hired. Planters in the area desiring laborers would hereafter apply to the superintendents of the home farms and all blacks over the age of twelve, who were capable of labor, would be required to work. The home farms themselves would provide employment for the newly arrived contrabands as well as surplus laborers. Lest the Negroes decide they preferred labor on the government farms to employment with Southern planters or Northern lessees, no wages would be allowed on the home farms. Food and clothing, however, would be provided by the government, and profits would be used to render the entire freedmen program self-supporting. Once the contrabands faced the alternative of working without wages on the home farms, it was assumed they would choose to accept contracts with planters.[12]

Yeatman was confident that "ample provision" had been made for "such Freedmen as desired to lease ground for themselves."[13] Believing that many of the injustices of Thomas' system were due to the predominance of large lessees seeking speculative fortunes at the expense of the freedmen, Yeatman sought to encourage small farmers, black as well as white, to engage in the leasing business. The Treasury program promised to give preference to applicants wishing to lease small tracts of land, and in no case would more than one plantation be leased to a single party or interest.

The wage system adopted by Yeatman and Mellen was based on a classification of contrabands according to their value as laborers. "Sound persons" between twenty and forty years old were designated number one hands. Younger blacks, from fifteen to nineteen, and older ones, from forty-one to fifty, were given a number two classification. Children between the ages of twelve and fourteen, and all blacks older than fifty, would be considered number three hands. In cases where physical disability was not complete, the superintendents were to use their own judgment concerning an adequate wage. For classified laborers, however, a scale of wages was provided which more than doubled the rates that had been authorized by General Thomas for the previous season. Number one males, under the Treasury plan, would receive twenty-five dollars per month; males in the second class, twenty; and third class males fifteen dollars. First, second, and third class females would receive eighteen, fourteen, and thirteen dollars, respectively. Equivalent sharecropping arrangements were allowed in place of wages as long as such contracts were approved by the home farm superintendent and the Treasury agent of the district.

Apparently to insure an equitable distribution of the field hands and to guard against overwork, the regulations required that one number one hand, "or the equivalent in other grades" (presumably two number two hands, or three of the third classification), be employed for every twelve acres of tillable land. The home farm superintendent would determine in each case the proportionate numbers and sex of each grade of laborers assigned to a lessee.

In addition to paying wages, lessees were taxed one cent per pound on all cotton raised and a proportionate rate on other crops for rent. An equal amount was required for the support of helpless and aged freedmen.

Yeatman was aware of the exploitative nature of the leasing system inaugurated by General Thomas. Accordingly, Yeatman sought to provide safeguards for the protection of the freedmen. Under Thomas' system, for example, hands were often paid for the days actually worked rather than by the month. Thus, in slack season, laborers received only a portion of their monthly wages. The Treasury system instead provided that hands receive their full monthly wage unless sick or idle through their own choice. In such cases, employers were required to report wage deductions to the local home farm superintendents within ten days after the end of the month. The superintendent's endorsement was necessary to change the contractual arrangement.

Lessees also were required to pay at least half of the monthly wages during each month. As Thomas' orders had contained no such provision, the planters understandably preferred to postpone payment until the end of the season in order to insure the faithful service of their hands and to minimize operating expenses. Yeatman had hoped to require the prompt payment of full monthly wages to encourage the freedmen in their new status. But half wages during the season and the balance after harvest represented an improvement over General Thomas' system. This new financial burden on the lessees was lightened somewhat with the provision that food, clothing, and other goods could be substituted for payment of wages during the season at the discretion of the laborer. In such cases, the lessees were instructed to provide articles of good quality and to charge no more than 15 percent above wholesale invoice prices. If a laborer received supplies at a cost exceeding his monthly half wage, the employer was to keep account of such debts. At the close of the season, individual accounts would be reviewed by farm superintendents and the balance due, if any, would be paid the freedmen.

Lessees were also expected to provide without charge a separate tenement for each laboring family, "with proper regard for sanitary conditions." Families of four or more could cultivate their own garden vegetables on a one-acre plot provided without charge by the lessee. The Treasury plan further promised that schools would be erected at convenient locations and that all children between the ages of six and twelve would be required to attend.[14]

These rules and regulations, Yeatman hoped, would protect freedmen from the "involuntary servitude" he discovered in General Thomas' leasing system. In the hands of benevolent men, and with effective enforcement, freedmen might indeed have been protected from the worst abuses of the previous system. Certainly, the relatively large increase in wages went a long way toward improving the status of such labor. But, as long as the major concern continued to be the renewed productivity of cotton plantations under loyal white management, there remained ample room for exploitation. Evidently Yeatman realized that the leasing system he proposed offered white employers an authority over blacks potentially as great as that of the slaveholders. Lessees were therefore prohibited from administering "the lash, paddle, and all other cruel modes of punishment" to discipline their labor force.[15]

To administer the new system, the Mississippi Valley was divided into four leasing districts stretching from the mouth of the St. Francis

River below Memphis to the mouth of the Red River below Natchez. The Treasury Department's agent in each district controlled all abandoned plantations and leasing arrangements. The agents appointed superintendents for the freedmen home farms established in their districts. Home farms were located at Helena, Arkansas, and Natchez, Mississippi, as well as at several locations in the Vicksburg area: Skipwith's Landing, Mississippi; Goodrich's Landing, Louisiana; Milliken's Bend, Louisiana; Vicksburg, Mississippi; and Davis Bend, Mississippi.

It soon became apparent, however, that this organization occurred too late in the season to transfer contrabands from military camps to home farms before lessees began hiring. Lessees therefore continued to apply to army contraband camps for laborers.[16] Since the army looked covetously upon all able-bodied black men, lessees could only complain that between Treasury wages and War Department recruitment, they would be ruined. Yeatman himself lamented that "there are but few men among the laborers," noting that unless the army would spare some men, the lessees "will have to rely mainly upon the labor of women." The army's vigorous policy of impressment, he argued, was self-defeating since it discouraged slave defection from the Confederacy. "The fear of being drafted," said Yeatman, "is preventing thousands from coming in." If army officers would protect lessees from Rebels as well as Yankee recruiters, Yeatman promised that thousands of blacks would no longer require the support of the government. In one season, he believed, their labor would add 8 million dollars to the federal treasury.[17]

III

Although Yeatman did his best to secure an adequate labor supply, Northern men who moved South to make their fortunes as lessees in General Thomas' attractive system tended to blame the new Treasury program rather than the army or the war for their troubles. Lessees who had made their arrangements with Thomas' commissioners and expected to hire Negroes at the old rates (seven dollars maximum for men, five for women) were predictably upset to discover they must renegotiate their leases and pay a maximum rate of twenty-five dollars for men and eighteen for women. Yeatman conceded that the lessees were "necessarily disappointed," but while many of them argued that the plantations could not be operated profitably with such wages, there were none, to Yeatman's knowledge, "that held back on this account" when the time came to sign the new leases.

Yeatman's only fear, he claimed, was that wages were too low considering the inflated price of cotton. But since wartime prices could not continue indefinitely, he thought it was best to begin the system of free labor with wages which would not be prohibitive once the market stabilized.[18]

The lessees necessarily accepted the requirements of the Treasury plan, but they remained dissatisfied with it. When many of them began to experience unanticipated difficulties, they blamed the new regulations. Alexander Winchell, president of the Ann Arbor Cotton Company of Ann Arbor, Michigan, which leased plantations in the Natchez area, was particularly critical of the new arrangements. Winchell was Professor of Geology, Zoology, and Botany at the University of Michigan. He represented the interests of several Ann Arbor businessmen, fellow faculty members, and Erastis Otis Haven, president of the University. Winchell believed that Yeatman's plan was framed "in the exclusive interest of the negro," and with utter disregard for the "moral sense and patriotism of the white man" who sacrificed life, limb, and fortune in his efforts to secure the loyalty of the Mississippi Valley to the federal union. Winchell's major investments were at Lake St. Joseph, Louisiana, a location continually exposed to guerrilla attack. As the Ann Arbor Company's capital (totaling $10,000) drained away and prospects for recouping the losses became increasingly dim, E. O. Haven lamented that "changes in policy and men" had embarrassed them. He hoped that Winchell could somehow get enough out of the venture to return the stock and "give yourself a little payment." For his part, Winchell hoped that in its concern over the massacre of blacks at Fort Pillow Congress would not forget "the massacre of patriotic and useful citizens" who were loyal lessees. In the end, it was Rebel guerrillas, not the Treasury's system, that convinced Winchell to forsake his patriotic and potentially profitable leasing venture.[19]

A group of Wisconsin lessees expressed similar complaints, abandoning their plantations in disgust after less than two months. These men apparently had been recruited by Lark S. Livermore, one of Thomas' original leasing commissioners. Livermore visited his Wisconsin home during the winter of 1863 and publicized the opportunities made available by Thomas' system.[20] Several of Livermore's Ripon neighbors ventured South in December. They soon lost heart, however, and were safely back in Wisconsin by the end of January, complaining that the "proportion of able bodied men to women, children and infirm persons" was altogether too small for the labor required. The necessity of renegotiating leases with Treasury agents seemed bothersome to them and the power of the home farm superintendents to "abrogate contracts and dispossess the Lessees upon the complaint of the laborers" threatened disaster to the entire program.[21]

Protection was the key to successful plantation operations under any program. As Yeatman noted, the lessees might complain of hardships imposed by the Treasury regulations, but it was the guerrillas rather than the powers of the home farm superintendents or the increased scale of wages that convinced many of them to write off their investments and return to the safety of the North.

As the 1864 season progressed, complaints of guerrilla harassment and pleas for protection came from all sides. Lessees at Helena, Arkansas, informed Treasury Agent Mellen early in February that guerrillas threatened to "annihilate" hands who continued to work for them.[22] As Rebels approached, lessees withdrew, leaving their hands to fend for themselves. After the removal of a federal garrison from Goodrich's Landing, near Vicksburg, a Treasury agent discovered that many of the lessees "all fearing the approach of Guerillas," had left the area. Lacking both protection and employment, the abandoned laborers were reported by the agent to be "wandering objects of pity, rapidly becoming demoralized and dying."[23] Conditions were similar in the Natchez district where the Treasury agent reported that not a day passed without a guerrilla raid somewhere in his district.[24]

The disruption of the plantation system not only discouraged lessees, but removed government controls over blacks as well. As a result, Negroes on the Louisiana bank of the river above Lake Providence reportedly formed marauding bands preying on local whites in the same manner that Rebel guerrillas harassed Negroes and lessees.

The Treasury agent feared that such conditions would be the ruin of the blacks. "They collect in abandoned Camps in large numbers," he wrote, and make a "precarious living" by chopping wood and stealing from the abandoned plantations. Many of them, continued the agent, were armed with government rifles, "and they not unfrequently resort to murder and all manner of personal violence upon unprotected white persons." In one such camp, the agent reported several hundred blacks living "in filth and disease with all manner of booty." Unprotected as well as undisciplined, they were subject to the vengeance of local whites. "Last Sunday Morning," wrote the agent, "thirty white men rode in upon them and fired indiscriminately." Four of the contrabands were killed and twelve seriously wounded.[25]

Loss of control over groups of contrabands was only one of the difficulties facing the Treasury agents. Since the organization of the Treasury system came too late in the season to enable Mellen's home farms to function as major suppliers of plantation hands, Treasury agents and lessees found themselves dependent on the goodwill of the contraband camp superintendents for their labor supply. Treasury authority over the contrabands was naturally undermined. The Treasury agent at Little Rock, Arkansas, for example, believed that the military authorities showed favoritism in granting laborers to lessees, but he lacked the authority to order blacks out of the contraband camps.[26]

Increasingly, the Treasury agents sought more coercive means to force freedmen onto the plantations. The Treasury agent at Natchez thus charged the army contraband superintendent with encouraging idleness among the blacks. "It appears to me," he wrote the superintendent in March, "that the time has come when it is necessary to compel these Freed people, who are under your Military Control and are able to work, to find employment either on Plantations or elsewhere." Blacks, he thought, must be made to understand that the government "does not intend to support in idleness any except the helpless." The army should therefore require all those fit for labor "to make their Contract" and go with planters offering fair wages.[27]

Indeed, Treasury agents throughout the Mississippi Valley were distressed and embittered by the open reluctance of the freedmen to leave the contraband camps for plantation employment. When a party of loyal planters visited the camp at Davis Bend, below Vicksburg, they found the blacks unwilling to follow them back to their estates. Moreover, the officers in charge of the camp did not force them to go. At the Natchez camp, the Treasury agent reported angrily that an army officer had told the freedmen that "they need not work unless they chose," that the government would take care of them, and that the army "would not let anyone force them to labor against their will."[28] Such talk seemed designed to destroy the Treasury labor system, although one agent felt sure that Colonel Eaton would order his men to "drive them out bye and bye."[29]

IV

The Treasury system had not worked in the manner Yeatman and Chase had intended. Lessees frequently proved to be faint of heart; Rebel guerrillas often succeeded in disrupting Union plantation operations; and the freedmen themselves had not found the lure of wages sufficient to encourage them to resume their plantation chores in the midst of war. Moreover, Colonel Eaton and General Lorenzo Thomas had not been idle in the face of competition. While conditions along the Mississippi frustrated Treasury attempts to control the contraband population, Eaton and Thomas devised the means to remove the Treasury Department entirely from the administration of Negro affairs.

In February 1864 Eaton and General Thomas met in Chattanooga, Tennessee, to discuss the challenge posed by the Treasury Department. Both men agreed that "the Military authorities must have command of the negroes, or there will be endless confusion." Thomas vowed to keep that control unless specifically ordered otherwise by Secretary Stanton. The general was particularly upset that Mellen, instead of accepting what had already been accomplished under his direction, had required all leases to be rewritten and had introduced an entirely new system which "men of experience" judged "impracticable." Thomas was confident that both his own system and the efforts of Colonel Eaton had proved successful. By overthrowing programs of established worth, the government invited disaster and would become burdened with thousands of blacks to feed and clothe. The proper field of the Treasury agents, Thomas and Eaton believed, was the leasing of abandoned plantations. The collection, care, and hiring of Negro contrabands was an army responsibility. If Mellen would acknowledge this distinction, Thomas promised to "furnish all the labor required" to run the plantations successfully.[30]

Congress was partly to blame for this administrative feud. Responsibility for the freedmen was not clearly fixed until the creation of the Bureau of Refugees, Freedmen and Abandoned Lands as part of the War Department in March 1865. However, General Thomas and Colonel Eaton did their best to discredit the Treasury system, and their stubbornness left the Treasury agents largely powerless. Moreover, although Stanton evidently supported Chase's labor reforms, President Lincoln did not. A week after conferring with Eaton at Chattanooga, Thomas wrote Stanton that he was proceeding to Vicksburg to continue consulting with Eaton "on the subject of the hire of the freedmen."[31] The general received an immediate reply from Lincoln. "I wish you would go to the Mississippi River at once," the president said, "and take hold of and be master in the contraband and leasing business." Lincoln thought Thomas understood the matter better than anyone. Mellen's system, he said, was "doubtless . . . well intended," but he feared it would "fall dead within its own entangled details." "Go there," were Lincoln's orders to Thomas, "and be the judge."[32] There was little in the matter that Thomas had not already judged. After reassuring Stanton that he still considered the organization of Negro troops his "paramount duty," Thomas left for Vicksburg to assume control of the contrabands once more.[33]

Consulting with Mellen at Vicksburg, Thomas constructed a new leasing program, the third in less than five months. The two men agreed on one matter at least: protection was necessary immediately or the leasing system would collapse. Thomas promised to establish garrisons—manned by fresh Negro troops—at Lake Providence, Goodrich's Landing, and Milliken's Bend on the west bank and Skipwith's Landing in Mississippi to protect lessees in the Vicksburg area from attack. The Natchez district would be similarly secured by garrisons at Vidalia and Lake St. Joseph in Louisiana.[34]

"For the sake of uniformity," Thomas, who had visited New Orleans in April 1864, adopted the plantation regulations issued by General N. P. Banks for the Department of the Gulf. Special provost marshals were appointed to each leasing district to insure "justice and equity" in relations between lessees and freedmen. Hands were prohibited from leaving their plantations without passes from the provost marshals. Freedmen who shirked labor by feigning sickness "or stubborn refusal of duty" would be arrested by the provost marshals "for labor upon the public works without pay." Labor was defined as a "public duty"; idleness and vagrancy were considered "a crime." Hands would provide ten hours in summer and nine in winter "of respectful, honest, faithful labor."

Only on the matter of wages did Thomas deviate significantly from Banks' example. Thomas adopted a somewhat higher pay scale, although one well below that imposed by the Treasury plan. Males over fourteen years of age would now receive ten dollars per month; females, seven. Children from twelve to fourteen, as well as those "too feeble" to perform a full day's labor, would receive half wages. Other rates of pay were permitted if agreed to by the employer, employee, and provost marshal. On the matter of deductions, however, Thomas returned once more to Banks' regulations. Wages would be deducted during sickness, and, if illness was "feigned," employers could withhold rations as well.[35]

V

The debate between Mellen and Thomas over the proper organization of freedmen labor in the Mississippi Valley reflected the larger conflict between Radical and Conservative forces within the Republican party. The debate, then, was a real one, but, on the loyal plantations lining the Mississippi, the Treasury Department's reforms had proved to be largely illusory.

Mellen had been aware of Thomas' views for some time before their meeting in Vicksburg. He realized that Thomas disapproved of the Treasury system in part for its high wage scale, but he also believed that the general was exclusively interested in the profits of the lessees. It was Thomas' argument, in fact, that Mellen's wage system was prohibitively high and that the leasing system was therefore failing and lessees returning North. Mellon, on the other hand, shared Yeatman's and Chase's conviction that the compensation Thomas proposed was insufficient to encourage contrabands to return to the plantations. Mellen agreed that the profits of the lessees should be sufficient to maintain the demand for labor, but that the government system should seek to "improve the negroes and fit them for free labor." Finally, Mellen was convinced that it was lack of military protection alone which forced the removal of most lessees. With cotton prices what they were, he was sure that planters could afford to pay the wages fixed by the Treasury plan, "provided there is such Military protection afforded as will induce planting on *any* terms."[36]

Thomas regarded Mellen's plea for protection as naive. Commanders were waging war and could not squander their time and resources protecting lessees. From time to time some lessees would necessarily be exposed to guerrilla attack. "These are great risks for men of capital to take," observed the general, and lessees could not be expected to pay the wages established in the Treasury plan. Mellen's and Yeatman's regulations were therefore "beautiful in theory, but utterly impracticable."[37] Thomas blamed much of the whole controversy on Yeatman, who, he claimed, never set foot on a leased plantation but obtained his information from Thomas' enemies, "and from negroes, who are very ready to make complaints."[38] Negroes, after all, had been slaves. To remove traditional controls immediately would simply invite social and economic chaos. The plantation system adopted by slaveholders, General Thomas pointed out, was the product of experience; the closer the free labor system approached it the better, "and the further we depart from it the worse."[39]

Mellen, to be sure, disagreed with such views, but his disagreements were not fundamental. While he took exception to the general's belief that government policy should approximate, as nearly as possible, the tried and true system of slavery, he acknowledged that the transition to freedom should not be rushed.[40] Assessments of the two leasing programs therefore varied with loyalties. Those sympathetic with Yeatman's report and the Treasury authorities could point to the higher scale of wages their system offered as evidence of its benevolent concern with the welfare of freedmen. Supporters of Eaton and the army, on the other hand, could point to the frantic efforts of Treasury agents to force contrabands onto unprotected plantations, placing them "in danger of oppression and in actual and present want."[41]

Given the limitations of both programs, it was fitting that General

William Tecumseh Sherman, whom no one could mistake as a friend of the slave, submitted a thoroughly radical solution to the contraband problem in the Mississippi Valley. Thomas had sought Sherman's aid in his battle with the Treasury plan, but Sherman refused to become embroiled in details. His objection to the leasing plan, he said, was purely military. As a line of supply, the Mississippi River was long and weak, easily approached from either side. Typical plantation populations of three whites and fifty blacks could be broken up by guerrilla bands of one hundred "with perfect impunity." "You and I," he wrote Thomas, "know the temper of the whites in the South." It was not reasonable to expect lessees, interspersed among native planters, to successfully protect the river, the plantations, or the contrabands. If the government's emancipation policy was to succeed, Sherman argued, "we have to combat not only with organized resistance . . . but the entire people of the South." Sherman therefore proposed that the "rich alluvial region" lying between Memphis and Vicksburg should either be confiscated or purchased by the federal government and settled exclusively and permanently with blacks.[42] Such a step—later executed by Sherman in South Carolina—carried the argument of military necessity to its logical conclusion.

Yeatman's reforms were largely illusory, despite the clear differences between Secretary Chase's interest in land redistribution and General Thomas' efforts to maintain the established antebellum plantation structure. Each system, in fact, viewed the Negro as a "mere appendage to the land,"[43] and adopted measures to tie him to it. General Sherman's bold proposal was simply incomprehensible to men preoccupied with balancing wages and profits, liberty and discipline.

9

Black Labor and

White Lessees

★

With the collapse of Treasury Department authority over blacks in
the Mississippi Valley, John Eaton again emerged as the freedmen's
guardian and governor. He enjoyed broad authority over matters ranging from freedmen education to contraband relief. At the center of
his responsibility lay the vital function of regulating labor contracts.
Although Eaton had opposed the Treasury labor system, he had always
accepted its basic premise. Like James Yeatman, Eaton believed that
blacks, as the newborn children of freedom, required the government's
paternal care and guidance. Indeed, paternalism characterized the
humanitarian impulse of the age. Those, like Eaton, who hoped to
improve the condition and status of the downtrodden slave generally
viewed their task in paternalistic terms.[1]

Sentiments of paternalism doubtless imposed severe limitations on
those involved in freedmen affairs, but the wartime failure of reform
programs owed far less to the attitudes of the contraband superintendents than to the nature of federal policy toward Southern blacks.
Although the federal labor programs in the South were not devoid
of benevolent concern for blacks, the plantation leasing system in the

153

Mississippi Valley undermined paternalistic plans for the freedmen's care.

Men of goodwill, concerned with the freedmen's welfare, found themselves incapable of improving the lot of the former slaves. Freedmen superintendents characteristically began their work with optimistic plans to uplift the oppressed blacks. But, by 1864, under the pressure of events and developing national policy, they found themselves simply serving the interests of the planters and the needs of the Union army. For the most part John Eaton and his counterparts elsewhere in the South permitted their early programs to die without a struggle. Yet, the defeat of paternalism in the administration of freedmen's affairs resulted not from individual weaknesses, but from the national government's unwillingness to provide for blacks any longer than the exigencies of war demanded. The contract labor system, begun in Louisiana in 1862, spread to every area of Union control by 1864 and foretold the postwar emergence of tenantry and sharecropping as the principal forms of black agricultural labor in the South. Thus, while paternalistic reforms suffered their most obvious and unequivocal defeats in the Mississippi Valley, conditions along the river from Memphis to Natchez illustrated the obstacles facing everyone who hoped to reconstruct the South.

Although the tenuousness of wartime reform programs would soon become apparent, Superintendent Eaton began his labors among the contrabands with dedication and hope. In November 1862, when General U. S. Grant appointed Chaplain Eaton superintendent of Negro affairs, the way seemed clear for the development of a contraband policy in the Mississippi Valley that would satisfy both the army's interests and Eaton's hopes for guided emancipation.

Eaton's work was diligent and systematic. He moved quickly to establish several contraband camps and to surround himself with fellow Ohioans who shared his sympathies regarding emancipation and the Negro. His plans for the freedmen closely resembled those of Charles B. Wilder and Orlando Brown in Virginia. The government, Eaton believed. should occupy abandoned lands for the benefit of blacks. The more capable freedmen would lease plots of their own, while those requiring government guidance and care could be employed in a traditional fashion under the direction of Eaton's

superintendents. The government would assume the role of a benevolent planter, leading its black charges to freedom. It was with such
a plan in mind that Eaton sought the support of several freedmen's
aid societies early in 1863.[2]

Nevertheless, when Adjutant General Lorenzo Thomas arrived in
March 1863 to mobilize contrabands as soldiers and plantation hands,
Eaton quickly subordinated his paternalistic plans to the army's needs.
Despite the obviously repressive nature of Thomas' labor system,
Eaton never ceased to defend it. The decision to mobilize blacks
brought with it an extension of Eaton's authority. By late 1863 his
control of freedmen extended from above Memphis, Tennessee, to
Natchez, Mississippi. Moreover, with the introduction of the contract
labor and leasing system, General Thomas empowered Eaton to
negotiate and enforce contracts between freedmen and planters.[3] While
Eaton continued to speak of the need for paternalistic programs, he
served as General Thomas' assistant, bitterly opposed Treasury
Department reforms, and insisted at every turn on the necessity of
army control over blacks.

Eaton may have hoped that lessees would be carefully screened and
restricted in the new system, leaving ample room for his own agricultural experiments under government auspices. But it soon became
clear that General Thomas' interest in the freedmen was limited to
their usefulness as soldiers and laborers. If Eaton was disappointed
by such developments, he did not show it. Apparently, it was compensation enough that his own responsibilities were greatly widened when
General Thomas placed the administration of Negro affairs on a
strictly military footing.

The creation of the 9th and 7th Regiments, Louisiana Volunteers
(later the 63rd and 64th Regiments, U.S. Colored Troops) was part
of General Thomas' plan to mobilize contrabands in the Mississippi
Valley. These two regiments, consisting of black men unfit for active
field duty but not wholly disabled, provided the means for maintaining
the entire contraband population under martial law. The 9th Louisiana
Regiment was organized in October 1863 with Eaton as colonel. Eaton
was now independent of General Grant's staff and, as general superintendent of freedmen, he administered Negro affairs throughout the
Mississippi Valley. In November, the 7th Louisiana Regiment was

organized with Eaton's chief assistant, Samuel Thomas, as colonel. When General Thomas regained military control of freedmen in March 1864 and adopted General Banks' labor system, he appointed Samuel Thomas provost marshal general of freedmen. Thereafter, Eaton and Samuel Thomas—the former with headquarters at Memphis, the latter at Vicksburg—commanded freedmen's affairs throughout the Mississippi Valley.[4]

The logic of the new arrangement pleased Eaton. Duties once vague and ill-defined were now clear. The surgeon of the new black regiment, as Eaton explained, "naturally became Medical Director of freedmen" while the quartermaster "naturally looks after all the property" involving contrabands. The new regiments increased the powers of Eaton and his officers, but it was not altogether clear why black men unfit for active duty, along with women, children, and the disabled, should be organized as military units. Eaton, however, had no doubts. "In the midst of social upheaval," he wrote, the freedmen of the Mississippi Valley required control and protection. "These people," he concluded, "must be under martial law."[5]

The Treasury Department's decision, late in 1863, to assume control of abandoned plantations and contraband labor clearly threatened Eaton's new powers. Eaton granted that the Treasury system was "theoretically" better than the army plan, but he insisted that it had serious, even disastrous, practical defects. His opposition to the Treasury plan was bureaucratic rather than theoretical, jealous rather than principled. He never successfully demonstrated that the Treasury system's shortcomings were greater than those he acknowledged in Thomas' plan.

By jealously guarding his own bureaucratic position, Eaton helped defeat the paternalistic programs he himself espoused. Once the Treasury plan had been defeated and General Thomas adopted General Banks' labor regulations for the Mississippi Valley, there was little Eaton and his officers could do but work to supply planters and lessees with hands as efficiently as possible. Thereafter, progress was measured not by those paternal concerns which motivated Northern reformers—the physical, intellectual, and moral improvement of the freedmen—but by decreasing issues of rations to destitute blacks and ever-smaller populations in contraband camps. Eaton and his officers worked simply to relieve the government of the economic burden which the care of contrabands imposed. "Our laboring force," Eaton remarked years later, was "composed largely of men deemed unfit for regular service, together with the women, the children, and those positively disabled." He took pride in the fact that "even with this crippled body of workers," free labor could be compared not unfavorably with slave labor.[6]

II

With the resolution of the conflict between Eaton and the Treasury agents in March 1864, thousands of hands were turned out of contraband camps for plantation labor. Typically, the camp at Helena, Arkansas, dropped from a peak of 3,300 early in 1864 to 1,290 by October. In the Skipwith's Landing district, well over 17,000 blacks were employed on plantations. Of these, 4,409 were rated as hands (the balance being dependent women, children, and the aged). A total of 55,000 acres were reported in cultivation. With each hand planting twelve and a half acres, the work was hard indeed. Few, if any, slaveholders required so much labor from their hands.[7]

In the Vicksburg district, matters were much the same. Several days after General Thomas regained control of contraband affairs, Colonel Samuel Thomas "transferred" 3,700 of the 13,665 blacks under his control to plantations. By the middle of June 1864, Colonel Thomas reported 11,117 freedmen on plantations. Almost 7,000 of these were rated as hands, and about 47,000 acres of cotton were reported in cultivation. Perhaps reflecting their awareness of the greater risk of guerrilla attacks, Vicksburg planters required one hand for every seven acres of cotton planted.[8] As the number of blacks on plantations increased, the population of the contraband camps in the Vicksburg area correspondingly decreased, falling from a peak of 13,665 in March to 8,465 in April. As a result, perhaps, of guerrilla activity, the number in camps exceeded 13,000 in May 1864, but then fell steadily (with a slight rise in December) to 405 in April 1865.[9]

The number of contrabands in the Natchez area was considerably smaller, but the pattern was generally the same. Samuel Shipley reported approximately 8,000 contrabands in the area in November 1863. By the middle of June 1864, 5,712 blacks were reported on plantations and 28,637 acres planted in cotton. Since more than half of the contrabands on plantations in this district were considered hands, each laborer cultivated nine and a half acres.[10] After December 1864, the population of the Natchez contraband camps declined steadily to 533 in April 1865.[11]

Severe labor was not the only hardship with which the freedmen had to contend. Guerrilla raids frequently sent lessees fleeing, leaving blacks to protect themselves and plantation supplies as best they could. The frequency of raids in many areas kept the hands in a constant state of alarm. While visiting plantations late in 1864, Eaton's superintendent, Reverend Asa S. Fiske, discovered that his party's approach on horseback was enough to send the hands "scattering to the weeds like frightened hares—so timid have they become on these haunted grounds."[12]

The security of the plantations to which the contrabands were sent depended on the character of the proprietor as well as the proximity of Union and Rebel troops. In the Memphis area where there were few lessees and few guerrillas, the plantations were safe. Local planters registered their loyalty and obtained the labor they needed. To the south, matters worsened progressively so that in the Natchez district lessees found it virtually impossible to operate save within easy reach of military garrisons. In reviewing the season's efforts, one of Eaton's assistants estimated that of the approximately 450 lessees who began the season, only 115 remained. During the year, guerrillas were credited with stealing over two thousand head of stock and nearly one thousand Negroes.[13]

Even in the relatively safe areas around Helena, Arkansas, guerrilla raids were frequent. The numerous lakes, swamps, bayous, and cane brakes made the district "impossible to guard" according to the commanding general there. During two weeks in March 1864, five raids were made on leased plantations. One white man, "many negroes and about 100 mules" were carried off by the marauders.[14] But most of the plantations in the Helena area were held by native whites. Only a few abandoned plantations were leased directly by the government. Guerrilla activity was therefore selective and conditions on most of the plantations were evidently good.

William F. Allen, who had taught blacks at Port Royal, South

Carolina, before beginning work among the freedmen at Helena, found the Negro quarters on the local plantations "much superior" to anything he had seen in the Sea Islands—"neat, roomy cottages, in almost every instance." There was work available for as many contrabands as would go, although he thought a great many of them, "like the Irish," preferred to "crowd together in the town and live miserably by pilfering and chance charity."[15]

In the Vicksburg and Natchez areas, plantation life was considerably more dangerous for blacks. Colonel Samuel Thomas, who as provost marshal general of freedmen was responsible for negotiating contracts between planters and hands, admitted that protection in the Vicksburg and Natchez areas was by no means complete. Leased plantations stretched from Lake Providence to Natchez. Most had been leased to Northern men by Treasury agents and were seldom more than three miles from the river. On the west bank, in the area of Goodrich's Landing and Milliken's Bend, above Vicksburg, plantations were relatively safe. Warren County, Mississippi, including Vicksburg, was also well-protected and successfully planted. But some areas were unsafe and others extremely dangerous. Washington County, Mississippi, above Vicksburg, was considered unsafe by June 1864, although a large number of plantations had been leased during the spring.[16]

Below Vicksburg, conditions deteriorated rapidly. Near Lake St. Joseph, Louisiana, about thirty miles south of Vicksburg, two Yankee lessees struggled unsuccessfully to raise a profitable cotton crop. Beginning their efforts in March 1864, they persevered for some time despite unnerving guerrilla raids and the murder of several hands. Colonel Thomas thought they deserved "great praise" for their determined efforts to raise cotton under adverse conditions. They needed more hands, he admitted, if they were to succeed, "but find trouble in getting them to go, owing to their exposed condition."[17]

Lessees in the area between Lake St. Joseph and Vidalia, Louisiana, were similarly discouraged. Troops had been stationed at Waterproof, Louisiana, during March and April, and six lessees began planting, expecting large returns. When the troops were moved to Vidalia, the lessees also withdrew. Plantations in the area were thereafter occupied by a few Negroes, mostly old men and women, considered, in Colonel Thomas' words, "too harmless" to interest Rebels or Yankees. On the east bank, outside the city of Natchez, protection simply did not exist, and little effort was made to lease plantations. A number of freedmen reportedly lived on abandoned plantations in the area, planting small gardens and subsisting on whatever their masters left behind.[18]

III

Where guerrillas failed to disrupt plantations, harsh weather and destructive insects generally succeeded. Administrative confusion and drought at the beginning of the season delayed planting in many cases until April. Unaccustomed to cotton planting, lessees often began with low-quality seed and were forced to replant large areas. By the first of September, the army worm attacked and all but destroyed the cotton crop throughout the valley. It was hard, as Samuel Thomas explained, for lessees "to see the whole crop snatched away, just as the dazzling dream of immense wealth began to look probable and real."[19] It proved harder still for the freedmen who had been made dependent on the lessees for their welfare. The government had abandoned programs of paternal guidance in order to promote the success of the leasing system. As events dispelled the planters' visions of vast profits, Eaton and his officers found themselves without the means to secure for the freedmen the most basic provisions of their contracts.

As the situation worsened, Colonel Samuel Thomas, who was responsible for seeing that justice prevailed in relations between lessees and freedmen, insisted that the planters were "as upright and just a body of men as can be found anywhere." With a few exceptions, he claimed that the lessees treated their hands "justly and humanely," and sought to instill their laborers with a sense of "manliness and self reliance." Thomas thought the Negro had no more right to expect ease and wealth than white laborers. The important thing was that blacks now labored for wages like whites. Colonel Thomas thought that the complaints of the hands themselves could lead to the mistaken belief that "serious abuses existed among them." He found that freedmen tended to "invent stories" to justify their desires to leave the plantations and avoid work.[20]

Blacks had reason to fear guerrilla attack, but there were other reasons for their reluctance to labor. As Colonel Thomas' reports indicate, planters did not fulfill their contracts. At the end of the season, Thomas' subordinates reviewed labor contracts to insure the payment of wages or the posting of adequate bond to cover their payment. In Vicksburg alone, more than two hundred of these bonds were filed amounting to an indebtedness of over $400,000. The provost marshal of freedmen at Natchez reported it necessary to require bonds as high as $10,000 in single cases.[21]

The reluctance of blacks to work and the failure of lessees to fulfill their contracts troubled Eaton. He hoped that the number of provost marshals would be expanded, allowing Colonel Thomas and his officers to supervise activities on the plantations. A group of lessees near Helena argued that a "tangible power" was needed to "compel all parties to fulfill their contracts." The lessees hoped Colonel Thomas' office would be granted the resources to travel from plantation to plantation "to compel laborers to render service; to decide upon all cases of minor importance; and to enforce discipline and order." Preferably a physician would be present on such visits to treat the sick, inspect quarters, "and determine who should be exempt from labor on account of sickness." The lessees confessed that they were frustrated by the feigned sickness of their hands. The delicacy of the matter, they thought, required "*just men*, and *business men*" as inspecting officers. An armed guard, it was hoped, would accompany the inspectors to execute their orders on the spot "with certainty and dispatch."[22]

Although the Treasury system had attracted the hostility of most lessees without noticeably inspiring the contrabands to labor, there were probably several lessees in the Mississippi Valley who successfully practiced the paternalism Yeatman and Mellen had preached.[23] The blacks, they believed, needed guidance rather than dictation, incentive rather than coercion. Willian F. Allen, Eaton's superintendent of colored schools at Helena, found several lessees in the area who were concerned for the welfare of their hands. But the humanity of the lessees could not be assumed. The major difficulty with the leasing system, Allen thought, affected the Treasury and army labor systems alike. "In scarcely any item," observed Allen, "was either

plan faithfully carried out." Even the best planters admitted that there
was nothing to prevent them from defrauding their hands. Promises
of garden plots, medical attention, and schooling were all largely for-
gotten.[24]

IV

The failure of planters to abide by the terms of the government's
labor system was widespread. Even in the most basic matters—food,
clothing, and wages—planters often failed to meet the very minimal
standards set by General Thomas' orders.

Eaton and his assistants had been aware of many shortcomings for
some time. As early as June 1864 Samuel Thomas reported to General
Lorenzo Thomas that it was impossible for his office to write contracts
for all the freedmen employed. The disruption of plantations by guerrillas and the consequent turnover of laborers in the Vicksburg and
Natchez districts made it impossible for him to provide the necessary
forms and supervision. As a result, planters in the area frequently did
not bind themselves by contract to individual laborers. Some blacks
complained that their monthly half wage was not paid, but Colonel
Thomas dismissed their charges feeling certain that "through stupid-
ity, or a desire to be finding fault" the blacks were telling "hard
stories of their treatment which are not founded on facts."[25]

As the army worm began destroying cotton crops in September
1864, planters systematically sought ways to minimize their labor
costs. Facing a meager harvest, some planters attempted to unburden
themselves of surplus hands. Rations were cut, harsh treatment
applied, and stories of impending guerrilla raids circulated—all in an
effort to force blacks off plantations and back into the contraband
camps. Eaton and his assistants reminded planters of their obligations
to employ freedmen until the first of January 1865. "Planters reaping
the benefit of freedmen's labor during the summer months," warned
Eaton in October, "will be compelled to live up to the requirements
of their contracts," and supply food, housing, and medical attention
to hands until contracts were renegotiated at the beginning of the
year.[26] Such directions did not always prove effective. When
Reverend Asa S. Fiske visited plantations in the Vicksburg district
in November, he reported numerous contract violations to Colonel

Thomas. Planters often provided insufficient rations and failed to support dependent blacks. Moreover, most deducted wages whenever bad weather or guerrilla raids kept hands out of the field.[27]

At the end of the 1864 season, Colonel Eaton questioned planters, superintendents, commanding officers, missionaries, and the freedmen themselves on matters relating to the employment and treatment of contrabands. Although he expressed general optimism in his review of the year's efforts, much of the testimony he collected indicated that the government had failed to protect freedmen in their first year of contractual labor.[28]

Although the planters universally claimed to provide their hands with all the food they wanted, Chaplain Fiske, interviewing laborers on ninety-five plantations, concluded that only ten planters provided full rations. Many hands received only a portion of the molasses and fresh pork required by the government. In some cases, according to Colonel Thomas, the amount of food supplied was "impossible to live on." The testimony of the freedmen and the planters themselves indicated that about half of the employers provided no rations to children, the infirm, and other dependent persons. Reverend Fiske found that rations for the sick had been stopped on more than a third of the plantations he visited. Fully a quarter of the planters themselves said they were not concerned with means by which the non-laboring freedmen subsisted.

Although half of the planters claimed to sell clothing to their hands at cost, the rest admitted to profits ranging from 15 to 25 percent. It was not a matter of defrauding blacks; goods at inflated prices simply replaced wages. Since the planters employed their hands, in effect, for room and board, as Colonel Thomas observed, "but little wool was left for the most expert shearer."

Only in exceptional cases had the planters taken steps to provide schooling or medical care for the blacks. The shortage of teachers and the insecurity of plantations made the establishment of schools difficult outside the cities and garrisons. The lack of medical attention, on the other hand, was simply a means of cutting labor costs. After deducting wages and often stopping rations, planters left the sick to the care of their families and friends.

Harsh punishment, of course, was prohibited by General Thomas' order, and the planters claimed to rely on "moral suasion" to discipline their labor force. However, on half of the plantations visited by Reverend Fiske the freedmen complained of rough treatment ranging from violent and insulting language to blows and kicks. Samuel Thomas admitted that, while none of the planters would admit they abused their hands, he was aware that "moral suasion sometimes consisted in the use of a club."

As Chaplain Fiske discovered, most of the planters deducted wages for lost time. Freedmen, Fiske found, were bitter about the loss of wages. They had begun the season, after all, under the Treasury plan which promised a maximum monthly wage of twenty-five dollars for men and sixteen for women. Although their obligations to the planters remained unchanged, they discovered in midseason that the planters' obligations to them were virtually removed. When Eaton asked his superintendents what progress they saw in the freedmen's disposition "to labor steadily; to remain home; and to be quiet," they replied that there was not much change. Samuel Thomas explained that the blacks remained restless because they hoped to become independent of the planters and the plantations.

V

Freedmen were predictably disheartened with the results of their first season as free laborers. Few received anything more for their efforts than shoddy room and board. "The actual amount of money paid to these people," admitted Samuel Thomas, "will be small." The cost of clothing alone absorbed most of their theoretical wage. As the season's accounts were closed at Helena, William F. Allen, superintendent of colored schools, noted that the blacks found they had bought on credit more from the planters than they had supposed. They consequently ended the year "with very narrow margins." Chaplain Fiske knew of only six plantations where the employees ended the season with any measurable profit. The firm of Ayres and Taylor at Helena was one exception. Its hands were provided with plots of land for their own use. In this way some Negroes reportedly earned hundreds of dollars beyond their wages.[29]

For most blacks, however, the free labor system imposed by the government simply foretold the perpetual dependency on landlords that characterized the tenant farming and sharecropping systems of the postwar era. After visiting freedmen on nearly a hundred plantations in November 1864, Chaplain Fiske drew up what he believed to be average accounts of first-class male and female hands after a season as free laborers. Under the most favorable circumstances, concluded Fiske, freedmen could do little better than break even with their employer.

Most hands in the Mississippi Valley began working in March. Their contracts extended through the first of January, providing ten months of wages, or gross earnings of $100.00. Since planters generally deducted for idle time, laborers lost about $8.25 for half-day Sunday vacations along with about $30.00 for time lost during bad weather, guerrilla raids, and sickness. Thus a hand's real wages before expenses amounted to something closer to $61.75. Fiske estimated that minimum expenses for a single man without dependents would amount to $36.00 for clothing, tobacco, candles, soap, and the like. If an able-bodied man had only himself to care for, he might end the season with a yearly salary of $25.75.

The fate of a first-class female hand—and the work force was composed largely of women—was worse still. If a woman did not become ill and did not have children or other dependents to care for, she might, after deductions and expenses end the year with $9.00.

Fiske argued that such accounts represented the maximum possible earnings of first-class hands. The mass of laborers fared considerably worse. Nearly all hands, after all, supported families. Where the wage system was taken seriously, many hands were in debt. One plantation manager told Fiske that he did not know what to do with his laborers at the end of the season: "they were so much in debt to him, and he had not paid them a dime of money."[30]

Extant plantation accounts with freedmen bear out Chaplain Fiske's conclusions. On the plantations of Dr. P. E. Buckner below Milliken's Bend, Louisiana, more than half of the laboring families ended the 1864 season in debt or with balances of less than $5.00.[31] Some accounts corresponded almost exactly with Fiske's estimates. Nancy Cooper, with only herself to support, ended the season with $9.65. Strother Thornton, also without dependents, earned $21.60 during the year.

For many laborers, however, deductions for lost time and charges for food and clothing absorbed their wages. Jim Coleman, whose wife and son also worked, ended the season with only $3.45. Together the family had been able to accumulate only eleven and a half months of labor. Since rations were provided only for days actually worked, the family's earnings went largely for food. Nor were the freedmen extravagant in their purchases. Relatively large sums went for tobacco (at $1.50 a pound) and flour (two pounds for 15 cents). An occasional pound of meat or butter appears in the accounts and a few pairs of shoes (at $3.50 a pair). Accounting errors (which were invariably in the planter's favor) further eroded earnings. Thus Jim and Francis Brown, who should have earned $26.75, were mistakenly credited with only $18.75. Since they had bought almost $30.00 worth of food and clothing on credit, they ended the season over $10.00 in debt. Less significant errors added to the expenses of several other hands.

Since the freedmen had little protection from excessive wage deductions, they necessarily relied on the honesty of their employers and the vigilance of government officers. But what troubled many provost marshals was not that laborers were ill-treated and ill-paid, but that discipline among them was difficult to maintain. Blacks frequently cursed their overseers, one officer reported, and refused to labor. The women, he found, were particularly troublesome since they could not be punished by forced labor on government works. Similarly, fines proved ineffective, except with the "most intelligent." Imprisonment, the provost marshal found, was also futile since black soldiers garrisoning posts along the river filled the minds of rebellious hands with "all kinds of abuse . . . respecting Plantations." In the minds of the soldiers, the planters and lessees alike were simply secessionists; such talk had a "very bad influence on the hands." One officer experimented with more effective means of enforcing plantation discipline. In July 1864 he informed Samuel Thomas that he had "bucked and gagged six persons," who were then returned to their plantation duties and seemed to be "doing nicely." However, one of the women who had been punished in this manner complained to Colonel Thomas and the officer was later removed.[32]

VI

The failure of the government to protect blacks as free laborers, or to improve their condition after a year's labor, contributed to the demoralization and restlessness that provost marshals reported. Freedmen, as Samuel Thomas noted, were unable to reason in such matters and looked "only at results." The freedmen, Thomas observed, see "that the white man has received his labor, and has paid him with food and clothing—about the same he used to get."[33]

Yet, blacks seemed fundamentally concerned with the form of their labor rather than the scale of their wages. Above all they sought independence from planters and plantations. The army temporarily offered a measure of independence in black regiments as well as in contraband camps. More significantly, the government leased plots of land to the few blacks it considered capable of independent farming. But for the mass of contrabands, it soon became clear that the North had no more interest than the South in uprooting the plantation system.

"Our country," wrote Samuel Thomas, "has enough to bear without undertaking the enormous task of starting out each freedman with a competency for the rest of his life." Black labor, although emancipated, could expect no more than white labor. "Capital does now, and will for some time to come," carry on the country's great enterprises. The war would not change this, and black men as well as white "must labor for this capital at regulated wages, without any direct interest in the result of the enterprise."[34] Cotton culture had become a capitalistic enterprise and few in positions of authority, as Colonel Thomas indicated, seriously considered abandoning it for the benefit of blacks. For those freedmen who temporarily enjoyed the status of independent farmers, the war years were a cruel delusion.

10

An Elusive Independence

I

The collapse of paternalistic programs in the Mississippi Valley indicated the magnitude of the problems facing those who hoped to uproot slavery and its effects. The contract labor system, as the foundation of federal contraband policy, insured the continued dependence of the mass of black laborers on white planters. But the federal labor system did not necessarily require the subordination and repression of all blacks. Some government officials in the Union-controlled South leased or rented farms to freedmen whom they considered capable of stocking and operating a few acres with little or no assistance. Reform-minded whites hoped thereby to encourage the development of an independent class of black farmers. "All that is needed to establish a truly loyal and prosperous community," announced Massachusetts Radical Francis W. Bird after touring government-operated plantations at Hampton, Virginia, "is that the men and women who have watered the soil with their tears and blood, should be allowed to own it."[1] Certainly the government had no intention of subsidizing masses of blacks as small farmers on fragmented plantations; most blacks under Union control continued to labor on large plantations as field hands. But for a few freedmen, federal occupation offered the hope of independence.

Interest in creating what missionaries and freedmen superintendents called a black "peasantry" was by no means universal in the occupied

South. In Louisiana and on Virginia's Eastern Shore, federal authorities dismissed as fanciful the notion of providing land for blacks. But in Tidewater Virginia plantation superintendents rented land directly to a handful of freedmen, and in South Carolina the Direct Tax Commission briefly permitted blacks to preempt plots on estates to be sold at public auction. The best conditions for settling blacks on the land as independent farmers existed in the Mississippi Valley from Memphis to Natchez. Here the effects of war left an abundance of abandoned and confiscated land in government control. Here, too, Union authorities made their most ambitious efforts to provide land for blacks.

General Lorenzo Thomas' leasing commissioners provided several blacks with farms during the 1863 season. George B. Field, apparently the most active figure in these efforts, aided black lessees in the Union-occupied areas above Vicksburg. Field reportedly helped black farmers obtain needed implements, seeds, and capital. Perhaps as many as thirty blacks leased farms from the government during 1863, and individual farmers were credited with raising anywhere from one to one hundred and fifty bales of cotton.[2] Encouraged by this early success, Treasury Secretary Salmon P. Chase drafted plans for a more general redistribution of confiscated lands among the freedmen.[3]

With the aid of Treasury agents, the number of freedmen farmers in the Mississippi Valley increased during the war years to about 250 in 1864 and to as many as 500 by 1865. But the number of such farmers always remained relatively small. Of the 100,000 acres of cotton reported to be under cultivation by loyal planters during 1864, only 7,000 acres were managed by blacks.[4] Only the "best" freedmen, former drivers, and others whose training as slaves seemed to qualify them for independent farming were permitted to demonstrate their agricultural skills.[5]

The independence of black lessees under wartime conditions was not absolute. Like white planters, black lessees depended on army protection to raise crops and on Treasury permission to market them. Black farmers were additionally hampered by their poverty. Those who possessed the means were able to lease respectable farms of a hundred acres or more, employ hands according to the government's labor system, and enjoy substantial profits. However, most relied on private loans and government rations to subsist until harvest. These freedmen seldom managed plots larger than forty acres. More often, they were limited to between ten and twenty acres.

Although restricted, the independence of these black lessees should not be underestimated. They controlled their own land, managed their own crops, and made their own bargains. By contrast, federal labor policies held most blacks in positions of dependence on white planters. In addition to contract labor, federal authorities promoted sharecropping arrangements between planters and laborers. Thus Superintendent John Eaton sponsored a system on the government home farms that allowed some freedmen to work ten-acre plots under their own supervision for shares. In other cases, planters and lessees employed blacks on a sharecropping basis.[6] But sharecroppers, as distinct from the black lessees, had no more control over the type of crop they worked or its marketing than the common contract laborer working for wages.

In many respects, the status of black lessees was comparable to that of tenant farmers. While black lessees were far less secure than Southern yeoman farmers, they differed from sharecroppers and contract laborers because they invested more in the agricultural enterprise than their physical labor. Frequently, black lessees owned mules and other stock. In all cases, they impressed government officials with their industry and skill. As a result, they succeeded in making arrangements which offered them a measure of independence.

II

The largest concentration of black lessees farmed in the areas near Helena, Arkansas, and Vicksburg, Mississippi. Elsewhere in the Mississippi Valley, conditions did not favor them. While the Natchez area was blessed with an abundance of abandoned land, it was plagued by guerrilla attacks and shunned by black and white lessees alike.[7] The Memphis area was safe, but Northern men eagerly leased government-controlled plantations, leaving little room for black farmers. At Helena and Vicksburg, federal authorities controlled more land than loyal whites were willing to lease. In these two areas, a few blacks controlled plots of land and provided for their own needs.

During the 1864 season, government agents at Helena divided two surplus plantations for lease to blacks. "Manageable" plots ranging from ten to fifty acres were leased to about forty freedmen who possessed, or could raise, the means to farm them. The army apparently supplied rations on credit to some, but government aid was not extensive. Freedmen gathered their stock and farming utensils where they could. They frequently obtained cash loans from whites in Helena and Vicksburg, using a portion of their expected crop as collateral.[8]

Lacking capital and in many cases the necessary equipment, black lessees were rarely in secure positions. Rivalries, incompetence, and corruption among the officers Colonel Eaton assigned to superintend Negro affairs added substantially to the difficulties of the black lessees.[9] Nonetheless, several in the Helena area were said to have ended the 1864 season quite successfully. Napoleon Bowman, who impressed William F. Allen as "a fine, manly seeming negro," farmed twenty-four acres. Owning a team to start with, he borrowed about two hundred dollars, hired one hand, and cleared six thousand dollars. Jerome Hubbard cultivated forty acres of cotton with a partner and made eight thousand dollars. Sam Bladen, with thirteen acres, earned two thousand dollars. A white lessee, observing the black farmers around him, believed that with their plots of ten to fifty acres, they could realize profits of at least two thousand dollars. Considering the indebtedness of many of the black lessees, however, such returns were probably exceptional. Even with seventy acres, "Aleck," who began the 1864 season in debt and with a large family to support, ended the year only "a little ahead."[10]

Prospects for a second season were further clouded by the expiration of existing leases. Many blacks who had held leases in 1864 lost them at the end of the season. Only a few successfully negotiated new agreements with the government. These few freedmen were reported "working with far more satisfaction and contentment" than those who necessarily labored "for wages or shares." But the relative success of black lessees in the Helena area during 1864 had falsely raised the hopes of many. "There are numbers," reported the superintendent at Helena in June 1865, "who have hired out that were compelled to do so, on account of not being able to obtain land for themselves and who are anxious and able to cultivate small tracts." Independent farming by blacks in the Helena area had been tenuous and short-lived.[11]

As a result in part of better administration and more effective government aid, the situation for black lessees was somewhat brighter in the Vicksburg area. Above the city, at Milliken's Bend, Louisiana, a group of fifteen black lessees cultivated nearly 1,500 acres of cotton in 1864, employed 126 hands, and supported an equal number of non-laboring dependents. Milliken's Bend, long occupied by Union troops and garrisoned with Negro soldiers who had demonstrated their mettle during the siege of Vicksburg, was relatively safe from guerrilla attack. A few blacks even managed sizable farms. Levi Parker, for example, farmed two hundred acres of cotton and employed twenty-five hands while his neighbor William Ashby managed one hundred acres with fourteen hands. The remaining thirteen black lessees worked more modest farms, generally in partnership. Thus Archer Watkins, Edward Leadbetter, and James Givens jointly farmed three hundred acres and employed twenty-five hands. Nearby, a group of six blacks jointly worked one hundred acres of cotton. How well these farmers fared is not known, but their holdings were among the largest managed by black men anywhere in the South.[12]

Directly across from Vicksburg, in an area known as Young's Point, several black lessees and a number of freedmen on home farms cultivated crops in 1864. Four Negroes leased land directly from the government, three of them in partnership with two hundred acres and twenty-six hands. The lessees' crops were reported "very promising" in June, and their management was judged "good and husbandman-like."[13]

Two miles west of DeSoto Landing, on a home farm supervised by Quaker missionary Elkanah Beard, four freedmen were allowed to lease farms and employ contrabands. Jacob Truman Hunter, the largest of these lessees, cultivated one hundred and seventy-five acres and employed thirty-seven hands at government rates. Hunter and his employees reportedly worked together "very harmoniously." On a lesser scale, Cutus Pollard farmed forty acres with twelve hands employed as sharecroppers. The remaining two black lessees under Beard's care farmed plots by themselves. One of them, David Thomas, cultivated twenty acres and his neighbor, Albert Barley, managed a ten-acre plot.[14]

In addition to the lessees, a number of freedmen on Young's Point worked garden plots. During 1864, nineteen blacks leased ten-acre plots on the Birney Plantation, and about one hundred families, mostly wives and children of soldiers, farmed small tracts of land under Beard's direction.[15] Early in 1865 one hundred more received plots of similar size on adjoining estates. Although the black farmers on Young's Point were considered industrious, their success was limited by their poverty. Industry, after all, was no substitute for capital, and the freedmen suffered from a shortage of teams and farming implements. They were too poor to buy what they needed, and the government did not supply it. The consequence was poor farming and unnecessarily small farms.[16]

Regardless of the difficulties and limitations, freedmen were anxious to farm land of their own. Colonel Samuel Thomas reported late in 1864 that the success of black farmers in the area encouraged a group of Vicksburg blacks to attempt a similar venture the following spring. "The more intelligent part of the negro population," thought Thomas, "are [sic] beginning to see the immense advantages of such a scheme." The Vicksburg group hoped to acquire a year's lease for a thousand-acre tract, and, if possible, title to it.[17] Likewise, freedmen on a home farm north of Vicksburg hoped to farm plots of their own during the 1865 season. James A. Hawley, a Congregationalist minister from Ripon, Wisconsin, and a former lessee himself, supervised this group of about four hundred freedmen just outside the city's picket lines. Many of his charges, he acknowledged, were a burden to the government, a heavy expense "which might be relieved by a judicious disposition of their labor." To make the contrabands self-sustaining, Hawley proposed that adjoining plantations be leased to them. The freedmen were hopeful for the future, he said. They had already built homes, erected a school, and were preparing gardens for planting.[18]

Hawley organized his charges into thirteen "squads or companies," assigning land according to their abilities. To finance the venture, Hawley negotiated a contract with a Memphis firm. The freedmen received seed, implements, and subsistence rations, and paid the "white capitalists" two-thirds of their net proceeds. Despite many hardships, Hawley reported that the blacks raised 233 bales of cotton during the 1865 season, worth nearly $36,000. Net profits approached $10,000, and the blacks' share was just over $3,000. Profits for the freedmen, however, were by no means uniform. One man received over $200 while six of the thirteen "squads" ended the year in debt to the Memphis capitalists. Hawley nonetheless thought the year successful since it saved the government the cost of supporting dependent blacks, and "it has given the people a lesson in independent labor."[19]

III

In general, black lessees in the Vicksburg area fared better than their Helena counterparts, but nowhere else were black farmers as successful as at David Bend, the antebellum home of Confederate President Jefferson Davis and his wealthy brother Joseph. The Davis brothers' estates, "Brierfield" and "Hurricane," dominated the peninsula formed by one of the long, involuted bends in the Mississippi River below Vicksburg. Here blacks established a self-sufficient and largely self-governing community under the protection of the Union army.

From the outset, the freedmen on Davis Bend distinguished themselves from ordinary contrabands. As the slaves of the Davis brothers and other planters on the Bend, they had been well-maintained and unusually well-educated. As Grant moved against Vicksburg, the slaves on the Bend were taken within the city's fortifications. During the siege, however, many escaped and returned to their homes. Several of the young men enlisted as sailors on federal gunboats, but most (about six hundred) remained on the plantations as independent farmers. Virtually surrounded by the river, the freedmen were protected by gunboats of the Mississippi Squadron. Navy officers drew up rules and regulations for them and placed "an old Patriarch" in charge of governing the population. The freedmen planned to begin planting cotton in the spring, and seemed capable of raising more than ever before.[20]

Although Northern whites interested themselves in the Bend as an experimental black community, the freedmen's success in establishing their independence resulted from their own actions rather than from benevolent aid. Visitors were always impressed with their relative intelligence and ability; they offered a refreshing contrast to the ragged and ignorant contrabands generally encountered along the river. They seemed particularly notable, moreover, for their efforts to organize

and govern themselves.[21] Yet, it was a measure of the paternalism
that characterized benevolent efforts that the Davis Bend freedmen
were not simply protected and encouraged in their own efforts.

James E. Yeatman, who toured the Mississippi Valley late in 1863
for the Western Sanitary Commission, hoped that the Bend would be
used permanently for "infirmary farms" employing old and disabled
blacks. He thought it "but right and proper" that the Davis brothers
should thus be made to provide for some of those they had enslaved.
He acknowledged that the freedmen had taken the initiative in occupying the area, but he evidently looked forward to government control.
"These plantations will be taken possession of by the Government,"
he reported, "and a regular camp established."[22]

While conferring with Superintendent John Eaton, Samuel Shipley
of the Friends' Association of Philadelphia proposed detailed plans
for the Bend. The area seemed an excellent place to initiate experiments in developing a class of independent black farmers. Shipley
and Eaton hoped to begin by providing about one hundred hands with
five or ten acres for their individual care, "subject in a measure to
the direction of a capable and faithful Friend." Since few blacks possessed the capital or, Shipley thought, the experience to become successful on their own, interested Philadelphia Quakers were urged "to
give them a helping hand."[23]

The paternal guidance Shipley and Eaton had in mind may have
been unnecessary, but the Davis Bend freedmen clearly did require
the protection of the federal government. When General Grant confiscated the several estates and placed the area under Eaton's control,
it could hardly be doubted that he acted in the best interest of the
blacks. But Eaton, claiming that the freedmen had "naturally submitted their affairs" to his direction, proceeded immediately to organize
the colony as an example of the civilizing progress to be expected
from his paternal care.[24] Eaton persistently saw the Bend in terms
of his own interests, and it was the efforts of the blacks themselves
that prevented Davis Bend from becoming just one more contraband
camp.

IV

Ironically, the adoption of the Treasury labor system, with its
promised reforms, most directly threatened the independence of the

Davis Bend freedmen. Despite the fact that Secretary Chase and Agent Mellen expressed interest in leasing directly to blacks wherever possible, one of the plantations on the Bend—the Quitman and Turner property—was returned to heirs who took the oath of allegiance. Moreover, Treasury agents leased a large portion of the "Joe" David plantation to whites, thus displacing several black farmers.[25] These actions, evidently taken without Mellen's approval, weakened the colony. "No white person," Mellen later wrote, "should ever have been permitted to lease any part of the Bend."[26] White planters nonetheless remained on the Bend throughout the 1864 season.

After General Lorenzo Thomas regained control of freedmen's affairs in March 1864, the Bend was turned over to Eaton's assistant, Colonel Samuel Thomas, who supervised the Vicksburg and Natchez districts. Since the season had begun and the white lessees had started planting, Colonel Thomas made no effort to displace them. He confined his efforts to the southern portion of the Bend, the "Jeff" Davis estate, which he thought would be sufficient to demonstrate the productivity of the blacks as independent farmers.[27] Here, the "best" Negroes were permitted to lease plots of land averaging thirty acres. Typically, the distribution of land was quite uneven. Some managed farms of a hundred acres while others were limited to ten. Mules, tools, wagons, and other farm implements which the blacks had appropriated from the abandoned plantations in 1863 were now confiscated by the government and rented to the black lessees. The object, explained Colonel Thomas, was to furnish everything necessary through the government and receive payment from the blacks at the end of the season.[28]

Eaton and Thomas wanted to develop the Bend as a self-sustaining and exclusively black community, isolated from the corruption and exploitation that frequently resulted from contact with white troops and lessees. Black troops guarded the neck of the peninsula, securing the Bend from guerrilla attack. By the end of the season, the colony was indeed self-sustaining and the black farmers, whose "energy, industry, and close calculation of results" surprised Colonel Thomas, were judged successful.[29] In November all whites were finally excluded, and the Bend, as well as three surrounding islands, was reserved for "military purposes," to be devoted to the "colonization,

residence and support of Freedmen." All whites not connected with
the army were ordered to leave the area by January 1, 1865.[30]

Colonel Thomas expected the Bend to show a sizable profit in 1864,
but the destructive work of the army worm left the black lessees with
substantially lower returns than they might reasonably have expected.
Nevertheless, the 180 lessees raised approximately 130 bales of cotton
which, according to Colonel Thomas' estimate, would allow them to
pay their debts and enjoy profits of $500 to $2,550. Their vegetables
and corn crops, moreover, would feed them through the winter and
keep their stock until spring. Several blacks had constructed comfortable houses. Thomas thought they all had "learned lessons they will
never forget;" their experience would be "worth much to them hereafter."[31]

The success of black lessees on Davis Bend amazed Eaton and
Samuel Thomas, and they were quick to point to the Bend as evidence
of their own success as administrators of Negro affairs. "The efforts
of the freedmen on Davis Bend were particularly encouraging," wrote
Eaton, "and this property, under Colonel Thomas' able direction,
became in reality the 'Negro Paradise' that General Grant had urged
us to make of it."[32] Confident that the success of the venture was
the product of their own efforts, Eaton and Thomas used the Bend
to demonstrate the wisdom of paternalism and the ability of the freedmen to develop social stability and economic prosperity when properly
guided.[33]

For Eaton and Thomas, the success of the Bend's black lessees
tended to obscure the fact that most blacks on Davis Bend fared no
better than contrabands throughout the Mississippi Valley. Most of
the Jefferson Davis plantation (comprising roughly the southern half
of the Bend) was used by the government as a home farm for disabled
and unemployed contrabands from other areas. Like similar farms
attached to contraband camps elsewhere, the Davis Bend farm served
as a point of collection for arriving blacks and as a labor depot for
local white planters. The population of the government farm rose from
nine hundred in January 1864 to a peak of four thousand in the first
half of March.[34]

The Bend's home farm thus functioned like any other contraband camp, unaffected by the good fortune of the local black lessees. As hands were forced off plantations by guerrillas and disgruntled lessees, hundreds were shipped to the Bend only to be hired again by white planters. In July five hundred hands arrived from St. Joseph, Louisiana, following a series of guerrilla raids. Within a month one hundred of them had been hired again by planters. In October eight hundred blacks were unceremoniously dropped when General N. J. T. Dana ordered rations stopped for nearly two thousand contrabands in the Vicksburg area and directed Samuel Thomas to compel them "to earn their own living."[35] With no land available, they could only enter into contracts with whites.

V

The success of the Davis Bend farmers in maintaining a measure of independence was largely the result of their own efforts and exceptional background. Nevertheless, early in 1865, Eaton and Thomas reorganized the colony on a "self-governing" basis under the direction of an army superintendent. A freedmen's court was established, composed of three black judges elected for three-month terms. Moreover, each plantation elected a sheriff to maintain order and bring all complaints and disputes before the court.[36]

Planting operations as well were reorganized for the new season. Those who were willing and able to farm "on their own account" were directed to form companies of three to twenty-five hands. Each company would choose a manager to transact its business and direct its affairs. The amount of land leased would be determined by the superintendent according to the size of the company. No individual rations would thereafter be issued, and each company would pay the government at the end of the season for all rations, mules, and farm utensils received.

The government's home farm continued to operate on the "Jeff" plantation. Hands who refused to work or were unable to do so were employed there. Once enrolled, no one could leave the new companies without the agreement of the members and the army superintendent. Finally, company managers were responsible for the good behavior of their hands. The superintendent hoped that this new arrangement would improve the "present disgraceful and bad conduct" of many of the freedmen who plundered the countryside and lived in "idleness and vagrancy."[37]

It seems doubtful that these new regulations substantially changed existing farming arrangements on the Bend. At the end of the 1865 season, when Samuel Thomas reported the results of the year's labor, he recorded 181 companies or partnerships, a figure nearly equal to the number of black lessees on the Bend in 1864.[38] Since the number of companies so nearly equaled the number of previous lessees, and since the government leased plots at the outset only to the "best" Negroes, it seems reasonable to conclude that the established lessees continued under the new system as "managers." If so, the new regulations served to strengthen the government's control over lessees and their hands, a change accounted for, perhaps, by the new superintendent's interest in suppressing "idleness and vagrancy."

"These people," claimed Samuel Thomas late in 1865, "were left free to manage their own affairs." Presumably, not even the army superintendent was allowed to "meddle with the pecuniary or domestic affairs" of the colony. Yet, the independence of the blacks on Davis Bend had always been closely circumscribed by the guiding influence of government superintendents. Blacks were required to plant at least two-thirds of their land in cotton and surrender their crop to Colonel Thomas' provost marshals for marketing. Thomas was not about to leave the community's financial success to the freedmen alone. And the Bend *was* financially successful. The freedmen raised 1,736 bales of cotton in 1865, worth nearly $350,000. After expenses, the blacks were credited with a combined profit of $159,200. "The people worked well," concluded Thomas, "and have shown by their industry, perserverance, and management, that they are capable of doing business for themselves." The Bend, he was sure, proved the success of government paternalism: the Negro "will do best where the greatest encouragement is held out of future reward."[39]

With the close of the war, however, the federal protection was withdrawn which had made a measure of independence possible. Following the 1865 season, four of the plantations on the Bend were restored to their antebellum owners by presidential pardon. Jefferson Davis remained beyond the pale, even for lenient Andrew Johnson, but the

"Brierfield" and "Hurricane" estates were gradually restored to his brother Joseph. The freedmen were required to rent the plantations in 1866, and by January 1867 Joseph Davis regained full possession.[40]

The federal government's inability to protect black lessees on Davis Bend and elsewhere from dispossession indicates the very limited alternatives open to those who would reconstruct the postwar South. Neither Eaton nor his superintendents displayed any interest in overturning the South's plantation system. Like Southern planters, they saw the mass of blacks as field hands necessary for the cultivation of cotton. Like their successors in the Freedmen's Bureau, they encouraged and, when necessary, forced blacks to accept plantation labor. Their aim, as the nation's aim, was not revolutionary. But they did hope that the "best" Negroes—those who in slavery already had formed a discernible elite—would be assisted and protected as a class of independent farmers. This too was the initial promise of the Freedmen's Bureau.

Conclusion:
The Transition to the
Freedmen's Bureau

★

I

It was a curious feature of the wartime administration of Negro affairs that Radical Republicans and abolitionists played such an inconspicuous and even inconsequential role. Although freedmen's aid societies proliferated during the war and generally represented Northern antislavery interests, freedmen's aid work was limited almost exclusively to relief, education, and religious training. Some missionaries (like C. B. Wilder in Virginia, Mansfield French in South Carolina, and James E. Yeatman in the Mississippi Valley) concerned themselves with broader questions involving the economic and social status of the blacks. But most missionaries found themselves overwhelmed with the task of feeding, clothing, and schooling their charges. Most displayed little interest in drafting fundamental reforms.

By and large, federal labor policies developed in contradiction to the humanitarian concerns of the Northern missionaries. Government contraband superintendents, regardless of their intentions, functioned as quartermasters of black labor. They consolidated, categorized, and dispensed freedmen as if they were mules or wagons. Certainly some superintendents expressed genuine concern for the plight of the former slaves, but men like Rufus Saxton, Thomas W. Conway, and John Eaton could not themselves soften the tone of federal policy or alter its purposes. And, in the final analysis, federal contraband policy served no higher purpose than that of securing Union victory. Thus the substance of federal policy toward Southern blacks throughout the occupied South varied little. Most blacks worked on large plantations for wages or shares. Only in exceptional cases did freedmen purchase or lease farms of their own. The Union army encouraged stability and continuity; dramatic changes in the status of blacks and in the conditions under which they labored were consciously avoided.

Under the circumstances, it seemed obvious that substantial changes in the status of Southern blacks would come gradually, if at all. Those who conceived of themselves broadly as the friends of the freedmen agreed that the first step to be taken involved a degree of land redistribution. There was never sufficient coordination among reform-minded politicians, freedmen superintendents, and missionaries to generate a comprehensive theory of social change. But taken together, wartime reform efforts revealed concrete interests which seemed to portend a Radical program for the social reconstruction of the South.

Reformist missionaries and superintendents generally envisioned a social and economic hierarchy among the freedmen. Federal authorities offered land only to an elite group of blacks—those whose antebellum experience and status impressed missionaries and superintendents as ample training for independence. In South Carolina, a few such blacks managed to purchase farms. More typically, as in Virginia and the Mississippi Valley, the government rented or leased farms to blacks it considered qualified. Only a few among this elite controlled farms exceeding forty acres, but their numbers seemed less important than the fact that they formed the nucleus of what might have become a class of black yeoman farmers. The largest part of the black elite rented or leased subsistence plots of five or ten acres from the government. This "peasantry," as reformers conceived it, could provide for its basic needs while laboring from time to time for wages on the large plantations. Below these two independent groups, the mass of freedmen continued their traditional plantation labors for wages or shares. However, it could be hoped that through diligence and thrift, individual plantation hands might rise from their dependent position and join a growing "peasantry," and perhaps eventually emerge as "yeoman" farmers.

Out of the carnage of war would rise a system of free labor, allowing blacks to make their way in the world as their ability, industry, and frugality permitted. With an infusion of Northern men and capital into the South and with the destruction of the planter aristocracy, blacks might emerge from the war with all the liberties and opportunities enjoyed by Northern white laborers. Although considerations of humanity, as the American Freedmen's Inquiry Commission insisted, demanded a period of paternal care and supervision, the freedmen essentially required only equal protection under the law to overcome oppression and the degrading influences of slavery.

Whatever its merits or shortcomings, this plan was overwhelmed by the magnitude of the contraband problem and was finally defeated by the purely military needs of the federal government. Emancipation came as a war necessity and the various contraband labor systems succeeded only to the extent that they usefully served the Union's military needs. The confiscation acts, the Direct Tax Law, and the commercial regulations of the Treasury Department all relied in large measure upon the arbitrary powers of martial law. Linked as they were to the military needs of the federal government, the Yankee-directed labor systems did not survive the war. Likewise, the alienation of Rebel property begun under martial law was quickly reversed by President Andrew Johnson with the return of peace and the restored sanctity of private property. To uproot the planter aristocracy required widespread and permanent confiscation. Congress, under Lincoln's restraining hand, had been unwilling to take such a step in the midst of civil war. It could hardly accomplish the task once civil government and constitutional procedures regained their traditional sway.

Under the circumstances, the Freedmen's Bureau, which paid lip service to the idea of creating a class of independent black farmers, could do little more than preside over the liquidation of wartime labor programs while facilitating the restoration of antebellum property rights and the institution of a contract labor system throughout the South. Denying the Bureau any real power and discarding the agricultural programs begun during the war, Congress replaced programs of government protection and support with hollow promises of land for freedmen and poor whites.[1]

II

The first Freedmen's Bureau bill was the work of Massachusetts Radical Thomas D. Eliot, and was brought before the House of Representatives in the winter of 1863-1864. The original bill contained no direct promise of land for blacks. Rather, it authorized officers to permit the occupation, cultivation, and improvement of abandoned and confiscated lands by freedmen. The settlement of blacks on government lands was not mandatory, and the terms under which freedmen would labor were not stated. The organization and direction of black labor nevertheless lay exclusively with the Bureau agents in Eliot's bill. By placing the Bureau in the War Department, moreover, Eliot evidently hoped to consolidate and strengthen existing labor programs. Bureau agents were therefore authorized to "adjust" wages for blacks and "receive all returns" resulting from their labor.[2]

Eliot's bill passed the House in March 1864, by a narrow margin of two votes. It was completely rewritten in the Senate by Charles Sumner who hoped to place the Bureau in the Treasury Department and expand its program of leasing abandoned and confiscated lands to Northern whites. Despite the fact that the Treasury leasing system had been defeated in the Mississippi Valley by March 1864, Sumner evidently hoped to make Yeatman's and Mellen's program the basis of the Bureau's agricultural policy. Abandoned and confiscated lands, according to Sumner's version of the bill, should be rented or leased. In all cases, Bureau officers would act as "advisory guardians" to aid the freedmen by establishing wages, and, in cases where blacks rented plots or farms on their own, to supervise the "organization of their labor." Despite warnings from abolitionists that the bill would simply delay the creation of a Freedmen's Bureau, Sumner pressed ahead and the Senate passed his bill in June 1864.[3]

Attempting to circumvent conflicts over administrative jurisdiction, the compromise bill which emerged from conference in February 1865 proposed the creation of an independent department. This bill passed the House, but despite Sumner's support failed in the Senate.[4] Pressure to keep the administration of freedmen's affairs in the War Department was strong. John Eaton, who lobbied in Washington for army control of contrabands, applauded the defeat of the compromise bill.[5] Sumner at last relented, and Congress created a Freedmen's Bureau in March 1865 as an agency of the War Department. In the final version, the Bureau bill authorized the division of confiscated lands, under the direction of the president, among freedmen and "loyal refugees." Individual families might lease up to forty acres for three years at an annual rate not exceeding 6 percent of the land's assessed value. During the leasing period, the tenants might "purchase the land and receive such title thereto as the United States can convey."[6]

On the face of it, the final Freedmen's Bureau bill, with its "promise" of land for blacks and poor whites, seemed to sanction the most radical wartime efforts to settle blacks on government-held lands as independent farmers. But in fact the Bureau bill was something of a defeat for those who hoped to guide and protect freedmen in the postwar years. Basic to the weaknesses of the Bureau bill was the nature of the title which the government could "convey" to those who settled on abandoned and confiscated lands. Since constitutional prohibitions against bills of attainder limited the effects of the confiscation acts, the federal government's "ownership" of Southern estates was far from absolute. It necessarily followed that the titles which blacks could obtain under the provisions of the Bureau bill would remain highly suspect and open to continual legal challenge.[7]

Of more immediate importance was the Bureau's status as a self-supporting agency without annual appropriations from the federal Treasury. The wartime emphasis on the self-sufficiency of freedmen continued, with one important addition. The only source of revenue for the Bureau would be the sale and rental of the very lands which Congress "promised" to the freedmen. The Bureau's educational and humanitarian work would be financed by the freedmen themselves; the Bureau would wither away as blacks and poor whites purchased the lands it controlled during the three-year leasing period. However, once President Johnson, with the liberal use of presidential pardons, began restoring property to former Rebels, the Bureau's power to divide government-held lands among blacks was effectively subverted. As the lands under its control diminished, the Bureau was reduced to the administration of a few home farms for dependent blacks. Without further confiscation, the Freedmen's Bureau in 1865 could provide land only for a black elite. Within a few short years, it could not do that. In the fall of 1865, the Bureau controlled about 800,000 acres of arable land, enough at most for 20,000 family farms of forty acres or 160,000 five-acre plots. By the end of 1868, the Bureau held only

140,000 acres.[8] President Johnson did his best to weaken the Bureau, but the virtual exclusion by Congress of white lessees made Johnson's task of restoration considerably easier. Moreover, the questionable legality of confiscation and the limited amount of available land demanded far more detailed plans for land divisions and sales than the Bureau bill provided.

Opponents of Radical Reconstruction charged that the Freedmen's Bureau served the political purposes of the Republican party. Doubtless there were those who wished it did. But the Bureau's administrators lacked the means to continue even the limited and quite modest labor programs of the war years. Wartime freedmen's programs were quickly discontinued under President Andrew Johnson's direction, and Radicals could do little to stop it. Senator Sumner confided to Salmon P. Chase in October 1865 that without an effective Freedmen's Bureau, "the victory of truth & great ideas . . . must be postponed,—perhaps, till the next generation."[9] As far as blacks were concerned, the Freedmen's Bureau hardly represented a bright beginning. Rather, it marked a discouraging end to the variety of alternatives which the Civil War seemed to make possible.

III

Congress created the Freedmen's Bureau as a part of the War Department, and the army superintendents continued their work for a time under Bureau auspices. Orlando Brown, who had worked among the freedmen in the Norfolk area since early in 1862, became assistant Bureau commissioner for Virginia and, except for a brief period, he remained at that post throughout the Bureau's existence. Similarly, Rufus Saxton continued to supervise freedmen's affairs in South Carolina until January 1866, and Thomas W. Conway remained at New Orleans as Bureau superintendent for Louisiana until October 1865. Horace James worked with the Bureau in the Newbern area of North Carolina until January 1866, and C. B. Wilder remained in Hampton, Virginia, as a Bureau agent until June 1866.

John Eaton, who had expected an important Bureau office, accepted the post of assistant commissioner for the District of Columbia, hoping to influence Bureau policy by his presence in Washington. The work proved discouraging, however, and Eaton left in December 1865 to establish the pro-Grant *Memphis Post* and to build a Republican party in western Tennessee. Eaton's wartime assistant, Samuel Thomas, supervised Bureau affairs in Mississippi until August 1866.[10]

Although many of the superintendents remained, the Bureau did not continue wartime programs. Conway in Louisiana and Saxton in South Carolina vainly opposed efforts to withdraw government aid to freedmen. Conway was dismissed in October 1865, and Saxton, while remaining at his post until January 1866, was unable to salvage any of the wartime programs in his area. Before he left his Washington post, John Eaton began to close contraband camps around the federal city and to return blacks to the nearby plantations as contract laborers.[11]

Throughout the South, the situation was the same. The attitude of Eliphalet Whittlesey, Bureau commissioner for North Carolina, illustrated the labor policy of the new Bureau as a whole. In a series of circulars issued during the summer and fall of 1865, Whittlesey left no doubt that federal aid to freedmen would cease. "Your freedom gives you new privileges," Whittlesey insisted in July. To "assist" blacks in obtaining fair wages, he promised to leave them "free to make their own bargains" with planters. In August Whittlesey stated flatly that no lands would be divided among blacks. "Vagrant idlers who try to live without any honest calling," the commissioner later promised, "will be promptly arrested and punished."[12]

Notwithstanding Orlando Brown's wartime efforts among the freedmen, the Virginia Bureau commissioner bluntly announced the withdrawal of government support for blacks under his care. In June 1865 Brown ordered government rations stopped for all but the totally dependent. Vagrants who remained unemployed would be forced to work under military guard, "until they are ready to work for themselves." The new commissioner understood that many blacks were reluctant to accept labor contracts, believing that the government intended to provide each family with a farm. Brown therefore took pains to explain that the Bureau controlled very little land in Virginia (about 86,000 acres for 500,000 freedmen), and that "no lands will be given . . . by the government." Under the circumstances, Brown believed that planters should rent small tracts to blacks on shares in order to "attach" them to the plantations and "counteract any temptation" on their part to break labor contracts.[13]

By the fall of 1865 Brown grew impatient with continued "idleness" among blacks and became somewhat fearful of the consequences. "You will please notify these headquarters," Brown directed his subordinates in September, "whether you have any evidence of suspicion that any insurrectionary movement has been thought of or contemplated by the freedmen within your district." In October, Brown authorized C. B. Wilder to use every means at his command to prevent destruction of property by blacks dispossessed of farms they had rented or leased in the Hampton area during the 1865 season. Anger among the freedmen ran deep. Commissioner Brown noted euphemistically in December that many of them were "in the habit of engaging in hunting with fire-arms on the Sabbath." Brown ordered Bureau agents to disarm blacks throughout the state.[14]

Alternatives to employment with white planters no longer existed even for a black elite, and Brown ordered his charges to accept contracts or face arrest as vagrants. At the same time, he warned his subordinates to refrain from arresting whites on "trivial or groundless" charges made against them by blacks. Only in "serious criminal cases," where "proof is clear," should Bureau officers disturb local whites. By late November Brown reported to Bureau Commissioner O. O. Howard that the migration of blacks from the countryside to the cities had been halted. The freedmen, Brown believed, were "generally contented," and now sought homes and employment "that promise to be permanent."[15]

Samuel Thomas became Bureau commissioner for Mississippi in June 1865. From the start, he worked under stern directions from the district's commanding general to keep blacks on the plantations of their former masters. Similarly, Bureau Commissioner O. O. Howard advised Thomas to abandon the wartime practice of fixing minimum wages for plantation hands. Defeat for wartime reform efforts was complete, and Thomas, like Bureau commissioners elsewhere, had little choice but to force former contrabands and the mass of new freedmen into contracts with white landowners. "Freedmen will be urged to remain at their old homes," Thomas dutifully announced. At the same time he warned blacks to remain respectful toward their former masters. "A good master is likely to prove a good employer," Thomas reasoned, "and is to be treated with respect and affection "[16]

Although the Freedmen's Bureau began its work in Mississippi with about 80,000 acres of land, restoration to antebellum owners came swiftly. By the end of 1865 only 35,000 acres remained, and after November 1867 the Bureau controlled no property in the state. The alternative of leasing land to blacks no longer existed. "Idleness and vagrancy will not be allowed," Thomas proclaimed when he announced that "no lands or property of any kind" would be divided among the blacks. Freedmen henceforth would support themselves by contracting to labor for whites. If they refused, "they will be compelled to go to work" by state law and Bureau regulations. Thomas directed his subordinates to suppress forcefully all acts of violence or destruction on the part of the freedmen, and to disarm any individuals or groups of blacks intending to impede a return to responsible employment and the restoration of civil government.[17]

IV

The weaknesses of the Freedmen's Bureau went well beyond the shortcomings of individuals like O. O. Howard and his assistant commissioners. At the close of the Civil War, the federal government had successfully organized and in a measure protected only 200,000 of the one million blacks within its lines.[18] Even with over a million Union troops mobilized against the South, and with a quarter of the slave population within Union lines, most freedmen remained untouched by the government's labor systems. Once the war ended, Union demobilization was swift and permanent, despite the army's responsibility through the Freedmen's Bureau for four million blacks. By the end of 1865 there were only 150,000 troops in the entire U.S. Army, many of them stationed in the West. Even after congressional Radicals began directing Reconstruction policies, the number of troops in the South did not substantially increase.[19] The Freedmen's Bureau, regardless of the shortcomings of its officers, lacked the means to affect the lives and labor of Southern blacks.

"Suffering and want," John Eaton wrote from Vicksburg late in 1864, "are great remedial agencies." The suffering of the contrabands, he admitted, "has been appalling." Although the outcome seemed uncertain, Eaton hoped that through the experience of war the nation would atone for past sins and would secure for the freedmen a just place in American society.[20] The country did not emerge from the conflict chastened and pure, but the war had inevitably brought change. Slavery, by whatever means, had been abolished and bondsmen had become freedmen.

APPENDIX

The following table presents estimates of the number of blacks organized by freedmen superintendents during the war and the total number within Union lines before the close of hostilities in the spring of 1865.

	UNDER ORGANIZED CONTROL	WITHIN UNION LINES
Tidewater Virginia	25,000[1]	70,000[2]
Eastern Shore, Virginia	13,000	13,000[3]
North Carolina	17,300	17,300[4]
South Carolina	15,000[5]	25,000[6]
Louisiana (Department of Gulf)	95,000[7]	106,000[8]
Mississippi Valley	72,500[9]	770,000[10]
Total	237,800	1,001,300

1. "Census Return of Negro Population," February 1, 1864, Old Military Records, Bureau of Negro Affairs.
2. Orlando Brown to General O. O. Howard, November 31, 1865, *Senate Executive Documents,* No. 37, 39th Cong., 1st sess. For Confederate estimates of the number of slaves lost to federal lines, see James H. Brewer, *The Confederate Negro: Virginia's Craftsmen and Military Laborers, 1861-1865* (Durham, N.C., 1969), 15.
3. The government labor system on the Eastern Shore included all blacks

in Accomac and Northampton counties. This figure is based on 1860 census returns for the two counties.

4. Horace James, *Annual Report,* 4. Since Union control in North Carolina was limited to the immediate vicinity of several fortified towns, freedmen were either under direct federal control or living in Rebel-held territory.

5. Rose, *Rehearsal,* 322.

6. Ibid. This figure includes 10,000 blacks who arrived in the Port Royal area in the wake of Sherman's march to the sea, but not the black population in the coastal areas through which Sherman's army marched in the final months of the war.

7. T. W. Conway to General N. P. Banks, September 8, 1864, USCC-DG, Bureau of Civil Affairs, Letters Received; Conway, *Annual Report for 1864,* 4; unsigned report, "Plantations Under Cultivation, Aug., 1864," USCC-DG, Provost Marshal General, Letters Received. This figure includes about 10,500 antebellum free Negroes living in New Orleans.

8. This figure represents the black population in the Louisiana parishes excluded from the Emancipation Proclamation, and is compiled from 1860 census returns.

9. John Eaton to Levi Coffin, July 5, 1864, in Warren, *Extracts from Reports,* second series, 50.

10. Eaton, *Autobiography,* 216. Eaton based his estimate on 1860 census returns for the areas nominally controlled by Union troops.

NOTES

INTRODUCTION

1. Recent studies of major importance are Joel R. Williamson, *After Slavery: The Negro in South Carolina During Reconstruction* (Chapel Hill, 1965); James M. McPherson, *The Struggle for Equality: Abolitionists and the Negro in the Civil War and Reconstruction* (Princeton, 1964); and Willie Lee Rose, *Rehearsal for Reconstruction: The Port Royal Experiment* (New York, 1964).

2. The recent work of Avery Craven illustrates quite well the continuity of the traditional emphasis on social upheaval during the Civil War. Craven easily accommodates current values, arguing that the North's task during Reconstruction "was not merely one of securing a satisfactory peace but one of consolidating a revolution." Avery O. Craven, *Reconstruction: The Ending of the Civil War* (New York, 1969), 2.

The vicissitudes of Reconstruction historiography are variously analyzed in W. E. B. DuBois, *Black Reconstruction in America*, Atheneum edition (New York, 1970), 711-29; Bernard Weisberger, "The Dark and Bloody Ground of Reconstruction Historiography," *Journal of Southern History*, XXV (1959), 427-47; Kenneth M. Stampp, *The Era of Reconstruction, 1865-1877* (New York, 1965), 3-23; and John S. Rosenberg, "Toward a New Civil War Revisionism," *American Scholar*, XXXVIII (1969), 250-72.

3. The theme of revolution has become pervasive. Margaret Shortreed, "The Antislavery Radicals: From Crusade to Revolution, 1840-1868," *Past and Present*, XVI (1959), 65-87, provided the first systematic treatment of the theme. Allan Nevins, *The War for the Union*, 2 vols. (New York, 1959-1960) entitled volume two "War Becomes Revolution." David Brion Davis, an expert on slave institutions, found the emphasis on "the revolutionary implications of mass emancipation" entirely justified, although "revolution" in the end "misfired." See Davis, "Abolitionists and the Freedmen: An Essay Review," *Journal of Southern History*, XXXI (1965), 169. C. Vann Woodward, *The Burden of Southern History*, rev. ed. (Baton Rouge, 1968), 70, argued that the North's war aims changed from a "pragmatic struggle for power to a crusade for ideals" embracing "revolutionary aims." Later studies of Northern racism, however, convinced Woodward that the North's

"revolutionary aims" did not encompass racial equality. See Woodward, "White Racism and Black 'Emancipation,' " *New York Review of Books*, February 27, 1969, 8.

The theme of Radical weakness and betrayal is developed in Patrick W. Riddleberger, "The Radicals' Abandonment of the Negro During Reconstruction," *Journal of Negro History*, XLV (1960), 88-102; Richard O. Curry, "The Abolitionists and Reconstruction: A Critical Appraisal," *Journal of Southern History*, XXIV (1968), 540; and William S. McFeely, *Yankee Stepfather: General O. O. Howard and the Freedmen* (New Haven, 1968), 119-20.

4. David M. Potter, *The South and the Sectional Conflict* (Baton Rouge, 1968), 114. For studies of white "racism" during the Civil War era, see V. Jacque Voegeli, *Free But Not Equal: The Midwest and the Negro During the Civil War* (Chicago, 1968); and Forrest G. Wood, *Black Scare: The Racist Response to Emancipation and Reconstruction* (Berkeley, 1969).

Of more value than studies cataloguing anti-Negro sentiments are detailed investigations of conditions among blacks. For an example of the type of work that needs to be done, see Edward H. Bonekemper III, "Negro Ownership of Real Property in Hampton and Elizabeth City County, Virginia, 1860-1870," *Journal of Negro History*, LV (1970), 165-81.

5. Eugene D. Genovese, *The Political Economy of Slavery*, Vintage edition (New York, 1965), 268.

6. See Abraham Lincoln to Cuthbert Bullitt, July 28, 1862, and Francis Lieber, "A Memoir on the Military Uses of Colored Persons . . .," both in the Benjamin F. Butler Papers, LC.

7. Stampp, *Reconstruction*, 129; Philip S. Foner, *The Life and Writings of Frederick Douglass* (New York, 1955), 200, 204.

8. Sherman to General N. W. Halleck, January 12, 1865, OR, I, xlvii, pt. 2, 36-7; Sherman to General O. O. Howard, May 17, 1865, OR, I, xlvii, pt. 3, 515-16.

9. Undated, unsigned manuscript, enclosed in Lt. Colonel James Hopkins to Brig. General James Bowen, September 2, 1863, USCC-DG, Bureau of Civil Affairs, Letters Received.

CHAPTER 1

1. Richard S. West, Jr., *Lincoln's Scapegoat General: A Life of Benjamin F. Butler, 1818-1893* (Boston, 1965), 70.

2. B. F. Butler to General Winfield Scott, May 24, 1861, OR II, i, 752; Edward L. Pierce, "The Contrabands at Fortress Monroe," *Atlantic*, VIII (1861), 626-40; Luther P. Jackson, "The Origin of Hampton Institute," *Journal of Negro History*, X (1925), 133.

3. B. F. Butler to Thomas Hicks, Governor of Maryland, April 22, 1861, and John A. Andrew to Butler, April 25, 1861, Butler Papers, LC.

4. West, *Butler*, 81-83.

5. B. F. Butler to General Winfield Scott, May 24, 1861, OR, II, i, 752.

6. B. F. Butler to General Winfield Scott, May 27, 1861, OR, II, i, 754; Butler, Special Order, May 29, 1861, Butler Papers, LC.

7. Montgomery Blair to B. F. Butler, May 29 and 30, 1861, Butler Papers, LC.

8. Secretary Cameron to B. F. Butler, May 30, 1861, Butler Papers, LC and published in OR, II, i, 754-55.

9. Pierce, "Contrabands at Fortress Monroe," 627; Charles Fairman, "Edward Lillie Pierce," *Dictionary of American Biography*, XIV, 575-76.

10. For figures on the contraband population at Fortress Monroe during the summer of 1861, see an unsigned report dated July 29, 1861 in the Butler Papers, LC.

11. Pierce, "Contrabands at Fortress Monroe," 633-36. Pierce mentions that his orders prohibited the use of free Negroes as laborers. The 1860 census recorded 201 free Negroes and nearly 2,500 slaves in Elizabeth City County, which included Fortress Monroe and the town of Hampton.

12. OR, II, i, 759; *U.S. Statutes at Large*, XII, 319; McPherson, *Struggle for Equality*, 70-72.

13. *U.S. Statutes at Large*, XII, 319.

14. Secretary Cameron to B. F. Butler, August 8, 1861, OR, II, i, 762.

15. James Redpath to Secretary Cameron, June 1, 1861, OR, III, i, 244-45; Benjamin Quarles, *The Negro in the Civil War* (Boston, 1953), 64-65. Quarles argues that Cameron followed a "wishy-washy" course concerning the contrabands, allowing each commander to act as he wished. It is true that commanders in the loyal slave states generally excluded fugitives or delivered them to their masters, but confiscation of contrabands could occur only in rebellious areas. On this point, Secretary Cameron was as unequivocal as political conditions permitted.

16. Lewis Tappan to B. F. Butler, August 8 and 14, 1861, Butler Papers, LC; Butler to Tappan, August 10, 1861, AMA Archives.

17. Concerning the removal of contrabands to the North, see, for example, B. F. Butler to C. B. Wilder, April 13, 1864, BRFAL-Va, Department of Negro Affairs.

Voegeli, *Free But Not Equal*, makes a good deal of Midwestern fears that blacks would inundate the North. A similar paranoia contributed to the anti-Negro hysteria of the New York draft riot. But as Albon P. Man, Jr. points out in "Labor Competition and the New York Draft Riots of 1863," *Journal of Negro History*, XXXVI (1951), 375-405, the fear of Negro migration existed in the absence of any real threat.

18. E. L. Pierce to B. F. Butler, August 10, 1861; Lewis Tappan to Butler, August 8, 1861; Elizure Wright to Butler, August 10, 1861, Butler Papers, LC.

19. Quoted in West, *Butler*, 84.

20. General John E. Wool to Secretary Cameron, September 8, 1861, and Cameron to Wool, September 20, 1861, OR, II, i, 770-71.

21. For the contraband population in the Hampton Roads area, see unsigned report dated July 29, 1861, Butler Papers, LC, and T. J. Cram et al., Report to General Wool, March 20, 1862, *House Executive Documents*, No. 85, 37th Cong., 2nd sess. How many blacks were shipped to Washington over the years has not been determined, but requests for labor were continuous. See, for example, General Dix, Special Orders No. 183, July 3, 1863, Wilder Papers.

22. General Wool, Special Orders No. 72, October 14, 1861, *House Executive Documents*, No. 85, 37th Cong., 2nd sess.

23. Black laborers were scheduled to receive five dollars a month, to be held by the quartermaster for the care of dependents. At the discretion of the chief of each department, however, laborers might receive monthly incentive payments (two dollars for men of the first class and one dollar for second-class hands). If individuals proved exceptionally diligent, bonuses (not to exceed one dollar per month) were permitted. General Wool, General Orders No. 34, November 1, 1861, OR, II, i, 774-75.

24. Lewis Tappan to B. F. Butler, August 17, 1861, and draft of letter to Lewis Tappan, August 19, 1861, Butler Papers, LC.

25. Jackson, "Origin of Hampton Institute," 131-33. See also the early correspondence of AMA teachers in Virginia, particularly M. L. Coan to "Dear Bretheren," December 26, 1861, and C. P. Day to S. S. Jocelyn, April 30, 1862, AMA Archives.

26. General Wool, General Orders No. 21, March 15, 1862, Wilder Papers.

27. General Wool, General Orders No. 22, March 18, 1862, *House Executive Documents*, No. 85, 37th Cong., 2nd sess.; C. B. Wilder to Wool, March 22, 1862, Wilder Papers.

28. General Wool, General Orders, No. 30, April 14, 1862, Wilder Papers; C. B. Wilder to Wool, April 15, 1862, USCC-DVa, Letters Received.

29. General Wool to Secretary Stanton, May 1, 1862, Wilder Papers.

30. C. B. Wilder to S. S. Jocelyn, May 4, 1862, AMA Archives.

31. Benjamin P. Thomas and Harold M. Hyman, *Stanton: The Life and Times of Lincoln's Secretary of War* (New York, 1962), 194; C. B. Wilder, letter dated August 29, 1863, in the *New York Independent*, October 15, 1863; Wilder to George Whipple, June 9, 1862, AMA Archives.

32. General Dix, "Proclamation to the People of Accomac and Northampton Counties, Va.," November 13, 1861, OR, I, v, 431-32; Dix to Major General George B. McClellan, August 21, 1861, OR, II, i, 763; Dix to Colonel Augustus Morse, October 14, 1861, OR, II, i, 773-74.

33. T. C. Cram et al., Report to General Wool, March 20, 1862, *House Executive Documents*, No. 85, 37th Cong., 2nd sess.; Major General John A. Dix to John A. Andrew, November 5, 1862, USCC-DVa-NC, Letters Sent, vol. 3; Orlando Brown to General Dix, November 7, 1862, and Brown to Colonel Hoffman, September 13, 1863, USCC-DVa-NC, Letters Received;

Thomas Tucker to S. S. Jocelyn, December 24, 1862, and N. S. Beals to S. S. Jocelyn, September 7, 1863, AMA Archives.

34. Thomas and Hyman, *Stanton*, 232-33.

35. Francis Lieber, "A Memoir on the Military use of Colored Persons, Free or Slave, that come to our Armies for Support or Protection; Written at the Request of Honorable Edwin M. Stanton, Secretary of War," copy of original in Butler Papers, LC; Thomas and Hyman, *Stanton*, 234. During the Civil War, Lieber was frequently consulted by the federal government on matters concerning the laws of war. See John Martin Vincent's biographical sketch in the *Dictionary of American Biography*, XI, 236-38, and Frank Freidel, *Francis Lieber: Nineteenth Century Liberal* (Baton Rouge, 1947), 331, 292-359.

36. George Whipple to S. S. Jocelyn, June 11, 1862; S. L. Sprague to Whipple, June 20, 1862; C. B. Wilder to Whipple, June 20, 1862, AMA Archives.

37. General Dix to Secretary Stanton, September 12 and November 22, 1862, OR, I, xviii, 391, 461.

38. General Dix to John A. Andrew, November 5, 1862, USCC-DVa-NC, Letters Sent, vol. 3; Dix to Stanton, November 22, 1862, OR, I, xviii, 461.

39. General Dix to Secretary Stanton, November 22, 1862, OR, I, xviii, 461; Thomas and Hyman, *Stanton*, 243.

40. General Dix to Secretary Stanton, September 12, 1860, OR, I, xviii, 391; C. B. Wilder, "Copy of Petition to General Dix," November 16, 1862, AMA Archives; Wilder to (George Whipple), November 16, 1862, AMA Archives; General Dix to Secretary Stanton, December 13, 1862, OR, I, xviii, 480-81. For Wilder's commission, see Stanton to Wilder, January 28, 1863, Wilder Papers.

41. C. B. Wilder to S. S. Jocelyn, December 28, 1862, AMA Archives.

42. General Dix to Secretary Stanton, November 22, 1862, OR, I, xviii, 461.

43. General Dix to Secretary Stanton, December 13, 1862, USCC-DVa-NC, Letters Sent, vol. 2.

44. John Oliver to S. S. Jocelyn, November 25, 1862, AMA Archives.

45. General Dix to General M. Corcoran, November 26, 1862, OR, I, xviii, 464.

46. Orlando Brown to General Dix, November 7, 1862, USCC-DVa-NC, Letters Received.

47. Palmer Litts to S. S. Jocelyn, December 1, 1861, AMA Archives.

48. Henry Lee Swint (ed.), *Dear Ones at Home: Letters from Contraband Camps* (Nashville, 1966), 24, 29. Hereafter cited as Swint, *Contraband Camps*.

49. Swint, *Contraband Camps*, 24, 89.

50. Ibid., 29.

51. Ibid., 40.

52. Ibid., 21.
53. Orlando Brown to S. S. Jocelyn, July 11, 1863, AMA Archives; *Senate Executive Documents*, No. 27, 39th Cong., 1st sess.; Orlando Brown, 18th Mass. Vols., 29th Mass. Vols., and 24th U.S. Colored Troops, AGO-MSR and CWPR.
54. Miss R. G. C. Pattern to George Whipple, and E. Frances Jencks to S. S. Jocelyn, both dated June 3, 1864, AMA Archives; M. L. Coan to S. S. Jocelyn, May 9, 1863, AMA Archives.
55. General A. E. Burnside to Secretary Stanton, March 21, 1862, OR, II, i, 812; Vincent Colyer, *Brief Report of the Services Rendered by the Freed People to the United States Army in North Carolina in the Spring of 1862, after the Battle of Newbern* (New York, 1864), 5. The reaction of the largely New England troops to the contrabands is described in James A. Emmerton, *A Record of the Twenty-Third Regiment Mass. Vol. Infantry in the War of the Rebellion 1861-1865* (Boston, 1886), 95.
56. Colyer, *Brief Report*, 6; General Burnside to Secretary Stanton, March 21 and 27, 1862, OR, II, i, 812-13; Colonel R. C. Hawkins, General Orders No. 2, March 12, 1862, OR, II, i, 810.
57. Colyer, *Brief Report*, 44, 47; J. G. deR. Hamilton, "Edward Stanly," *Dictionary of American Biography*, VII, 515-16.
58. Horace James, *The Two Great Wars of America. An Oration Delivered in Newbern, North Carolina, Before the Twenty-Fifth Regiment Massachusetts Volunteers, July 4, 1862* (Boston, 1862), 27.
59. Chaplain Horace James, 25th Mass. Vols., AGO-MSR and CWPR. See also James' correspondence in the AMA Archives.
60. Howard K. Beale (ed.), *Diary of Gideon Welles; Secretary of the Navy Under Lincoln and Johnson*, 3 vols. (New York, 1960), I, 324.
61. *House Executive Documents*, No. 1, 38th Cong., 1st sess., 8.

CHAPTER 2

1. Joel Cook, *The Siege of Richmond: A Narrative of the Military Operations of Major General George B. McClellan During the Months of May and June, 1862* (Philadelphia, 1862), 73-74.
2. Swint, *Contraband Camps*, 47.
3. C. B. Wilder to William Whiting, July 18, 1862, AMA Archives.
4. Rev. Horace James, *Annual Report of the Superintendent of Negro Affairs in North Carolina, 1864. With an Appendix Containing the History and Management of the Freedmen in this Department up to June 1st, 1865* (Boston, 1865), 44.
5. Secretary Stanton to Robert Dale Owen et al., March 16, 1863, OR, III, iii, 73; McPherson, *Struggle for Equality*, 183.
6. Robert Dale Owen et al., "Preliminary and also the Final Report of the American Freedmen's Inquiry Commission," *Senate Executive Docu-*

ments, No. 53, 38th Cong., 1st sess., 13-15. Hereafter cited as AFIC, "Preliminary," or "Final Report."

7. AFIC, "Preliminary Report," 3-4.

8. AFIC, "Final Report"; John G. Sproat, "Blueprint for Radical Reconstruction," *Journal of Southern History*, XXIII (1957), 25-44; McPherson, *Struggle for Equality*, 185-86.

9. C. B. Wilder to General Wool, April 15, 1862, USCC-DVa-NC, Letters Received.

10. Thomas A. Scott to E. M. Stanton, March 22, 1862, Stanton Papers, LC.

11. Secretary Stanton to General M. C. Meigs, January 28, 1863, Wilder Papers.

12. General Dix to George Whipple, March 1, 1863, AMA Archives; Orlando Brown, testimony, AGO-AFIC.

13. General Dix to C. B. Wilder, March 28, 1863, Wilder Papers; C. B. Wilder to Secretary Stanton, August 1, 1863, AGO-DCT, Adjutant General, Letters Received; C. B. Wilder, letter dated August 29, 1863, published in the *New York Independent*, October 15, 1863.

14. C. B. Wilder to Lt. Colonel Hoffman, September 18, 1863, USCC-DVa-NC, Letters Received.

15. S. S. Jocelyn, article in the *New York Independent*, August 20, 1863.

16. General B. F. Butler, General Orders No. 46, December 5, 1863, OR, III, iii, 1139-44.

17. Ibid. Soldiers and laborers received rations plus ten dollars per month, three dollars of which was deducted for clothing.

18. Ibid. Butler replaced Kinsman as general superintendent in November 1864 with Major General George J. Carney. Carney held the office until the establishment of the Freedmen's Bureau and Orlando Brown's appointment as assistant commissioner for Virginia.

19. General U. S. Grant to B. F. Butler, August 22, 1864, and Butler to Grant, August 22, 1864, OR, I, xlii, pt. 3, 411; Asst. Adjutant General J. A. Judson to Colonel D. W. Wardrup, August 29, 1864, OR, I, xlii, pt. 2, 590; General I. N. Palmer to Major R. S. Davis, September 1, 1864, and Frederick Martin to B. F. Butler, September 1, 1864, OR, I, xlii, pt. 2, 653-54.

20. "Census Return of Negro Population in Dept. Va. and N. Carolina," February, 1864, Old Military Records, Bureau of Negro Affairs; Orlando Brown to O. O. Howard, November 31, 1865, *Senate Executive Documents*, No. 27, 39th Cong., 1st sess.

21. F. W. Bird, testimony, AGO-AFIC.

22. Testimony of F. W. Bird, C. B. Wilder, and Orlando Brown, AGO-AFIC.

23. Orlando Brown, testimony, AGO-AFIC; Lt. Colonel Hoffman to C. B. Wilder, August 23, 1863, Wilder Papers; *Second Annual Report of the New England Freedmen's Aid Society* (Boston, 1864), 28; *Extracts from Let-*

ters of Teachers and Superintendents of the New England Educational Commission for Freedmen (Boston, 1864), 11-12. Brown apologized for the use of local white overseers, but insisted that Northern men could not be located quickly enough to manage estates as they were occupied.

24. William Wakefield, testimony, AGO-AFIC.

25. C. B. Wilder, testimony, AGO-AFIC; Wilder to George Whipple, August 19, 1863, AMA Archives; Wilder to Lt. Colonel Hoffman, September 18, 1863, USCC-DVa-NC, Letters Received.

26. For Wilder's summary of planting operations during 1864, see his report to Major George J. Carney, December 30, 1864, QMG, Annual Reports. See also Edward W. Coffin to Major Theodore Reed, March 27, 1865, and B. F. Davis to E. W. Coffin, March 27, 1865, USCC-DVa-NC, Letters Received.

27. Luther P. Jackson, *Free Negro Labor and Property Holding in Virginia, 1830-1860* (New York, 1942), 105-111, Appendix II.

28. It is at least curious that the number of blacks reportedly settled on farms in Princess Anne and Norfolk counties early in 1865 (2,846) corresponded almost exactly with the number of free Negroes residing in those counties in 1860 (2,998). Wilder and Brown recorded nearly 9,000 "free" Negroes in the seven occupied counties, somewhat more than the 7,500 recorded in the 1860 census. While slaves doubtless claimed antebellum free Negro status, the increase could also have resulted from migration. See "Census Return of Negro Population," February 1, 1864, Old Military Records, Bureau of Negro Affairs; Lorenzo Thomas to Secretary Stanton, June 5, 1865, AGO, Letters Sent, vol. 3.

29. C. B. Wilder to Major George J. Carney, December 30, 1864, QMG, Annual Reports.

30. Orlando Brown to Colonel Kinsman, June 22, 1864, BRFAL-Va, Department of Negro Affairs.

31. Lorenzo Thomas to Secretary Stanton, June 5, 1865, AGO, Letters Sent, vol. 3; "Census Return of Negro Population," February 1, 1864, Old Military Records, Bureau of Negro Affairs.

32. C. B. Wilder to General E. O. C. Ord, January 23, 1865, CWSAR, Supervising Special Agent, Norfolk District, Letters Received; "Census Return of Negro Population," February 1, 1864, Old Military Records, Bureau of Negro Affairs.

33. B. F. Butler, Circular, February 2, 1864, BRFAL-Va, Department of Negro Affairs.

34. C. B. Wilder to General E. O. C. Ord, January 23, 1865, CWSAR, Supervising Special Agent, Norfolk District, Letters Received.

35. Major George J. Carney to General E. O. C. Ord, April 7, 1865, USCC-DVa-NC, Letters Received.

36. General E. O. C. Ord to General George H. Gordon, May 12, 1865, BRFAL-Va, Assistant Commissioner, Letters Received.

37. Edward W. Coffin to General Ludlow, April 21, 1865, Old Military Records, Bureau of Negro Affairs.

38. General Hartsuff, General Orders No. 11, April 24, 1865, OR, I, xlvi, pt. 3, 1291.

39. D. Heaton, report to Secretary of the Treasury W. P. Fessenden, February 11, 1865, printed copy in Banks Papers, LC; James, *Annual Report*, 4-5, 21-25, 56.

40. General Schofield, General Orders No. 32, April, 27, 1865, OR, I, xlvii, pt. 3, 331.

41. Schofield, General Orders No. 46, May 15, 1865, OR, I, xlvii, pt. 3, 505. Concern with keeping freedmen out of the cities and employed in the countryside pervaded the War Department. See General H. W. Halleck to General A. H. Terry, June 22, 1865, OR, I, xlvi, pt. 3, 1291; Lorenzo Thomas to Secretary Stanton, June 5, 1865, AGO, Letters Sent, vol. 3.

42. General A. H. Terry to General Ruggles, September 15, 1865, USCC-DVa-NC, Letters Sent, vol. 14.

43. Secretary Stanton to General Terry, June 17, 1865, OR, I, xlvi, pt. 3, 1283.

44. Lorenzo Thomas to Secretary Stanton, June 5, 1865, AGO, Letters Sent, vol. 3; General E. O. C. Ord to Secretary Stanton, March 5, 1865 and C. B. Wilder to George Whipple, March 20, 1865, AMA Archives.

45. Roster of Officers on Duty, BRFAL-Va. For Wilder's career after leaving the Hampton area, see his correspondence with the American Missionary Association, AMA Archives.

46. Agricultural activities in North Carolina during the war were evidently not extensive. The settlement of some blacks on abandoned lands near the town of Washington is mentioned in Horace James to Colonel J. B. Kinsman, February 15, 1864, Old Military Records, Bureau of Negro Affairs.

47. Although there were no written contracts, James agreed to pay his 150 hands from five dollars per month for boys to fifteen dollars for able-bodied men. Rations and garden plots were provided for each family, and some blacks were permitted to rent land for one-third of the crops they raised.

For a discussion of the incident which ended James' postwar efforts, see William S. McFeely, *Yankee Stepfather: General O. O. Howard and the Freedmen* (New Haven, 1968), 250-54. The victim, who had been placed by James at hard labor under an armed guard for stealing, was killed by a Negro guard while trying to escape. James justified the killing and Whittlesey felt sure the matter would be covered over. See also Whittlesey to James, September 5, Richard O'Flynn Papers, Holy Cross College Library, Worcester, Massachusetts.

48. Bonekemper, "Negro Ownership of Real Property," 165-81.

49. Edith Armstrong Talbot, *Samuel Chapman Armstrong: A Biographical Study* (New York, 1904), 142.

50. Richard L. Morton, " 'Contraband' and Quakers in the Virginia Penin-

sula, 1862-1869,'' *Virginia Magazine of History and Biography*, LXI (1953), 419-29.

CHAPTER 3

1. C. B. Wilder, letter dated August 29, 1863, published in the *New York Independent*, October 15, 1863.

2. Brig. General T. W. Sherman to Adjutant General Lorenzo Thomas, November 11, 1861, OR, I, vi, 5-6. ''The effect of this victory is startling,'' wrote Sherman. ''Every white inhabitant has left.''

In the discussion of the administration of freedmen's affairs in the Sea Islands which follows, I have relied heavily on Willie Lee Rose, *Rehearsal for Reconstruction: The Port Royal Experiment*, Vintage ed. (New York, 1967), a detailed and careful study of the important reform efforts in this area. I have already taken issue with the notion, shared by Rose, that the Civil War involved revolutionary change for blacks. But the author's assertion that ''by the close of 1862,'' the war had ''indeed become a social revolution,'' (170) is less crucial to her study than the details and observations which indicate that reform measures failed to alter the condition of the islands' laborers.

Less complete treatments of the Port Royal Experiment can be found in William H. and Jane H. Pease, *Black Utopia: Negro Communal Experiments in America* (Madison, 1963), 123-59; and Bell I. Wiley, *Southern Negroes, 1861-1865* (New Haven, 1938), 177-78 and passim.

3. Rose, *Rehearsal*, 15-16; Brig. General T. W. Sherman, ''Proclamation to the People of South Carolina,'' November 8, 1861, OR, I, vi, 4-5.

4. Quoted in Rose, *Rehearsal*, 26-27.

5. Elizabeth Ware Pearson (ed.), *Letters from Port Royal Written at the Time of the Civil War* (Boston, 1906), 12-13; Rose, *Rehearsal*, 65, 80, 83.

6. Rose, *Rehearsal*, 79, 81-82, 174, 203-4, 302-4; Kenneth Stampp, *The Peculiar Institution: Slavery in the Ante-Bellum South* (New York, 1956), 56. Under favorable conditions, antebellum planters cultivated ten acres of cotton for every prime field hand.

7. Major General David Hunter, General Orders No. 11, May 9, 1862, OR, I, xiv, 341.

8. Edward L. Pierce to Secretary Chase, May 12, 1862, OR, III, ii, 52-53; Rose, *Rehearsal*, 147.

9. Secretary Stanton to Brig. General Rufus Saxton, April 29, 1862, OR, III, ii, 27-28.

10. Rose, *Rehearsal*, 152-55, 203-4.

11. ''Letter from the Secretary of the Treasury,'' February 18, 1863, *House Executive Documents*, No. 72, 37th Cong., 3rd sess.; Rose, *Rehearsal*, 206n.

12. Secretary Stanton to General Saxton, August 25, 1862, OR, I, xiv, 377-78; Rose, *Rehearsal*, 191, 205.

13. Rose, *Rehearsal*, 82, 255.

14. Pearson, *Letters from Port Royal*, 231; Rose, *Rehearsal*, 235. For an analysis of the various factions among the missionaries and superintendents, and the role of the direct tax commission, see Rose, *Rehearsal*, 272-96.

15. Ibid., 285, 290, 296.

16. Ibid., 215.

17. See figures in Rose, *Rehearsal*, 300, 305, 434, and *Second Annual Report of the New England Freedmen's Aid Society* (Boston, 1864), 61-62.

18. Farm hands in eastern Virginia received shares rather than wages. For wage levels elsewhere in the occupied South, see below.

19. Quoted in Pease, *Black Utopia*, 151.

20. General William T. Sherman, Special Field Orders No. 15, January 16, 1865, OR, I, xlvii, pt. 2, 60-62; Rose, *Rehearsal*, 330.

Although Sherman made his decision with the full support of Secretary of War Stanton, he had contemplated the move for some time. Before beginning his Atlanta campaign a year earlier, Sherman suggested to Adjutant General Lorenzo Thomas that the east bank of the Mississippi River from Memphis to Vicksburg should be settled exclusively with blacks. Such a measure, the general argued, would solve the growing contraband problem and secure the river from Rebel attack. While Sherman's recommendations were ignored in the West, Secretary Stanton apparently found the plan useful in South Carolina and Georgia. See General William T. Sherman to General Lorenzo Thomas, April 12, 1864, OR, III, iv, 225.

21. Rose, *Rehearsal*, 396; see McFeely, *Yankee Stepfather*, 130-48, for a discussion of dispossession in the Sea Islands in the immediate postwar years.

22. Susie M. Ames, "Federal Policy Toward the Eastern Shore of Virginia in 1861," *Virginia Magazine of History and Biography*, LXIX (1961), 432-59.

23. Major General John A. Dix, "Proclamation to the People of Accomac and Northampton Counties, Va.," November 13, 1861, OR, I, v, 431-32; Ames, "Eastern Shore," 442. The order prohibiting blacks from entering Union camps was carefully followed. Commanding General Henry E. Lockwood ordered one slave flogged for repeatedly entering federal camps. Ibid., 452.

24. Reverend C. S. Henry supervised the Fourth District, Department of Negro Affairs, consisting of Accomac and Northampton counties in Virginia, and St. Mary's County, Maryland. Henry was appointed on January 9, 1864, and was assisted by William G. Leonard, assistant superintendent for St. Mary's County. See General B. F. Butler, Special Orders No. 9, January 9, 1864, BRFAL-Va, Department of Negro Affairs.

25. C. S. Henry to Colonel J. B. Kinsman, March 23 and February 29, 1864, Old Military Records, Bureau of Negro Affairs.

26. Jackson, *Free Negro in Virginia*, 111.

27. Lt. Colonel Frank J. White, 10th New York Vols., AGO-MSR and

CWPR; Colonel White, "Report; 4th Dist.: Negro Affairs," February 1, 1865, USCC-DVa-NC, Letters Received, filed under 'R' (hereafter cited Colonel White, "Report").

28. Colonel White, "Report."

29. Colonel White, Special Orders No. 81, November 4, 1864, USCC-DVa-NC, Letters Received, filed under 'R'. Announcing his labor plan, White wrote that "complaints have been made . . . that many of the *freed slaves* and colored inhabitants . . . are living in idleness." [Emphasis added.] Accomac and Northampton counties were excluded from the Emancipation Proclamation and slavery theoretically continued to exist until the ratification of the 13th Amendment in December 1865. But, as Colonel White's statement indicates, the contract labor system brought practical emancipation.

30. Ibid.; Colonel White to Thomas R. Joynes, November 1, 1864, USCC-DVa-NC, U.S. Forces, Eastern Shore, vol. 246.

31. Colonel White, Special Orders No. 81, November 4, 1864, USCC-DVa-NC, Letters Received.

32. Colonel White, Circular, December 23, 1864, USCC-DVa-NC, Letters Received, filed under 'R'.

33. Colonel White to G. C. Tyler, February 7, 1865, USCC-DVa-NC, U.S. Forces, Eastern Shore, vol. 246.

34. Colonel White, "Report."

35. Farm laborers in Tidewater Virginia worked for shares. Hands at Port Royal worked at a basic rate of 25¢ per day, or $6.50 per month, although real wages were considerably lower. For reported and real wages in the Department of the Gulf and the Mississippi Valley, see Chapters 5 and 10.

36. See Jackson, *Free Negro in Virginia*, 103 n. Jackson used postwar freedmen contracts to suggest that antebellum free Negro farm laborers seldom earned more than $40.00 a year. There is, then, no accurate way of comparing wartime wages with antebellum rates.

37. Old Military Records, Bureau of Negro Affairs. The total of 175 extant contracts falls into three groups: 1) labor contracts negotiated during November and December 1864, most of which expired during January 1865; 2) labor contracts negotiated for the 1865 season; and 3) rental contracts negotiated for the same period. The 1865 labor contracts, unfortunately, are of little use since the period for which wages were paid is not consistently recorded. Of the ninety-two contracts negotiated during November and December 1864, forty involved men, fifty-two women. Of the men, eight earned monthly wages of over ten dollars, although five of these were required to provide their own room and board. Eighteen men earned less than five dollars a month and three received no compensation about their maintenance. Women, predictably, earned considerably less. Only four earned more than five dollars each month above their room and board, while twenty-two earned less than one dollar.

38. Ironically, the Eastern Shore suffered from a shortage of labor. In

January 1865 White requested that some fifty black families be transferred to the Eastern Shore from Tidewater Virginia. The colonel promised immediate employment. See Colonel White to Major George J. Carney, January 31, 1865, USCC-DVa-NC, U.S. Forces, Eastern Shore, vol. 246.

39. Objectively, conditions for blacks on the Eastern Shore were no better as a result of federal occupation, but they were probably no worse. A number of freedmen, probably former free Negroes, rented farms as tenants. Existing contracts record eight farms rented by blacks for cash payments ranging from twenty to thirty-five dollars yearly. In three cases, black tenants labored a certain number of days each week on the landlord's farm. Most tenants, however, paid a portion of their seasons' produce as rent. Typically, one-third to two-fifths of the various crops were claimed by the landlords, although occasionally one-half of certain crops was required. In one case a landlord provided his tenant with a team and took two-thirds of the year's crops. Twenty-six rental contracts signed early in 1865 can be found in Old Military Records, Bureau of Negro Affairs.

For a discussion of the status of antebellum free Negro tenant farmers, see Jackson, *Free Negro in Virginia*, 104-5.

40. Colonel White to Major George J. Carney?, February 16, 1865, USCC-DVa-NC, Misc. Records, 1864-1865.

41. Unsigned and undated endorsement on ibid.; Jackson, *Free Negro in Virginia*, 250. Aside from Thomas Cropper in Accomac County, who owned 150 acres, the Collinses were the only blacks on Virginia's Eastern Shore with farms of this size. Together they owned 252 acres.

CHAPTER 4

1. By the end of the war, the number of blacks within Union lines at Hampton Roads, Newbern, Port Royal, and on the Eastern Shore numbered about 125,000. By contrast, there were approximately 770,000 freedmen within federal lines in the lower Mississippi Valley, and over 100,000 more in the occupied parishes of Louisiana.

2. B. F. Butler to Secretary Stanton, May 25, 1862, OR, I, xv, 439-40.

3. *New Orleans Daily Picayune*, May 2, 1862, quoted in Wiley, *Southern Negroes*, 187.

4. *Daily Picayune*, May 29, 30, 1962; Wiley, *Southern Negroes*, 187-88.

5. B. F. Butler to Count Mejan, French Consul, August 14, 1862, USCC-DG, Letters Sent, vol. 2.

6. *Daily Picayune*, June 10, 1862.

7. B. F. Butler to Secretary Stanton, May 25, 1863, OR, I, xv, 440-41.

8. Thus, when three fugitives belonging to the city's gas works sought protection within Union lines, Butler ordered them returned. Similarly, he ruled that while the state of Louisiana could no longer enslave children of

female convicts, "possibly the master might have some claim." B. F. Butler
to Moses Bates, August 20, 1862, and Butler to Brig. General J. W. Phelps,
September 8, 1862, USCC-DG, Letters Sent, vol. 2.

   9. B. F. Butler to J. W. Phelps, May 9 and May 10, 1862, OR, I, xv,
442-43.

   10. W. Mithoff, President of Police Jury, Jefferson Parish, to B. F. Butler,
May 20, 1862, Butler Papers, LC.

   11. B. F. Butler to J. W. Phelps, May 20, 1862, draft of letter, and Report
of Provost Marshal at Camp Parapet, May 22, 1862, Butler Papers, LC; Butler
to Phelps, May 23, 1862, USCC-DG, Letters Sent, vol. 2, also published
in OR, I, xv, 442.

   12. Captain Edward Page to B. F. Butler, May 27, 1862, Butler Papers,
LC.

   13. Butler to Captain Haggerty, May 27, 1862, USCC-DG, Letters Sent,
vol. 2.

   14. Captain Edward Page to B. F. Butler, June 1 and June 19, 1862, Butler
Papers, LC.

   15. J. W. Phelps to Captain R. S. Davis, June 16, 1862, OR, I, xv, 485-
90.

   16. B. F. Butler to Secretary Stanton, June 18, 1862, USCC-DG, Letters
Sent, vol. 2; also published in OR, I, xv, 485.

   17. Secretary Stanton to B. F. Butler, July 3, 1862, Butler Papers, LC,
also published in OR, III, iii, 200; Thomas and Hyman, *Stanton*, 242.

   18. George S. Denison to D. C. Denison, July 29, 1862, Denison Papers,
LC; J. W. Phelps to Adjutant General Lorenzo Thomas, August 2, 1862,
copy of letter in Butler Papers, LC; West, *Butler*, 179-80.

   The War Department accepted Phelps' resignation effective August 21,
1862.

   19. Butler to S. P. Chase, July 10, 1862, Chase Papers, Historical Society
of Pennsylvania; Chase to George S. Denison, September 8, 1862, Denison
Papers, LC; Chase to Butler, September 23, 1862, Butler Papers, LC.

   20. Lincoln rejected complaints lodged against Phelps by loyal planters in
Louisiana as mere "pretense." The president's growing weariness with arguments of loyal slaveholders had become evident by the summer of 1862.
". . . it is their own fault, not mine," wrote Lincoln, "that they are annoyed
by the presence of General Phelps. They also know the remedy . . . Remove
the necessity of his presence . . . I distrust the *wisdom* if not the *sincerity*
of friends, who would hold my hands while my enemies stab me. This appeal
of professed friends had paralyzed me more in this struggle than any other
one thing . . ." Lincoln to Reverdy Johnson, July 26, 1862, Butler Papers,
LC.

   21. B. F. Butler, General Orders No. 91, November 9, 1862, AGO-AFIC;
also published in OR, I, xv, 592-95.

   22. B. F. Butler to Maj. Gen. Henry W. Halleck, September 1, 1862,

and Butler to Brig. Gen. Weitzel, November 2, 1862, Butler Papers, LC.

23. Memorandum of contract with planters, enclosed in B. F. Butler to President Lincoln, November 28, 1862, AGO-AFIC.

24. B. F. Butler to President Lincoln, November 28, 1862, AGO-AFIC.

25. Fred Harvey Harrington, *Fighting Politician: Major General N. P. Banks* (Philadelphia, 1948), 88-89; B. F. Butler, Testimony, AGO-AFIC.

26. See Carl Russell Fish's biographical sketch of Butler in the *Dictionary of American Biography*, III, 357 ff.; T. Harry Williams, "General Banks and the Radical Republicans in the Civil War," *New England Quarterly*, XII (1939), 268; Harrington, *Banks*, 52.

27. *Daily Picayune*, December 25, 1862, quoted in Wiley, *Southern Negroes*, 210-11.

28. George H. Hepworth, *The Whip, Hoe, and Sword; or, the Gulf-Department in '63* (Boston, 1864), 27; Harris Elwood Starr, "George Hughes Hepworth," *Dictionary of American Biography*, VII, 569-70; Harrington, *Banks*, 93.

29. Draft of report, January 1863, Banks Papers, LC.

30. R. B. Irwin, endorsement entered in ledger, January 1863, USCC-DG, Letters Sent, vol. 2.

31. N. P. Banks, General Orders No. 12, January 29, 1863, OR, I, xv, 666-67.

32. Colonel E. G. Beckwith, president of the Sequestration Commission, printed announcement, February 5, 1863, USCC-DG, Provost Marshal General, Letters Received; Orders of the Sequestration Commission, approved by General Banks February 6, 1863, BRFAL, Louisiana, vol. 540.

33. N. P. Banks to "all Commanding Officers, Provost Marshals, Judges, etc., etc.," February 6, 1863, USCC-DG, Defenses of New Orleans, Provost Marshal General, Letters Received.

34. George S. Denison to Salmon P. Chase, March 14, 1863, "Diary and Correspondence of Salmon P. Chase," in *American Historical Association Report for 1902*, II, 366-67; Harrington, *Banks*, 105-7; Hepworth, *Whip, Hoe and Sword*, 25-28; Samuel W. Cozzens to Colonel S. B. Holabird, May 15, 1863, USCC-DG, Bureau of Civil Affairs, Letters Received.

35. *Daily Picayune*, January 31, 1863.

36. *L'Union*, April 7, June 16, 1863.

37. N. P. Banks to Lieutenant G. H. Hanks, April 21, 1863, USCC-DG, Letters Sent, vol. 5.

38. *Second Annual Report of the New England Freedmen's Aid Society*, (Boston, 1864), 46.

39. James McKaye, *The Mastership and its Fruits: The Emancipated Slave Face to Face with his Old Master*, (New York, 1864), 16-18, 25-27; N. P. Banks to James McKaye, March 29, 1864, and McKaye to Banks, April 29, 1864, Banks Papers, LC.

40. Speech delivered by Douglass, published in the *Liberator*, February

10, 1865, and quoted in James M. McPherson, *The Negro's Civil War: How American Negroes Felt and Acted During the War for the Union* (New York, 1965), 129. See also McPherson, *Struggle for Equality*, 290.

41. Abraham Lincoln to N. P. Banks, August 5, 1863, Banks Papers, LC.

42. N. P. Banks to James Bowen, December 26, 1863, USCC-DG, Provost Marshal Records, vol. 309.

43. Gerald M. Capers, *Occupied City: New Orleans Under the Federals, 1862-1865* (Lexington, 1965), 221-24; Harrington, *Banks*, 113.

44. N. P. Banks, General Orders No. 23, February 3, 1864, OR, I, xxxiv, pt. 2, 227-31.

45. Superintendent Hanks was permitted by Banks in May 1863 to negotiate contracts with planters outside Union-controlled areas "under such regulations as may be just." Evidently designed to provide laborers for planters beyond the jurisdiction of the provost marshals, Hanks' contracts set a somewhat higher rate of pay. He scheduled men to receive ten dollars per month, women six dollars, and children over twelve, two dollars. "Suitable" clothing and rations were to be provided by employers and the cost of clothing deducted from wages. Since the planters involved lived outside federal jurisdiction, there was apparently no way to enforce these provisions. A copy of the contract used by Hanks appears in BRFAL, Louisiana, Department of Plantations, vol. 93. See also N. P. Banks to G. H. Hanks, May 20, 1863, USCC-DG, Letters Sent, vol. 5.

46. In fact, planters sold laborers food and clothing on credit. These expenses, combined with wage deductions, eroded the laborers' meager wages and kept many continually in debt. See Captain James M. White to Captain Albert Stearns, and Lieutenant W. W. Mason to Stearns, August 23, 1864, USCC-DG, Defenses of New Orleans, Provost Marshal General, Letters Received.

47. N. P. Banks, General Orders No. 23, February 3, 1864, OR, I, xxiv, pt. 2, 227-31.

48. Ibid.

49. Ibid.

50. Edwin M. Wheelock to General Hurlbut, January 3, 1864, and E. M. Gregory to Colonel Whittlesey, September 15, 1865, E. M. Wheelock, 15th New Hampshire Volunteers and 76th U. S. Colored Troops, AGO-MSR; Wheelock to Captain Wage, May 13, 1865, USCC-DG, Defenses of New Orleans, Provost Marshal General, Letters Received. For Hanks' dismissal, see E. D. Townsend, Special Order No. 163, April 7, 1865, George H. Hanks, 12th Connecticut Volunteers and 99th U. S. Colored Troops, AGO-MSR.

51. T. W. Conway to Major George B. Drake, November 2, 1864, USCC-DG, Bureau of Civil Affairs, Letters Received; George R. Bentley, *A History of the Freedmen's Bureau* (Philadelphia, 1955), Appendix.

52. T. W. Conway, *The Freedmen of Louisiana. Final Report of the*

Bureau of Free Labor, Department of the Gulf to Major General E. R. S. *Camby, Commanding* (New Orleans, 1865), 4-6.
   53. Hepworth, *Whip, Hoe, and Sword*, 27.

CHAPTER 5

   1. George H. Hanks to Captain M. Hawes, July 1, 1863, and Hanks to N. P. Banks, July 12, 1863, USCC-DG, Bureau of Civil Affairs, Letters Received; Captain Samuel W. Cozzens to Colonel S. B. Holabird, May 15, 1863, USCC-DG, Bureau of Civil Affairs, Letters Received.
   2. George H. Hanks to Colonel John S. Clark, October 16, 1863, Banks Papers, LC.
   In September 1863, Hanks transferred the plantations under his control to Treasury Agent Benjamin F. Flanders and S. W. Cozzens, who then served as Flanders' assistant. Although Flanders expressed contempt for Banks' labor system and vainly sought to alter the plan of organization, he quickly discovered that the Treasury Department lacked the power to regulate plantation labor independently of the army. Whatever independent authority Flanders might have had to start with was undermined in October by orders from the War Department which directed General Banks to ''assume control over all such plantations, houses, funds and sources of revenue'' that seemed necessary for the care and support of blacks. See General H. W. Halleck to N. P. Banks, October 26, 1863, Banks Papers, LC.
   3. Thomas W. Conway to Major George B. Drake, October 3, 1864, USCC-DG, Bureau of Civil Affairs, Letters Received; N. P. Banks, General Orders No. 23, Feburary 3, 1864, OR, I, xxiv, pt. 2, 230.
   4. T. W. Conway to N. P. Banks, September 9, 1864, USCC-DG, Bureau of Civil Affairs, Letters Received; T. W. Conway, *Annual Report of Thomas W. Conway, Superintendent Bureau of Free Labor, Department of the Gulf, to Major General Hurlbut Commanding, for the Year 1864* (New Orleans, 1865), 3-4. The manuscript as well as a copy of the published report is filed in USCC-DG, Bureau of Civil Affairs, Letters Received.
   5. These totals are extracted from George H. Hanks to N. P. Banks, July 27, 1864, and T. W. Conway to Banks, October 10, 1864, Banks Papers, LC; Conway to Banks, September 9, 1864, USCC-DG, Bureau of Civil Affairs, Letters Received; ''Plantations Under Cultivation, August 1864,'' unsigned Report in USCC-DG, Provost Marshal General, Letters Received.
   6. Brig. General James Bowen to Captain Paige, June 10, 1863, USCC-DG, Provost Marshal Records, Letters Sent, vol. 297; Amadeo Landry to N. P. Banks, December 22, 1863, USCC-DG, Bureau of Civil Affairs, Letters Received.
   7. George H. Hanks to N. P. Banks, June 30 and July 12, 1863, USCC-DG, Bureau of Civil Affairs, Letters Received; Hanks to Captain George S.

Darling, July 29, 1864, USCC-DG, Defenses of New Orleans, Provost Marshal General, Letters Received.

8. Brig. General James Bowen to Captain G. S. Darling, April 14, 1864, USCC-DG, Defenses of New Orleans, Provost Marshal General, Letters Received.

9. Captain James M. White to Captain Albert Stearns, and Lieutenant W. W. Mason to Albert Stearns, August 23, 1864, USCC-DG, Defenses of New Orleans, Provost Marshal General, Letters Received; Printed circular to planters from the office of the Provost Marshal, Brashear City, 1864, ibid.

10. N. P. Banks, General Orders No. 92, July 9, 1864, ibid.

11. N. P. Banks to Colonel R. B. Brown, August 20, 1864, USCC-DG, Provost Marshal General, Letters Received.

12. T. W. Conway to N. P. Banks, September 9, 1864, USCC-DG, Bureau of Civil Affairs, Letters Received.

13. Conway to Major George B. Drake, September 20, 1864, and Conway to Major General S. A. Hurlbut, November 12, 1864, ibid.; Conway, *Annual Report for the Year 1864*, 6-7.

14. Captain Nelson Kenyon to Captain C. H. Miller, March 8, 1865, USCC-DG, Defenses of New Orleans, Misc. Letters Received; T. W. Conway, *Annual Report for the Year 1864*, 8-10.

15. Frank F. Barclay to N. P. Banks, February 22 and March 5, 1863, USCC-DG, Bureau of Civil Affairs, Letters Received. Barclay edited the New Orleans *L'Union*, a journal which included among its readership the New Orleans free Negro population. Interestingly, the publication used as its motto a French rendition of President Lincoln's famous response to Horace Greeley: "'L'Union'. . . . l'union avec des esclaves, l'union sans esclaves,—l'union quand meme.' " The editor also printed ads for runaway slaves. See *L'Union*, December 18, 1862.

16. Walter Prichard, "The Effects of the Civil War on the Louisiana Sugar Industry," *Journal of Southern History*, V (1939), 315-32.

17. Bell I. Wiley, "Vicissitudes of Early Reconstruction Farming in the Lower Mississippi Valley," *Journal of Southern History*, III (1937), 449, argues that the sudden removal of traditional controls had a "deleterious" effect on blacks. The same argument is made in Wiley, *Southern Negroes*, passim. The fact that traditional controls were maintained, particularly during the first year of occupation, is largely overlooked.

18. Frank F. Barclay to N. P. Banks, March 5, 1863, USCC-DG, Bureau of Civil Affairs, Letters Received.

19. L. Millandon to N. P. Banks, February 1, 1863, ibid.

20. Captain Samuel W. Cozzens to Colonel S. B. Holabird, May 15, 1863, ibid.

21. Captain Edward Page to Captain Henry S. Pierson, June 16, 1863; Captain Lawrence O'Brien to Pierson, June 10, 1863; Captain J. W. Rudyard to Pierson, June 1, 1863, USCC-DG, Provost Marshal General, Misc. Records.

Although enforcement of the labor regulations improved matters, the need for labor remained chronic throughout the war. Early in 1864, a planter near New Orleans requested permission to secure surplus blacks from federal authorities at Natchez or Vicksburg. And, in the last days of the war, Superintendent of Labor Conway reported thousands of applications for laborers in excess of the supply. "I could give work to five thousand more," he reported. See T. W. Conway to Colonel George B. Drake, March 29, 1865, and J. W. Austin to George H. Hanks February 22, 1864, USCC-DG, Bureau of Civil Affairs, Letters Received.

22. John T. Wood et al. to N. P. Banks, [February 1863?], USCC-DG, Bureau of Civil Affairs, Letters Received. A similar petition was received from planters in St. Mary's Parish.

23. Fred H. Knapp to N. P. Banks, April 1, 1863, ibid.

24. Dr. I. Zacharie to N. P. Banks, February 19, 1863, Banks Papers, LC.

25. Unsigned, undated letter to N. P. Banks [February 1863?], USCC-DG, Bureau of Civil Affairs, Letters Received.

26. William W. Pugh to Captain C. W. Rudyard, May 26, 1863, USCC-DG, Provost Marshal General, Misc. Records.

27. A. Robinson to N. P. Banks, (Received February 26, 1863), USCC-DG, Provost Marshal General, Letters Received.

28. Lieutenant Enoch Foster to Captain Henry S. Pierson, June 8, 1863, USCC-DG, Provost Marshal General, Misc. Records.

29. Rev. G. H. Hepworth to N. P. Banks, March 5, 1863; Hepworth and E. M. Wheelock to Banks, April 9, 1863, Banks Papers, LC.

30. *New Orleans Times*, November 22, 1864, cited in Wiley, "Early Reconstruction Farming," 450-51; W. J. Strictland to Lieutenant Van Ornum, July 13, 1865, USCC-DG, Defenses of New Orleans, Provost Marshal General, Letters Received.

31. Alexander F. Pugh, diary, quoted in John D. Winter, *The Civil War in Louisiana* (Baton Rouge, 1963), 410.

32. *Daily Picayune*, February 20, 1863; Harrington, *Banks*, 105.

33. Harry McCall to Major H. M. Porter, March 26, 1863, and "Proceedings, Meeting of Planters," March 19, 1863, USCC-DG, Defenses of New Orleans, Misc. Letters Received.

34. Captain John W. Ela to Brig. General James Bowen, May 27 and June 10, 1863, USCC-DG, Defenses of New Orleans, Provost Marshal General, Letters Received.

35. Captain Wickham Hoffman to John W. Ela, April 29, 1863, and General T. W. Sherman to General W. H. Emory, June 22, 1863, ibid.

36. C. W. Killborn to Captain Brown, March 5, 1863, ibid.

37. Ephraim L. Patterson, special investigating officer, to Brig. General James Bowen, July 8, 1863, USCC-DG, Provost Marshal General, Letters Received. A similar episode is attributed to a "Capt. Vander" in Hepworth, *Whip, Hoe, and Sword*, 232-37.

Apparently, Sawyer's brutality was exceptional. When he and his men punished a thief by binding him naked to a tree and leaving him helplessly exposed to the swarms of evening mosquitoes, the Vermont-born provost marshal was arrested and eventually dismissed from the service. Patterson to Bowen, July 8, 1863, USCC-DG, Provost Marshal General, Letters Received; Silas W. Sawyer, 9th Connecticut Volunteers, AGO-MSR.

38. Brig. General James Bowen, Circular No. 2, February 2, 1863, USCC-DG, Defenses of New Orleans, Provost Marshal General, Letters Received.

39. George H. Hanks to Brig. General James Bowen, March 16, 1863, USCC-DG, Defenses of New Orleans, Provost Marshal General, Letters Received.

40. C. W. Killborn to Captain Chapman, March 17, 1863, USCC-DG, Provost Marshal Records, New Orleans, vol. 345. The provost guard was directed at one point to "cause the negroes who may be pointed out by Mr. Stackhouse to be arrested as vagrants and deliver them to Lieutenant Hanks." See also Lieutenant James F. Miller to Captain A. W. Miller, April 4, 1863, USCC-DG, Defenses of New Orleans, Provost Marshal General, Letters Received.

41. George H. Hanks to N. P. Banks, April 8, 1863, USCC-DG, Bureau of Civil Affairs, Letters Received; George H. Hepworth and E. M. Wheelock to N. P. Banks, April 10, 1863, Banks Papers, LC.

The government itself was not particularly scrupulous in recruiting labor for particular tasks. In the winter of 1863-1864, when levees in the department required extensive repairs to contain the spring flood, labor camps and jails were emptied, and "vagrants" pulled off the streets. As many as 2,000 hands were thus worked under army direction. Similarly, officers arbitrarily arrested "idle" blacks in Brashear City to unload military stores. See Brig. General Stone to Brig. General James Bowen, December 18, 1863; Bowen to Hanks, February 9, 1864, USCC-DG, Provost Marshal Records, vols. 298 and 309.

42. George H. Hanks to Captain Albert Stearns, July 18, 1864; Stearns to Colonel C. L. Harris, July 18, 1864; Stearns to Hanks, July 15, 1864; Stearns to provost guard, July 11, 1864, USCC-DG, Defenses of New Orleans, Provost Marshal St. Mary's Parish, Letters Sent and Provost Marshal General, Letters Received.

43. Thomas W. Conway to Major George B. Drake, September 29, 1864; N. P. Banks to Colonel Robinson, September 9, 1864, USCC-DG, Provost Marshal General, Letters Received. Conway to Captain Darling, August 30, 1864, USCC-DG, Defenses of New Orleans, Provost Marshal General, Letters Received.

44. Captain Samuel W. Cozzens to Colonel S. B. Holabird, May 15, 1863, USCC-DG, Bureau of Civil Affairs, Letters Received.

45. S. W. Cozzens, "Regulations! To Govern Hands," undated, USCC-DG, Bureau of Civil Affairs, Letters Received. Filed with correspondence J-P, 1864.

46. S. W. Cozzens to S. B. Holabird, May 15, 1863, USCC-DG, Bureau

of Civil Affairs, Letters Received. See also Cozzens to Brig. General James Bowen, September 5, 1863, USCC-DG, Provost Marshal General, Letters Received.

47. Lieutenant Colonel A. J. N. Duganne to N. P. Banks, March 1, 1863, USCC-DG, Bureau of Civil Affairs, Letters Received.

48. Major H. M. Porter to Brig. General James Bowen, March 17, 1863, USCC-DG, Provost Marshal General, Letters Received.

49. Wadsworth, testimony, AGO-AFIC.

50. Captain Sylvester Cogswell to Captain John W. Ela, June 11, 1863, USCC-DG, Defenses of New Orleans, Provost Marshal General, Letters Received.

51. Lieutenant William B. Bragg, "To the residents of these Parishes," September 1, 1864, USCC-DG, Provost Marshal General, Letters Received.

52. Major T. H. Bradley to Lieutenant C. D. Wright, April 10, 1864, USCC-DG, Defenses of New Orleans, Provost Marshal General, Letters Received.

CHAPTER 6

1. Augustus S. Montgomery to Major General Foster, May 12, 1863, OR, I, xviii, 1067-69; Jefferson Davis to Z. B. Vance, May 30, 1863, OR, I, xviii, 1077.

The document which fell into Confederate hands bore the endorsement of Major C. Marshal, aide-de-camp, Department of North Carolina, who noted that "the plan is being generally adopted." General N. P. Banks, commanding the Department of the Gulf, received several letters from Montgomery, but seems to have ignored them. See Montgomery to Banks, June 4, June 8, and June 12, 1863, Banks Papers, LC.

2. Preliminary and Final Report of the American Freedmen's Inquiry Commission, *Senate Executive Documents*, No. 53, 38th Cong., 1st sess.

3. Wiley, *Southern Negroes*, 37, 67-68.

4. Ibid., 81-83; Herbert Aptheker, *American Negro Slave Revolts*, (New York, 1943), 359-67; Aptheker, "Notes on Slave Conspiracies in Confederate Mississippi," *Journal of Negro History*, XXIX (1944), 75-79.

5. T. W. Conway to N. P. Banks, September 9, 1864, USCC-DG, Bureau of Civil Affairs, Letters Received; Capers, *Occupied City*, 5.

6. B. F. Butler to S. P. Chase, July 10, 1862, Chase Papers, Historical Society of Pennsylvania, Philadelphia, Pennsylvania.

7. Dr. I. Zacharie to N. P. Banks, February 22, 1863, Banks Papers, LC.

8. W. H. Gray to N. P. Banks, January 17, 1863, USCC-DG, Bureau of Civil Affairs, Letters Received.

9. See, for example, Rachel Cosley to N. P. Banks, February 22, 1863, ibid.

10. Major General J. J. Reynolds, General Order No. 12, March 24, 1864,

and George H. Hanks, "Circular to the Colored People," March 26, 1864, Banks Papers, LC.

11. George H. Hanks to Lt. Col. R. B. Irwin, July 11, 1863, Banks Papers, LC.

12. T. W. Conway to George H. Hanks, April 25, 1864, USCC-DG, Defenses of New Orleans, Provost Marshal General, Letters Received.

13. L. Lofficial, W. Magruder et al. to Lieutenant Colonel Pardee, (received November 1863), USCC-DG, Bureau of Civil Affairs, Letters Received. Colonel Pardee admitted that there were many abuses committed against free blacks and forwarded the letter to General Banks. See also G. H. Hanks to N. P. Banks, August 5, 1863, Bureau of Civil Affairs, Letters Received.

14. Despite its general support of federal policies, L' Union bitterly protested the arrest and harassment of free Negroes, as did its successor, the Radical Negro journal, the Tribune. See L'Union, August 20, 1863; Tribune, August 13, 1864. See also C. W. Killborn to Provost Guard, First District, March 10, 1863; Brig. General James Bowen to N. P. Banks, March 12, 1864, USCC-DG, Provost Marshal Records, Letters Sent, vols. 298 and 345.

15. James H. Ingram and A. W. Lewis, committee representing a mass meeting of "Colored Citizens of New Orleans" to Major General S. A. Hurlbut, March 21, 1865, USCC-DG, Bureau of Civil Affiars, Letters Received; New Orleans Tribune, August 13 and December 8, 1964, quoted in McPherson, The Negro's Civil War, 129.

Adequate treatment of New Orleans free Negroes during the Civil War requires separate study. Capers, Occupied City, 214, 231, gives the topic superficial treatment. Donald E. Everett's "Demands of the New Orleans Free Colored Population for Political Equality, 1862-1865," Louisiana Historical Quarterly, XXXVII (1955), 43-64, is more detailed, but intent on proving that blacks sought political supremacy. Charles Barthelemy Rousseve, The Negro in Louisiana: Aspects of His History and His Literature (New Orleans, 1937), is best on the literary achievements of New Orleans free Negroes.

16. T. W. Conway to Lieutenant Colonel George B. Drake, March 29, 1865, USCC-DG, Bureau of Civil Affairs, Letters Received.

17. Samuel W. Cozzens to Colonel S. B. Holabird, May 15, 1863, USCC-DG, Bureau of Civil Affairs, Letters Received.

18. Thomas W. Conway to N. P. Banks, "Report on the Condition of the Freedmen of the Department of the Gulf," September 9, 1864, ibid.

19. T. W. Conway to N. P. Banks, August 29, 1864, enclosing Conway's published letter to the editor of the New York Times, Banks Papers, LC.

20. Captain James M. White to Captain Albert Stearns, and Lieutenant W. W. Mason to Stearns, August 24, 1864, USCC-DG, Defenses of New Orleans, Provost Marshal General, Letters Received; printed circular to planters from the office of the provost marshal, Brashear City, 1864, ibid.

21. Major W. W. Howe, Circular, June 28, 1864, USCC-DG, Defenses of New Orelans, Provost Marshal General, Letters Received. For a planter's

complaint concerning the laxness of federal controls, see William W. Pugh to Captain Rudyard, May 26, 1863, USCC-DG, Provost Marshal General, Misc. Records.

22. G. H. Hanks, endorsement on letter from Captain Thomas Tileston to Major W. W. Howe, June 29, 1864, USCC-DG, Defenses of New Orleans, Provost Marshal General, Letters Received.

23. Captain Edward Bigelow, Circular, December 31, 1864, Defenses of New Orleans, Records of the Provost Marshal, Lafourche Parish.

24. Provost Marshal's Office, Ascension Parish, transcript dated April 4 and April 8, 1863, USCC-DG, Defenses of New Orleans, Misc. Letters Received.

25. "Depty [*sic*] Sheriff Vs. the Slave Jasmin," April 1863, USCC-DG, Defenses of New Orleans, Provost Marshal General, Letters Received.

26. T. W. Conway to N. P. Banks, September 9, 1864, USCC-DG, Bureau of Civil Affairs, Letters Received.

27. N. P. Banks to Brig. General James Bowen, 1863, USCC-DG, Provost Marshal Records, vol. 309.

28. Major B. Rush Plumly to Major Yarrington, August 29, 1863, USCC-DG, Provost Marshal General, Letters Received.

29. S. B. Bevanst and Company to Colonel G. H. Hanks, August 2, 1864, and endorsement of N. P. Banks, August 9, 1864, USCC-DG, Bureau of Civil Affairs, Letters Received; Lieutenant Colonel Banks to Provost Marshal, Defenses of New Orleans, December 24, 1863, USCC-DG, Defenses of New Orleans, Misc. Letters Received. See also T. W. Conway to N. P. Banks, September 9, 1864, USCC-DG, Bureau of Civil Affairs, Letters Received.

30. N. P. Banks, General Orders No. 64, August 29, 1863, OR, I, xxvi, pt. 1, 704. Families were restricted from visiting soldiers, allegedly to maintain morale and protect the men from venereal diseases. See Captain Albert Stearns to Colonel G. H Hanks, July 15, 1864, USCC-DG, Defenses of New Orleans, Provost Marshal, St. Mary's Parish, Letters Sent.

31. Harrington, *Banks*, 112-13.

32. B. F. Butler, testimony, Boston, May 1, 1863, AGO-AFIC.

33. Harrington, *Banks*, 111.

34. Ibid.

35. Fred Harvey Harrington, "The Fort Jackson Mutiny," *Journal of Negro History*, XXVII (1942), 420-31; Harrington, *Banks*, 111.

36. Charles P. Stone to James Bowen, December 9, 1863, USCC-DG, Provost Marshal Records, vol. 309; Harrington, *Banks*, 113.

37. N. P. Banks to General H. W. Halleck, December 11, 1863, OR, I, xxvi, pt. 1, 456; Harrington, *Banks*, 111.

38. N. P. Banks to Brig. Gen. James Bowen, December 14, 1863, USCC-DG, Provost Marshal Records, vol. 309; Harrington, "Fort Jackson Mutiny," 420-31.

39. Colonel Charles Drew to Brig. General James Bowen, April 7, 1863, USCC-DG, Provost Marshal General, Letters Received.

40. Captain James N. White to Captain Albert Stearns, August 23, 1864, and Lieutenant W. W. Mason to Stearns, August 23, 1864, USCC-DG, Defenses of New Orleans, Provost Marshal General, Letters Received.

41. Lieutenant Enoch Foster to Captain Henry Pierson, August 3, 1863, USCC-DG, Provost Marshal General, Letters Received.

42. Captain George G. Davis to Brig. General James Bowen, August 21, 1863, ibid.

43. Captain Silas W. Sawyer to Lieutenant H. Kallenstroch, August 21, 1863, ibid.

44. Lt. Colonel A. P. Hawkins to Brig. General James Bowen, September 1863, enclosing undated and unsigned manuscript, USCC-DG, Bureau of Civil Affairs, Letters Received.

45. C. C. Porter to Captain R. B. Brown, October 1, 1863, and Captain B. Owen to Captain C. W. Killborn, August 6, 1863, USCC-DG, Defenses of New Orleans, Provost Marshal General, Letters Received. Eli T. Hazeur et al. to Colonel Beckwith, October 28, 1863, and Colonel William K. Kimball to Lieutenant Crawford Williams, November 3, 1863, USCC-DG, Bureau of Civil Affairs, Letters Received.

46. For a specific case, see Private F. Tennelli to Captain A. T. Vaughn, January 17, 1864, USCC-DG, Provost Marshal General, Misc. Records.

47. T. W. Conway to N. P. Banks, September 9, 1864, USCC-DG, Bureau of Civil Affairs, Letters Received. See also Lieutenant Charles Dewey to Brig. General James Bowen, February 19, 1864, USCC-DG, Provost Marshal General, Letters Received.

48. Captain John W. Ela to Provost Marshal's Office, June 22, 1863, USCC-DG, Defenses of New Orleans, Provost Marshal General, Letters Received.

49. Lieutenant Charles Brooks to T. W. Conway, April 2, 1865, USCC-DG, Provost Marshal General, Letters Received.

50. Captain R. B. Brown to Brig. General James Bowen, and Captain John W. Ela to Bowen, February 23, 1863, USCC-DG, Defenses of New Orleans, Provost Marshal General, Letters Received.

This episode gave rise to charges that Provost Marshal Ela's men had forcibly returned slaves to their master. Ela denied that this was so, arguing that his men had simply "witnessed the punishment but took no part in it."

51. Joshua Baker to Brig. General James Bowen, May 4, 1864, USCC-DG, Provost Marshal General, Letters Received.

52. James Aiken, overseer, to Provost Marshal's Office, August 30, 1864, USCC-DG, Defenses of New Orleans, Provost Marshal General, Letters Received.

53. A. B. Tripler to Colonel R. B. Brown, March 11, 1864, USCC-DG, Defenses of New Orleans, Provost Marshal General, Letters Received; Captain F. R. Clark to Brig. General James Bowen, May 3, 1864, Provost Marshal General, Letters Received.

54. Citizens of Vermilionville, Lafayette Parish to N. P. Banks, (Received

April 26, 1863), USCC-DG, Bureau of Civil Affairs, Letters Received. Original in italics.

55. Captain L. H. Stone to Provost Marshal A. B. Long, April 25, 1863, and Colonel S. G. Jerrard to Asst. Adjutant General R. B. Irwin, April 28, 1863, Banks Papers, LC; John D. Winter, *The Civil War in Louisiana,* (Baton Rouge, 1963), 238.

56. Captain Silas W. Sawyer to General T. W. Sherman, May 19, 1863, and Sawyer to Brig. General James Bowen, June 3, 1863, USCC-DG, Provost Marshal General, Letters Received.

CHAPTER 7

1. Hurlbut to Lincoln, March 27, 1863, OR, I, xxiv, pt. 3, 149-50.

2. Maria R. Mann to "Elisa," February 10, 1863; Maria Mann to "Miss Peabody," April 19, 1863; Maria Mann to unknown, undated slip of paper, [April 1863?] Maria Mann Papers, LC.

3. Eaton to Robert W. Carroll, March 10, 1863, BRFAL-GSC, Letters Sent, vol. 74; John Eaton, *Grant, Lincoln and the Freedmen, Reminiscences* (New York, 1907), 155-56. Hereafter cited as Eaton, *Autobiography.*

4. Eaton to Coffin, March 27, 1863, BRFAL-GSC, Letters Sent, vol. 74.

5. Beale, *Diary of Gideon Welles,* I, 219.

6. Secretary Stanton to Lorenzo Thomas, March 25, 1863, War Department, Letters Sent by the Secretary of War, Military Affairs, 1800-1889.

7. General Thomas' program is outlined in two letters: Thomas to Stanton, April 1 and April 12, 1863, AGO-GP, Lorenzo Thomas, Letter Book.

8. Thomas to Stanton, April 12, 1863, AGO-GP, Lorenzo Thomas, Letter Book.

9. Eaton to James M. Alexander, June 22, 1863, BRFAL-GSC, Letters Sent, vol. 74.

10. Samuel R. Shipley, "Visit to the Camps of the Freedmen on the Mississippi River," in *Statistics of the Operations of the Executive Board of the Friends' Association of Philadelphia, and its Vicinity, for the Relief of Colored Freedmen* (Philadelphia, 1864), 18-19.

11. Thomas, Special Orders No. 45, August 18, 1863, OR, III, iii, 686; Grant, General Orders No. 51, August 10, 1863, OR, I, xxiv, pt. 3, 585.

12. Lincoln to Stanton, July 21, 1863, Stanton Papers, LC.

13. Stanton to Lorenzo Thomas, August 24, 1863, OR, III, iii, 710; Thomas and Hyman, *Stanton,* 163. Stanton suspected Thomas of disloyalty and characterized the general as "only fit for presiding over a crypt of Egyptian mummies like himself." To get him out of the way, Stanton sent him on frequent trips, assigning Assistant Adjutant General E. D. Townsend to his duties in the War Department. See also A. Howard McNelly's biographical sketch of Thomas in the *Dictionary of American Biography,* XVII, 441-42.

14. Lorenzo Thomas, Special Orders No. 85, October 24, 1863, OR, III

iii, 917-18; Lorenzo Thomas, Circular, October 27, 1863, copy in CWSAR, General Agent, Letters Received.

15. Lorenzo Thomas, Special Orders No. 94, November 3, 1863, USCC, District of West Tennessee, Letters Received. For Eaton's appointment, see John Eaton, 27th Ohio, 63rd U.S. Colored Troops, AGO-MSR. For Thomas' appointment, see Samuel Thomas, 27th Ohio, 64th U.S. Colored Troops, AGO-MSR.

16. Thomas W. Knox, *Camp-Fire and Cotton-Field: Southern Adventures in Time of War. Life with the Union Armies, and Residence on a Louisiana Plantation* (Philadelphia, 1865), 312. A war correspondent in the Mississippi Valley for the *New York Herald*, Knox joined with a fellow correspondent to lease a plantation opposite Natchez, between Vidalia and Waterproof, Louisiana.

17. General John P. Hawkins to Gerrit Smith, October 21, 1863, included in AGO-AFIC; Wadsworth, testimony, ibid.; Abraham E. Strickle, CWPR; Chaplain Lark S. Livermore, 16th Wisconsin Volunteers, AGO-MSR; Eaton to Lt. Colonel J. A. Rawlins, April 29, 1863, AGO-AFIC.

General Thomas' original commissioner appointments are included in Thomas to Stanton, April 12, 1863, AGO-GP, Lorenzo Thomas, Letter Book. For the later appointments, see Thomas to George S. Denison, October 21, 1863, Denison Papers, LC.

18. Knox, *Camp-Fire,* 316.

19. Shipley, "Camps of the Freedmen," 23.

20. Yeatman, *A Report on the Conditions of the Freedmen of the Missis-sippi, presented to the Western Sanitary Commission, December 17, 1863* (St. Louis, 1864), 6.

21. Shipley, "Camps of the Freedmen," 23.

22. Yeatman, *Report,* 8; Knox, *Camp-Fire,* 316.

23. Hunter to Stanton, January 27, 1864, Stanton Papers, LC.

24. Porter to Lorenzo Thomas, October 21, 1863, AGO-DCT, Adjutant General, Letters Received.

25. Hawkins to Gerrit Smith, October 21, 1863, included in AGO-AFIC.

26. Yeatman, *Report,* 16.

27. *New York Independent,* January 28, 1864.

28. Wadsworth, testimony, AGO-AFIC. See also Thomas H. Spaulding's biographical sketch of Wadsworth in the *Dictionary of American Biography,* XIX, 308-9.

29. Wadsworth, testimony, AGO-AFIC; Wadsworth to War Department, December 16, 1863, copy in CWSAR, General Agent, Letters Received.

30. Wadsworth to War Department, December 16, 1863, CWSAR, General Agent, Letters Received.

31. Yeatman, *Report, 1,* 13, 15-16.

32. Ibid., 7-9.

33. Ibid., 10.

34. Ibid. Samuel Shipley was also encouraged to see evidence on every

side that "the negro will work far better under the stimulus of wages than by the compulsion of the lash." Shipley, "Camps of the Freedmen," 20.
35. Thomas to Stanton, August 23, October 15, and November 16, 1863, AGO-GP, Lorenzo Thomas, Letter Book.

CHAPTER 8

1. *U.S. Statutes at Large,* XIII, 255-58.
2. Ibid., XII, 319, 589; James G. Randall, *The Confiscation of Property During the Civil War* (Indianapolis, 1913), 12-14.
3. *U.S. Statutes at Large,* XII, 820; Randall, *Confiscation,* 44.
4. Chase to Mellen, October 19, 1863, CWSAR, General Agent, Letters Received.
5. General Wadsworth, testimony, AGO-AFIC; Thomas to Stanton, December 9, 1863, AGO, Letters Sent, vol. 2.
6. Chase to Mellen, December 17, 1863, CWSAR, General Agent, Letters Received.
7. Ibid.
8. Ibid.
9. Ibid.
10. Yeatman, *Report to the Western Sanitary Commission in Regard to Leasing Abandoned Plantations with Rules and Regulations Governing the Same* (St. Louis, 1864), 3-4.
11. Although the leasing plan adopted by the Treasury Department was essentially the same as the plan proposed by Yeatman in his report, there were certain differences. Yeatman had proposed that freedmen receive their full monthly wage each month while paying for their own food and clothing. The Treasury Department plan provided for half wages during each month, the balance to be paid at the end of the year. Likewise, Yeatman's suggestion that laborers on the home farms receive half the regular wage was excluded, as was his proposal that regular medical personnel be employed to care for freedmen. Compare the discussion below with Yeatman, *Suggestions of a Plan of Organization for Free Labor, and the Leasing of Plantations under a Bureau or Commission to be Appointed by the Government; Accompanying a Report Presented to the Western Sanitary Commission* (St. Louis, 1864).
12. "Rules and Regulations for Leasing Abandoned Plantations and Employing Freedmen," in Yeatman, *Report in Regard to Leasing,* 12, 13.
13. Yeatman, "Rules for Leasing," 4-5.
14. Ibid., 11-15.
15. Ibid.
16. Yeatman, *Report in Regard to Leasing,* 6, 8.
17. Ibid., 8-9.
18. Ibid., 2-4.
19. E. O. Haven to A. Winchell, February 9, July 22, 1864, Alexander

Winchell Papers, Michigan Historical Collections, University of Michigan, Ann Arbor, Michigan; Martha M. Bigelow (ed.), "Plantation Lessee Problems in 1864," *Journal of Southern History,* XXVII (1961), 354-67, prints the draft of Winchell's letter to Zachariah Chandler from the Winchell Papers. See also George P. Merrill's biographical sketch of Winchell in the *Dictionary of American Biography,* XX, 373-74.

20. David H. Overy, *Wisconsin Carpetbaggers in Dixie* (Madison, 1961), 17.

21. E. S. Burr et al. to Secretary Chase, January 30, 1864, Treasury Department Records, Misc. Letters Received, 'K' Series.

22. E. L. Floyd, W. Warnick, J. G. Tobias to William P. Mellen, February 18, 1864, CWSAR, General Agent, Letters Received.

23. A. McFarland to William P. Mellen, February 11, 1864, CWSAR, General Agent, Letters Received.

24. William Burnet to W. P. Mellen, March 10, 1864, BRFAL-Miss., vol. 237-1/2.

25. McFarland to Mellen, March 11, 1864, CWSAR, Mellen Papers.

26. Loyal Case to W. P. Mellen, February 16, 1864, CWSAR, General Agent, Letters Received.

27. William Burnet to Major George W. Young, March 10, 1864, BRFAL-Miss., vol. 237-1/2.

28. Burnet to J. H. Weldon, March 2, 1864, BRFAL-Miss., vol. 237-1/2; Burnet to W. P. Mellen, March 1, 1864, CWSAR, General Agent, Letters Received; Burnet to Mellen, March 12, 1864, CWSAR, Mellen Papers; A. McFarland to W. P. Mellen, March 11, 1864, ibid.

29. C. A. Montross to Burnet, April 9, 1864, CWSAR, Burnet Papers.

30. Thomas to Stanton, February 20, 1864, AGO, Letters Sent, vol. 2. Eaton printed the letter with some alterations in his *Autobiography,* 152-53, although he mistakenly dated it February 30, 1864.

31. Thomas to Stanton, February 27, 1864, OR, III, iv, 139.

32. Lincoln to Thomas, February 28, 1864, ibid., 143.

33. Thomas to Stanton, February 29, 1864, ibid., 144.

34. Thomas to Stanton, March 14, 1864, AGO, Letters Sent, vol. 2; also printed in OR, III, iv, 176-77.

35. Thomas, Orders No. 9, March 11, 1864, OR, III, iv, 166-170.

36. Mellen to McFarland, March 8, 1864, CWSAR, General Agent, Letters Received. A similar letter, requesting information to substantiate his opinions, was sent to each of Mellen's assistant agents.

37. Lorenzo Thomas to E. D. Townsend, April 19, 1864, OR, III, iv, 235.

38. Thomas to Stanton, March 18, 1864, AGO, Letters Sent, vol. 2.

39. Lorenzo Thomas to W. P. Mellen, February 22, 1865, CWSAR, General Agent, Letters Received.

40. W. P. Mellen to Lorenzo Thomas, March 22, 1864, and March 9, 1865, AGO-DCT, Adjutant General, Letters Received.

41. Eaton, *Autobiography,* 151.
42. Sherman to Lorenzo Thomas, April 12, 1864, OR, III, iv, 225; Thomas to Sherman, March 30, 1864, AGO, Letters Sent, vol. 2.
For Sherman's attitudes toward slavery and the Negro, see Robert K. Murray, "General Sherman, The Negro, and Slavery: The Story of an Unrecognized Rebel," *Negro History Bulletin,* XXII (1959), 125-30. Murray overlooks Sherman's interest in settling blacks on land in the Mississippi Valley and South Carolina.
43. Eaton, *Autobiography,* 151. Eaton used the phrase to condemn the Treasury plan.

CHAPTER 9

1. This point of view was most prominently developed by the American Freedmen's Inquiry Commission, but it permeated humanitarian concern for the freedmen. However, the Civil War years were a period of intellectual transition from early nineteenth century humanitarianism to late nineteenth century individualism. During the Civil War, benevolent paternalism dominated emancipationist thinking, but such powerful figures as Frederick Douglass and Wendell Phillips strongly opposed paternalistic sentiments as oppressive to blacks. Similarly, but with less sensitivity to the freedmen's condition, Horace Greeley voiced the nineteenth century liberal fear that government care of blacks—even in the form of destitute rations—destroyed incentive. See the Preliminary and Final Report of the American Freedmen's Inquiry Commission, *Senate Executive Documents,* No. 53, 38th Cong., 1st sess., and McPherson, *Struggle for Equality,* 392, 397.
2. John Eaton to Senator Henry Wilson, undated, and Eaton to Robert W. Carroll, undated, BRFAL-GSC, vol. 74. Since both letters make no mention of a plantation leasing system, they were evidently written before General Thomas arrived in March 1863. See also John Eaton to American Missionary Association, March, [1863?], AMA Archives.
3. Eaton, *Autobiography,* 24.
4. General Lorenzo Thomas, Special Orders No. 94, November 5, 1863, in John Eaton, 27th Ohio Vols. and 63rd U.S. Colored Troops, AGO-MSR; Major General McPherson, Special Orders No. 80, March 24, 1864, in Samuel Thomas, 27th Ohio Vols. and 64th U.S. Colored Troops, AGO-MSR.
5. Eaton, printed letter, February 6, 1864, AMA Archives. This letter was apparently sent to a number of freedmen's aid societies.
6. Eaton, *Autobiography,* 60, 217, 19. Eaton did not allow logical consistency to interfere with his denunciation of the Treasury system. For example, he insisted that the minimum wage provided by Agent Mellen was "higher than the industrial situation could sustain," but blandly charged that by expanding the leasing system the Treasury Department opened the door to speculators who "availed themselves recklessly" of the opportunity offered.

The lessees were perhaps reckless, but they evidently did not find higher wages prohibitive.

7. Stampp, *The Peculiar Institution*, 56: "Cotton growers on flat prairies and river bottoms planted as many as ten acres per hand but rarely more than that." For statistics on Helena and Skipwith's Landing district, see William F. Allen, diary, October 4, 1864, SHSW; A. McFarland to W. P. Mellen, March 11, 1864, CWSAR, General Agent, Letters Received.

8. Colonel Samuel Thomas, "Consolidated Morning Report of Freedmen Department March 14th, 1864," Old Military Records, Bureau of Negro Affairs; Samuel Thomas to Lorenzo Thomas, June 15, 1864, AGO-DCT, Adjutant General, Letters Received.

9. Consolidated Reports of Freedmen's Department, Vicksburg District, January 4, 1864—June 30, 1865, BRFAL-Miss., Records of Freedmen's Department. These figures are substantiated by the record of destitute rations issued from January 1864 to October 1864. See Rations Issued by Acting Assistant Quartermaster, 1864, BRFAL-Miss., vol. 76.

10. Samuel R. Shipley, "Camps of the Freedmen," 18-19; Samuel Thomas to Lorenzo Thomas, June 15, 1864, AGO-DCT, Adjutant General, Letters Received.

11. Reports of Freedmen on Vidalia Home Farm, Natchez District, April 30, 1864—September 29, 1864, and Tri-Monthly Reports of Freedmen's Department at Natchez and Vicinity, September 20, 1864—January 10, 1865, BRFAL-Miss., Records of Freedmen's Departments.

12. Quoted in Eaton, *Report for 1864*, 53.

13. Chaplain Asa S. Fiske, report to Colonel Eaton, December 8, 1864, included in Eaton, *Report for 1864*, 49.

14. Brig. General N. B. Buford to Lorenzo Thomas, April 1, 1864, AGO-DCT, Adjutant General, Letters Received. See also M. D. Landon to W. P. Mellen, May 12, 1864, CWSAR, General Agent, Letters Received.

15. William F. Allen, diary, October 4, November 13, 1864, SHSW.

16. William Burnet to W. P. Mellen, March 23, 1864, CWSAR, General Agent, Letters Received; C. A. Montross to W. P. Mellen, March 26, April 26, April 28, 1864, ibid.; Samuel Thomas to Lorenzo Thomas, June 15, 1864, AGO-DCT, Adjutant General, Letters Received.

17. Samuel Thomas to Lorenzo Thomas, June 15, 1864, AGO-DCT, Adjutant General, Letters Received; James A. Hawley, 63rd U.S. Colored Troops, AGO-MSR.

18. Samuel Thomas to Lorenzo Thomas, June 15, 1864, AGO-DCT, Adjutant General, Letters Received; Knox, *Camp-fire*, 441-50.

19. Quoted in Eaton, *Report for 1864*, 34-35.

20. Samuel Thomas to Lorenzo Thomas, June 15, 1864, AGO-DCT, Adjutant General, Letters Received.

21. Eaton, *Report for 1864*, 28.

22. Ibid., 38-39.

23. For one avowed "anti-slavery planter," see M. D. Landon to W. P. Mellen, May 12, 1864, CWSAR, General Agent, Letters Received.

24. Allen, diary, December 25, 1864, SHSW; Major General A. McCook, to Reverend J. H. Nixon, March 26, 1865, BRFAL-Ark., Letters Received from Helena.

25. Samuel Thomas to Lorenzo Thomas, June 15, 1864, AGO-DCT, Adjutant General, Letters Received.

26. John Eaton, General Orders No. 2, October 17, 1864, CWSAR, Letters Received, Assistant Special Agent, Memphis District; Eaton, *Report for 1864*, 35.

27. Asa S. Fiske to Samuel Thomas, November 28, 1864, BRFAL-Miss., Records of the Freedmen's Department.

28. Eaton submitted his questions in November. See printed letter in USCC, Department of Mississippi, Letters Received, A-M, 1864-1865. The results were published in his *Report for 1864*, 28-80.

29. Eaton, *Report for 1864*, 36, 47; Allen, diary, December 25, 1864, SHSW.

30. Fiske's summary appears in Eaton, *Report for 1864*, 46-47.

31. Buckner Plantation Records, Vicksburg District, 1864. These records, apparently torn from the plantation account books for review by the district provost marshal, contain the season's accounts with fifty-one hands employed on the Orkney and Oak Grove plantations. Although filed among the records of the Bureau of Negro Affairs, USCC-DVA-NC, the plantations were located opposite the mouth of the Yazoo River in Madison Parish, Louisiana.

32. Dougal McCall to Samuel Thomas, July 11, 1864, BRFAL-Miss., Records of Freedmen's Department; Samuel Thomas, Orders No. 14, October 6, 1864, in McCall, 72nd Illinois Vols. and 66th U.S. Colored Troops, AGO-MSR.

33. Quoted in Eaton, *Report for 1864*, 36.

34. Samuel Thomas to Lorenzo Thomas, June 15, 1864, AGO-DCT, Adjutant General, Letters Received.

CHAPTER 10

1. F. W. Bird, testimony, AGO-AFIC.

2. General James S. Wadsworth to War Department, December 16, 1863, copy in CWSAR, General Agent, Letters Received; Shipley, "Visit to the Camps of the Freedmen," 10; Yeatman, *Report of the Conditions of the Freedmen*, 20; Yeatman, *Report to the Western Sanitary Commission*, 4-5; General Lorenzo Thomas to Secretary Stanton, October 15, 1863, AGO-GP, Letter Book of Lorenzo Thomas.

3. S. P. Chase to W. P. Mellen, December 27, 1863, CWSAR, General Agent, Letters Received.

4. Rev. Joseph Warren, *Extracts from Reports of Superintendents of Freedmen*, second series (Vicksburg, 1864), 50.

5. Wadsworth to War Department, December 16, 1863, CWSAR, General Agent, Letters Received. Wadsworth described the type of freedmen allowed to lease lands in 1863 as follows: "Several Plantations and parts of Plantations have been leased by Colored Lessees, who have been previously slaves, employed by their masters as overseers or Drivers." Later observers were less explicit, referring to the lessees as the "best" Negroes, or a "better class." See below.

6. See, for example, copy of lease with Thomas W. Jordan, negotiated by William P. Mellen, March 5, 1864, CWSAR, Mellen Papers.

7. Army and Treasury officials mentioned but a single black lessee in the Natchez district: John Wilson, who marketed five bales of cotton in 1864, receiving one-half of the net proceeds from the Treasury agent. See William Burnet to Colonel Riggin, May 15, 1864, BRFAL-Miss., William Burnet, Letters Sent, vol. 237-1/2.

8. James R. Locke to William G. Sargent, July 1864, BRFAL-Ark., Letters Received from Helena; M. D. Landon to William P. Mellen, May 12, 1864, CWSAR, General Agent, Letters Received; William F. Allen, diary, October 2, 1864, SHSW; Eaton, *Autobiography*, 164; Eaton, *Report for 1864*, 37.

9. For the administrative battles at Helena and evidence of official corruption, see particularly AGO-MSR for John I. Herrick, 29th Wisconsin Vols.; Albert L. Thayer, 35th Missouri Vols. and 63rd U.S. Colored Troops; and Jonathan E. Thomas, 56th Ohio Vols. See also William F. Allen, diary, October 2 and December 11, 1864, SHSW; Eaton, *Autobiography*, 164.

10. Allen, diary, December 11 and 12, 1864, SHSW; M. D. Landon to W. P. Mellen, May 12, 1864, CWSAR, General Agent, Letters Received.

11. Henry Sweeney, report, June 30, 1865, BRFAL-Ark., Letters Received from Helena; John I. Herrick to W. P. Mellen, October 12, 1864, CWSAR, General Agent, Letters Received; William F. Allen, diary, undated entry, typescript copy, pp. 75-78, SHSW.

12. Dougal McCall, "List of Plantations and No. of Acres in Cultivation at this date August 1st, 1864," and Benjamin F. Cheney, "Report of Freedmen Employed on Plantations," October 31, 1864, BRFAL-Miss., Records of Freedmen's Department.

13. Moses Proctor, Report of Lessees and Planters on Young's Point, June 1864, BRFAL-Miss., Records of Freedmen's Department.

14. Proctor, Report of Lessees; Shipley, "Camps of the Freedmen," 13; Samuel Thomas to John Eaton, March 14, 1864, BRFAL-Miss., misfiled in Natchez District.

15. Warren, *Extracts from Reports*, second series, 5-8.

16. Proctor, Report of Lessees; Stuart Eldridge to W. H. Morgan, February 23, 1865, CWSAR, Supervising Special Agent, Second District, Letters

Received; Brig. General N. C. S. Smith, Special Orders No. 52, March 4, 1865, BRFAL-Miss., Records of Freedmen's Department.

17. Samuel Thomas' report is quoted in Eaton, *Report for 1864*, 41.

18. James A. Hawley to W. P. Mellen, January 14, 1865, CWSAR, General Agent, Letters Received.

After a dispute with white lessees, the army assumed control of the plantations specified by Hawley and reserved them for the freedmen, to be leased to them in "small pieces." Brig. General N. C. S. Smith, Special Orders No. 52, March 4, 1865, BRFAL-Miss., Records of Freedmen's Department; C. A. Montross to Major General C. C. Washburn, February 24, 1865, and Stuart Eldridge to W. H. Morgan, February 23, 1865, CWSAR, Supervising Special Agent, Second District, Letters Received.

19. James A. Hawley to Samuel Thomas, December 5, 1865, *Senate Executive Documents*, No. 27, 39th Cong., 1st sess., 39-40.

20. Admiral Davis D. Porter to Lorenzo Thomas, October 21, 1863, AGO-DCT, Adjutant General, Letters Received.

21. Admiral Porter to Lorenzo Thomas, ibid.

22. Yeatman, *Conditions of the Freedmen on the Mississippi*, 13.

23. Shipley, "Camps of the Freedmen," 24-25.

24. Eaton, *Autobiography*, 163-64.

25. Eaton, *Report for 1864*, 39.

26. William P. Mellen to William W. Orme, November 21, 1864, CWSAR, Supervising Special Agent, Second District, Letters Received; Mellen to David G. Bernitz, November 21, 1864, CWSAR, General Agent, Letters Received.

27. Lorenzo Thomas, Special Orders No. 51, March 28, 1864, BRFAL-Miss., Records of Freedmen's Department.

28. Quoted in Eaton, *Report for 1864*, 39-40.

29. Lorenzo Thomas to Secretary Stanton, September 11, 1864, OR, III, iv, 708; Samuel Thomas to Lorenzo Thomas, June 15, 1864, AGO-DCT, Adjutant General, Letters Received.

30. Major General N. J. T. Dana, Special Orders No. 120, November 5, 1864, quoted in Eaton, *Report for 1864*, 40-41.

31. Quoted in Eaton, *Report for 1864*, 40.

32. Eaton, *Autobiography*, 165.

33. Few reformers would have disagreed with Eaton and Thomas. The escaped slave and well-known abolitionist William Wells Brown visited Davis Bend to celebrate the Fourth of July, 1864 and evidently concurred with the gathered superintendents and missionaries that the Davis Bend freedmen were too important to be left to themselves. See William Wells Brown, *The Negro in the American Rebellion* (Boston, 1867), 298-308.

34. For statistics on the Davis Bend home farm and black lessees, see Samuel Thomas to Lorenzo Thomas, June 15, 1864, AGO-DCT, Adjutant General, Letters Received; Consolidated Reports of Freedmen's Department,

Vicksburg District, January 4, 1864—June 30, 1865, BRFAL-Miss., Records of Freedmen's Department; Rations Issued by Acting Assistant Quartermaster, 1864, BRFAL-Miss., vol. 76.

35. General N. J. T. Dana to Samuel Thomas, October 12, 1864, USCC-DT, Vicksburg District, Letters Sent, vol. 18; Captain Fox to Samuel Thomas, November 28, 1864, USCC-DT, Vicksburg District, Letters Sent, vol. 18; Eaton, *Report for 1864*, 35-36.

36. Record, Court of Freedmen at Davis Bend, BRFAL-Miss., vol. 124; Eaton, *Autobiography*, 165-66.

37. Rules and Regulations for the Government of the Freedmen at Davis Bend, undated, Records of Captain [Gaylord B.] Norton's Business, Davis Bend, BRFAL-Miss., vol. 122.

A captain in the 64th U.S. Colored Troops, Norton had supervised contrabands on Young's Point and the Davis Bend home farm before being appointed superintendent of the colony in February 1865. He served with the Freedmen's Bureau at the Bend until March 1866. See Gaylord B. Norton, 27th Ohio Vols., and 64th U.S. Colored Troops, AGO-MSR and CWPR.

38. Samuel Thomas, report to General O. O. Howard, December 1865, *Senate Executive Documents*, No. 27, 39th Cong., 1st sess., 38.

39. Ibid.; Office of Provost Marshal of Freedmen to Superintendent of Colonies, Davis Bend, April 7, 1865, Records of Captain Norton's Business, Davis Bend, BRFAL-Miss., vol. 122; Samuel Thomas to John Eaton, July 16, 1865, Eaton Papers, University of Tennessee Library, Knoxville, Tennessee; Samuel Thomas, Circular, September 16, 1864, BRFAL-Miss., Records of Freedmen's Department.

40. Samuel Thomas, report to General O. O. Howard, *Senate Executive Documents*, No. 27, 39th Cong., 1st sess., 39; Thomas J. Wood, report to O. O. Howard, October 31, 1866, *Senate Executive Documents*, No. 6, 39th Cong., 2nd sess., 99; Vernon Lane Wharton, *The Negro in Mississippi, 1865-1890* (Chapel Hill, 1947), 39-42.

The government did not sustain its policy of wartime confiscation, but the Davis Bend lessees found other means to keep their land. Before regaining full control, Joseph Davis leased the two plantations for a period of years to Benjamin T. Montgomery, his former slave and plantation manager. Under Montgomery's direction, the plantations were operated successfully and when the lease expired, the former slave undertook to buy the property. Over the years, Montgomery became quite wealthy, paying taxes in 1873 in excess of twelve thousand dollars.

When Montgomery died in 1878, his son Isaiah continued the enterprise. Five years later, however, repeated flooding forced the abandonment of the Bend. The colony thus ended, but the black community in large measure continued when, in 1887, Isaiah Montgomery founded a new town, present day Mound Bayou, in Boliver County, Mississippi.

CONCLUSION

1. At least in theory, the Southern Homestead Act, passed in February 1866, provided a more hopeful vehicle for land reform in the South. Drafted by the Indiana Radical George W. Julian, the act provided that remaining federal lands in Alabama, Arkansas, Florida, Louisiana, and Mississippi should be sold only to settlers, initially in units no larger than eighty acres. Although nearly 50 million acres were covered by the act, much of the land was timbered, swampy, or poorly drained. Nevertheless, 40,000 homestead entries were made before the repeal of the act in 1876. The extent to which blacks profited by the act requires separate study. It is clear that lumber interests filed a large number of dummy entries. But some of the 40,000 entries must have been filed by actual settlers. While lack of capital prevented most freedmen from homesteading, some black yeoman might have acquired farms through the act. See Paul W. Gates, "Federal Land Policy in the South 1866-1888," *Journal of Southern History*, VI (1940), 303-30.

2. Quoted in LaWanda Cox, "The Promise of Land for the Freedmen," *Mississippi Valley Historical Review*, XLV (1958), 413-39. The discussion of the Freedmen's Bureau bill which follows relies heavily upon this legislative history, although the conclusions presented here differ considerably from Cox's. Cox argues that the final version of the bill was "designed deliberately to eliminate Northern speculation in Southern lands and the abuse of Negroes by Northern lessees." The final bill seemingly offered the promise of reform. McFeely's *Yankee Stepfather*, a study of O. O. Howard's leadership during the first years of the Bureau, concludes that individual weakness in the face of Andrew Johnson's hostility accounted for the Bureau's failure to fulfill its original promise. Both Cox's and McFeeley's interpretations rest on the assumption, disputed here, that the promise of land for freedmen was real.

3. McPherson, *Struggle for Equality*, 189-90.

4. George R. Bentley, *A History of the Freedmen's Bureau* (Philadelphia, 1955), 48.

5. John Eaton to "Alice," February 3, 1865, John Eaton Papers, University of Tennessee Library, Knoxville, Tennessee.

6. *U.S. Statutes at Large*, XIII, 507; McPherson, *Struggle for Equality*, 190.

7. The confiscation acts specifically did not apply beyond the life of the rebellious owner. Estates could thus be claimed by "loyal" heirs. The same was not the case with the Direct Tax laws, which provided for the permanent alienation of property. Tax commissioners appointed by the president collected taxes or sold property in lieu of payment. *U.S. Statutes at Large*, XII, 294, 319, 422, 589.

The Direct Tax laws, however, were very unevenly applied. Almost $400,000 worth of property was sold in South Carolina, but only about

$300,000 was collected from sales elsewhere—in Virginia, Tennessee, Florida, and Arkansas. Apparently, no property was sold elsewhere in the former Confederacy. Although the Direct Tax laws were challenged by dispossessed landowners during Reconstruction, they were upheld by the Supreme Court in 1878. Randall, *Confiscation During the Civil War,* 34; Rose, *Rehearsal,* 397.

8. Martin Abbott, "Free Land, Free Labor, and the Freedmen's Bureau," *Agricultural History,* XXX (October, 1956), 150-56.

9. Charles Sumner to S. P. Chase, October 17, 1865, Chase Papers, Historical Society of Pennsylvania, Philadelphia, Pennsylvania.

10. Bentley, *Freedmen's Bureau,* 215-16; Colonel John Eaton, 63rd U.S. Colored Troops, AGO-MSR; Donald L. McMurry, "John Eaton," *Dictionary of American Biography,* V, 608-9; E. Whittlesey, Circular No. 2, July 15, 1865, *House Executive Documents,* No. 70, 39th Cong., 1st sess.; McFeely, *Yankee Stepfather,* 250-51; C. B. Wilder to American Missionary Association, March 28, 1865, AMA Archives; Roster of Officers on Duty, BRFAL; Orlando Brown, Special Orders No. 36, August 21, 1865, *House Executive Documents,* No. 70, 39th Cong., 1st sess.

After leaving Virginia, Wilder worked among freedmen at Jacksonville, Florida, until 1869. See his correspondence with the American Missionary Association, AMA Archives.

11. John Eaton to General O. O. Howard, December 15, 1865, *Senate Executive Documents,* No. 27, 39th Cong., 1st sess.; Conway, *Report for 1865.* Conway had planned to divide some 60,000 acres into plots of forty acres and less for sale to freedmen.

McFeely, *Yankee Stepfather,* argues that the Bureau offered real hope for reform, but finds that it "served to preclude rather than promote Negro freedom." It seems unlikely that the Bureau had the power to preclude anything, but the result was the same.

12. E. Whittlesey, Circular No. 1, July 1, 1865, *House Executive Documents,* No. 70, 39th Cong., 1st sess.; Circular No. 2, July 15, 1865, ibid.; Circular No. 3, August 15, 1865, ibid.; Circular No. 4, November 10, 1865, ibid.

13. Orlando Brown, Circular Letter, June 15 and September 19, 1865, *House Executive Documents,* No. 70, 39th Cong., 1st sess. See also Major General Alfred Terry to Brig. General Ruggles, September 15, 1865, USCC-DVa-NC, Letters Sent, vol. 14.

14. O. Brown, Circular Letter, December 8, 1865, *House Executive Documents,* No. 70, 39th Cong., 1st sess.; Brown, Circular Letter, September 10, 1865, ibid.; Brown to C. B. Wilder, October 21, 1865, ibid.

15. O. Brown to O. O. Howard, November 31, 1865, *Senate Executive Documents,* No. 27, 39th Cong., 1st sess.; O. Brown, Circular Letters, November 4, November 13, 1865, *House Executive Documents,* No. 70, 39th Cong., 1st sess.

16. S. Thomas, Circular No. 1, June 20, July 3, and July 29, 1865, *House Executive Documents*, No. 70, 39th Cong., 1st sess.; Brig. General J. P. Osterhaus, Printed Instructions, June 1865, BRFAL-Miss., Assistant Commissioner, Letters Received.

17. S. Thomas, General Orders No. 13, October 31, 1865, *House Executive Documents*, No. 70, 39th Cong., 1st sess.; S. Thomas, Circular No. 14, November 13, 1865, ibid.; Wharton, *Negro in Mississippi*, 58.

18. This figure does not include Southern blacks in the Union army. About 180,000 blacks served in the army. About 110,000 of these were recruited in the South. See Dudley Taylor Cornish, *The Sable Arm: Negro Troops in the Union Army, 1861-1865* (New York, 1966), 388. For estimates of the number of blacks in the various areas of federal occupation, see Appendix.

19. John Hope Franklin, "Reconstruction and the Negro," 69-71, in Harold M. Hyman (ed.), *New Frontiers of the American Reconstruction* (Urbana, 1966).

20. John Eaton to Jacob S. Wellits, November 1863, BRFAL-GSC, Letters Sent, vol. 74.

BIBLIOGRAPHY

PRIMARY SOURCES

Manuscripts

Adjutant General's Office, American Freedmen's Inquiry Commission Records, Record Group 94, National Archives, Washington, D. C.

————, Division of Colored Troops, Record Group 94, National Archives, Washington, D. C.

————, Generals' Papers, Record Group 94, National Archives, Washington, D. C.

————, Military Service Records, Record Group 94, National Archives, Washington, D. C.

Allen, William F., Papers, State Historical Society of Wisconsin, Madison, Wisconsin.

American Missionary Association Archives, Amistad Research Center, Dillard University, New Orleans, Louisiana.

Banks, Nathaniel P., Papers, Library of Congress, Washington, D. C.

Bureau of Refugees, Freedmen, and Abandoned Lands, Arkansas, Assistant Commissioner, Letters Received, Record Group 105, National Archives, Washington, D. C.

————, General Superintendent of Contrabands, Letters Received, Record Group 105, National Archives, Washington, D. C.

————, Louisiana, Assistant Commissioner, Letters Received, Record Group 105, National Archives, Washington, D. C.

————, Mississippi, Assistant Commissioner, Letters Received, Record Group 105, National Archives, Washington, D. C.

————, Virginia, Assistant Commissioner, Letters Received, Record Group 105, National Archives, Washington, D. C.

Butler, Benjamin F., Papers, Library of Congress, Washington, D. C.

Chase, Salmon P., Papers, Historical Society of Pennsylvania, Philadelphia, Pennsylvania.

————, Papers, Library of Congress, Washington, D. C.

Civil War Pension Records, Record Group 15, National Archives, Washington, D. C.

Denison, George S., Papers, Library of Congress, Washington, D. C.

Eaton, John, Jr., Papers, University of Tennessee Library, Knoxville, Tennessee.

Eliot, William Greenleaf, Papers, Missouri Historical Society, St. Louis, Missouri.

James, Horace E., Papers, in Richard O'Flynn Papers, Holy Cross College Library, Worcester, Massachusetts.

Mann, Mary Tyler, Papers, Library of Congress, Washington, D. C.

Quartermaster General's Office Records, Record Group 92, National Archives, Washington, D. C.

Stanton, Edwin M., Papers, Library of Congress, Washington, D. C.

Treasury Department, Civil War Special Agency Records, Record Group 366, National Archives, Washington, D. C.

————, General Records, Miscellaneous Letters Received, 'K' Series, 1863-1864, Record Group 56, National Archives, Washington, D. C.

————, Letters Sent by the Secretary of the Treasury Relating to Restricted Commercial Intercourse, 1861-1887, Record Group 56, National Archives, Washington, D. C.

United States Army Continental Commands, 1821-1920, Department of the Gulf, Record Group 393, National Archives, Washington, D. C.

————, Department of the Tennessee, Record Group 393, National Archives, Washington, D. C.

————, Department of Virginia and North Carolina, National Archives, Washington, D. C.

Western Sanitary Commission Papers, Missouri Historical Society, St. Louis, Missouri.

Wilder, Charles Baker, Papers, in John Augustus Wilder Papers, Yale University Library, New Haven, Connecticut.

Winchell, Alexander, Papers, Michigan Historical Collections, University of Michigan, Ann Arbor, Michigan.

Autobiographies, Reminiscences, Printed Diaries, and Letters

Ames, Mary, *From a New England Woman's Diary in Dixie in 1865.* Springfield, Mass., 1906.

Beale, Howard K. (ed.), *Diary of Gideon Wells: Secretary of the Navy under Lincoln and Johnson,* 3 vols. New York, 1960.

Billington, Ray Allen (ed.), *The Journal of Charlotte L. Forten.* New York, 1953.

Brown, William Wells, *The Negro in the American Rebellion.* Boston, 1867.

Butler, Benjamin F., *Private and Official Correspondence During the Period of the Civil War.* Norwood, Mass., 1917.

Chase, Salmon P., "Diary and Correspondence of Salmon P. Chase," in *American Historical Association Report for 1902.* 2 vols. Washington, D. C., 1903.

Coffin, Levi, *Reminiscences of Levi Coffin.* Cincinnati, 1880.

Cook, Joel, *The Siege of Richmond: A Narrative of the Military Operations of Major General George B. McClellan During the Months of May and June, 1862.* Philadelphia, 1862.

Donald, David (ed.), *Inside Lincoln's Cabinet: The Civil War Diaries of Salmon P. Chase.* New York, 1954.

Eaton, John, Jr., *Grant, Lincoln and the Freedmen, Reminiscences.* New York, 1907.

Emmerton, James A., *A Record of the Twenty-Third Regiment Mass. Vol. Infantry in the War of the Rebellion 1861-1865.* Boston, 1886.

Franklin, John Hope (ed.), *The Diary of James T. Ayers, Civil War Recruiter.* Springfield, Ill., 1947.

Gregg, J. Chandler, *Life in the Army in the Departments of Virginia and the Gulf*. Philadelphia, 1866.

Hepworth, George H., *The Whip, Hoe, and Sword; or, the Gulf-Department in '63*. Boston, 1864.

Howard, O. O., *Autobiography of Oliver Otis Howard, Major General United States Army*. 2 vols. New York, 1907.

Knox, Thomas W., *Camp-Fire and Cotton-Field: Southern Adventure in Time of War. Life with the Union Armies, and Residence on a Louisiana Plantation*. Philadelphia, 1865.

Putnam, Samuel H., *The Story of Company A, Twenty-Fifth Regiment, Mass., Vols., in the War of Rebellion*. Worcester, Mass., 1886.

Rogers, Reverend J.[ames] B., *War Pictures: Experiences and Observations of a Chaplain in the U.S. Army, in the War of Southern Rebellion*. Chicago, 1863.

Swint, Henry Lee (ed.), *Dear Ones at Home: Letters From Contraband Camps*. Nashville, 1966.

Government Documents and Published Reports

Boston Emancipation League, *Facts Concerning the Freedmen, Their Capacity and their Destiny. Collected and Published by the Emancipation League*. Boston, 1863.

Colyer, Vincent, *Brief Report of the Services Rendered by the Freed People to the United States Army in North Carolina in the Spring of 1862, after the Battle of Newbern*. New York, 1864.

Conway, Thomas W., *Annual Report of Thomas W. Conway, Superintendent Bureau of Free Labor, Department of the Gulf, to Major General Hurlbut, Commanding, for the Year 1864*. New Orleans, 1865.

————, *The Freedmen of Louisiana. Final Report of the Bureau of Free Labor, Department of the Gulf to Major General E. R. S. Canby, Commanding*. New Orleans, 1865.

Eaton, John, Jr., *Report of the General Superintendent of Freedmen, Department of the Tennessee and State of Arkansas for 1864*. Memphis, 1865.

Equal Suffrage, Address from the Colored Citizens of Norfolk, Va.

to the People of the United States. Also an Account of the Agitation Among the Colored People of Virginia for Equal Rights, with an Appendix Concerning the Rights of Colored Witnesses Before the State Courts. New Bedford, Mass., 1865.

Graham, George, and Hartwell, John W., *Report by the Committee of Contrabands' Relief Commission of Cincinnati, Ohio. Proposing a Plan for the Occupation and Government of Vacated Territory in the Seceded States.* Cincinnati, 1863.

James, Rev. Horace, *Annual Report of the Superintendent of Negro Affairs in North Carolina. 1864. With an Appendix Containing the History and Management of the Freedmen in this Department up to June 1st, 1865.* Boston, 1865.

———, *The Two Great Wars of America. An Oration Delivered in Newbern, North Carolina, Before the Twenty-Fifth Regiment Massachusetts Volunteers, July 4, 1862.* Boston, 1862.

McKaye, James, *The Mastership and its Fruits: The Emancipated Slave Face to Face with his Old Master.* New York, 1864.

Mellen, William P., *Report Relative to Leasing Abandoned Plantations and Affairs of the Freed People in First Special Agency.* Washington, 1864.

New England Educational Commission for Freedmen, *Extracts from Letters of Teachers and Superintendents of the New England Educational Commission for Freedmen.* Boston, 1864.

New England Freedmen's Aid Society, *Second Annual Report of the New England Freedmen's Aid Society.* Boston, 1864.

Pierce, Edward L., "The Contrabands at Fortress Monroe, *Atlantic,* VIII (1861), 626-40.

Plumly, B. Rush, and Wheelock, E. M., *Report of the Board of Education for Freedmen, Department of the Gulf, for the year 1864.* New Orleans, 1864.

Scott, R. N., et al. (eds.), *War of the Rebellion: A Compilation of the Official Records of the Union and Confederate Armies.* 130 vols. Washington, D. C., 1880-1901.

Shipley, Samuel R., "Visit to the Camps of the Freedmen on the Mississippi River," in *Statistics of the Operation of the Executive Board of Friends' Association of Philadelphia, and its Vicinity, for the Relief of Colored Freedmen.* Philadelphia, 1864.

United States, *House Executive Documents,* No. 85, 37th Cong., 2nd
sess.
————, *House Executive Documents,* No. 72, 37th Cong., 3rd sess.
————, *House Executive Documents,* No. 1, 38th Cong., 1st sess.
————, *House Executive Documents,* No. 3, 38th Cong., 2nd sess.
————, *House Executive Documents,* No. 70, 39th Cong., 1st sess.
————, *House Miscellaneous Documents,* No. 14, 39th Cong., 2nd
sess.
————, *Population of the United States in 1860; Compiled from the
Original Returns of the Eighth Census.* Washington, D. C., 1864.
————, *Senate Executive Documents,* No. 1, 38th Cong., 1st sess.
————, *Senate Executive Documents,* No. 53, 38th Cong., 1st sess.
————, *Senate Executive Documents,* No. 27, 39th Cong., 1st sess.
————, *Senate Executive Documents,* No. 6, 39th Cong., 2nd sess.
————, *Senate Reports,* No. 108, 37th Cong., 3rd sess.
————, *Statutes at Large of the United States of America, 1789-1873.*
17 vols. Boston, 1850-1873.
Warren, Reverend Joseph, *Extracts from the Reports of Superintend-
ents of Freedmen Compiled from Records in the Office of
Colonel John Eaton, Jr. General Superintendent of Freedmen,
Department of the Tennessee and State of Arkansas.* 1st and 2nd
series. Vicksburg, 1864.
Yeatman, James E., *A Report on the Conditions of the Freedmen of
the Mississippi, Presented to the Western Sanitary Commission,
December 17th, 1863.* St. Louis, 1864.
————, *Suggestions of a Plan of Organization for Free Labor, and
the Leasing of Plantations under a Bureau or Commission to be
Appointed by the Government; Accompanying a Report Presented
to the Western Sanitary Commission.* St. Louis, 1864.

Newspapers

New Orleans L'Union.
New Orleans Daily Picayune.
New Orleans Tribune.
New York Independent.
New York Tribune.

SECONDARY WORKS

BOOKS

Aptheker, Herbert, *American Negro Slave Revolts*. New York, 1943.
———, *The Negro in the Civil War*. New York, 1938.
Bartlett, John Russell, *Literature of the Rebellion. A Catalogue of Books and Pamphlets Relating to the Civil War in the United States, and on Subjects Growing out of that Event, Together with Works on American Slavery, and Essays from Reviews and Magazines on the Same Subjects*. Boston, 1866.
Beard, Augustus F., *Crusade of Brotherhood: The History of the American Missionary Association*. Boston, 1909.
Belz, Herman, *Reconstructing the Union: Theory and Policy during the Civil War*. Ithaca, 1969.
Bentley, George R., *A History of the Freedmen's Bureau*. Philadelphia, 1955.
Bernstein, Barton J. (ed.), *Towards a New Past: Dissenting Essays in American History*. New York, 1968.
Bragg, Jefferson Davis, *Louisiana in the Confederacy*. Baton Rouge, 1941.
Brewer, James H., *The Confederate Negro: Virginia's Craftsmen and Military Laborers, 1861-1865*. Durham, N. C., 1969.
Brown, Ira V., *Lyman Abbott, Christian Evolutionist: A Study in Religious Opinion*. Cambridge, 1953.
Capers, Gerald M., *Occupied City: New Orleans under the Federals, 1862-1865*. Lexington, Ky., 1965.
Cornish, Dudley Taylor, *The Sable Arm: Negro Troops in the Union Army, 1861-1865*. New York, 1966.
Coulter, E. Merton, *Travels in the Confederate States: A Bibliography*. Norman, Okla., 1948.
Curry, Leonard P., *Blueprint for Modern America, Nonmilitary Legislation of the First Civil War Congress*. Nashville, 1968.
Donald, Henderson N. *The Negro Freedman: Life Conditions of the American Negro in the Early Years After Emancipation*. New York, 1952.
DuBois, W. E. B., *Black Reconstruction: An Essay Toward a History*

of the Part which Black Folk Played in the Attempt to Reconstruct Democracy in America, 1860-1880. Philadelphia, 1935.

Dyer, Frederick H., *A Compendium of the War of the Rebellion.* 3 vols. New York, 1959.

Franklin, John Hope, *Reconstruction: After the Civil War.* Chicago, 1961.

Fredrickson, George M., *The Inner Civil War: Northern Intellectuals and the Crisis of the Union.* New York, 1965.

Freidel, Frank, *Francis Lieber: Nineteenth-Century Liberal.* Baton Rouge, 1947.

Handlin, Oscar, et al. (eds.), *Harvard Guide to American History.* Cambridge, 1954.

Harrington, Fred Harvey, *Fighting Politician: Major General N. P. Banks.* Philadelphia, 1948.

Harris, William C., *Presidential Reconstruction in Mississippi.* Baton Rouge, 1967.

Hyman, Harold M. (ed.), *New Frontiers of the American Reconstruction.* Urbana, 1966.

Jackson, Luther P., *Free Negro Labor and Property Holding in Virginia, 1830-1860.* New York, 1942.

Johnson, Allen and Malone, Dumas (eds.), *Dictionary of American Biography,* 22 vols. New York, 1928-1944.

McFeely, William S., *Yankee Stepfather: General O. O. Howard and the Freedmen.* New Haven, 1968.

McPherson, James M., *The Negro's Civil War: How American Negroes Felt and Acted During the War for the Union.* New York, 1965.

————, *The Struggle for Equality: Abolitionists and the Negro in the Civil War and Reconstruction.* Princeton, 1964.

Meier, August and Rudwick, Elliott M., *From Plantation to Ghetto: An Interpretive History of American Negroes.* New York, 1966.

Nevins, Allan, *The War for the Union.* 2 vols. New York, 1959-1960.

Overy, David H., *Wisconsin Carpetbaggers in Dixie.* Madison, 1961.

Pease, William H. and Jane H., *Black Utopia: Negro Communal Experiments in America.* Madison, 1963.

Quarles, Benjamin, *Lincoln and the Negro.* New York, 1962.

————, *The Negro in the Civil War*. Boston, 1953.

Randall, James G., *The Confiscation of Property During the Civil War*. Indianapolis, 1913.

Rollin, Frank A., *Life and Public Service of Martin R. Delany*. Boston, 1883.

Rose, Willie Lee, *Rehearsal for Reconstruction: The Port Royal Experiment*. New York, 1964.

Smith, Timothy L., *Revivalism and Social Reform in Mid-Nineteenth-Century America*. New York, 1957.

Stampp, Kenneth M., *The Era of Reconstruction, 1865-1877*. New York, 1965.

Swint, Henry Lee, *The Northern Teacher in the South, 1862-1870*. Nashville, 1941.

Talbot, Edith Armstrong, *Samuel Chapman Armstrong: A Biographical Study*. New York, 1904.

Taylor, Alrutheus Ambush, *The Negro in the Reconstruction of Virginia*. Washington, D. C., 1926.

Thomas, Benjamin P. and Hyman, Harold M., *Stanton: The Life and Times of Lincoln's Secretary of War*. New York, 1962.

Voegeli, V. Jacque. *Free But Not Equal: The Midwest and the Negro During the Civil War*. Chicago, 1967.

Wesley, Charles H., *Negro Labor in the United States, 1850-1925*. New York, 1927.

West, Richard S., Jr., *Lincoln's Scapegoat General: A Life of Benjamin F. Butler, 1818-1893*. Boston, 1965.

Wharton, Vernon Lane, *The Negro in Mississippi, 1865-1890*. Chapel Hill, 1947.

Wiley, Bell Irvin, *Southern Negroes, 1861-1865*. New Haven, 1938.

Williamson, Joel, *After Slavery: The Negro in South Carolina During Reconstruction, 1861-1877*. Chapel Hill, 1965.

Winter, John D., *The Civil War in Louisiana*. Baton Rouge, 1963.

Wood, Forrest G., *Black Scare: The Racist Response to Emancipation and Reconstruction*. Berkeley, 1969.

Woodward, C. Vann, *The Burden of Southern History*, rev. ed. Baton Rouge, 1968.

Articles and Dissertations

Abbott, Martin, "Free Land, Free Labor, and the Freedmen's Bureau," *Agricultural History*, XXX (1956), 150-56.

Abbott, Richard H., "Massachusetts and the Recruitment of Southern Negroes, 1863-1865," *Civil War History*, XIV (1968), 197-210.

Alderson, William T., "The Freedmen's Bureau and Negro Education in Virginia," *North Carolina Historical Review*, XXIX (1952), 64-90.

———, "The Influence of Military Rule and the Freedmen's Bureau on Reconstruction in Virginia, 1865-1870," Ph.D. dissertation, Vanderbilt Univ., 1952.

Ames, Susie M., "Federal Policy Toward the Eastern Shore of Virginia in 1861," *Virginia Magazine of History and Biography*, LXIX (1961), 432-59.

Aptheker, Herbert, "Notes on Slave Conspiracies in Confederate Mississippi," *Journal of Negro History*, XXIX (1944), 75-79.

Armstrong, Warren B., "The Organization, Function, and Contribution of the Chaplaincy in the United States Army, 1861-1865," Ph.D. dissertation, Univ. of Michigan, 1964.

———, "Union Chaplains and the Education of the Freedmen," *Journal of Negro History*, LII (1967), 104-15.

Bahney, Robert S., "Generals and Negroes: Education of Negroes by the Union Army, 1861-1865," Ph.D. dissertation, Univ. of Michigan, 1965.

Beck, Warren A., "Lincoln and Negro Colonization in Central America," *Abraham Lincoln Quarterly*, VI (1950), 162-83.

Bigelow, Martha M., "Freedmen of the Mississippi Valley, 1862-1865," *Civil War History*, VIII (1962), 38-47.

———, (ed.), "Plantation Lessee Problems in 1864," *Journal of Southern History*, XXVII (1961), 354-67.

———, "The Significance of Milliken's Bend in the Civil War," *Journal of Negro History*, XLV (1960), 156-63.

———, "Vicksburg: Experiment in Freedom," *Journal of Mississippi History*, XXVI (1964), 28-44.

Bonekemper, Edward H., III, "Negro Ownership of Real Property in Hampton and Elizabeth City County, Virginia, 1860-1870," *Journal of Negro History*, LV (1970), 165-81.

Brown, Ira V., "Lyman Abbott and Freedmen's Aid, 1865-69," *Journal of Southern History*, XV (1949), 22-38.

Cox, LaWanda, "The Promise of Land for the Freedmen," *Mississippi Valley Historical Review*, XLV (1958), 413-39.

Curry, Richard O., "The Abolitionists and Reconstruction: A Critical Appraisal," *Journal of Southern History*, XXXIV (1968), 527-45.

Davis, David Brion, "Abolitionists and the Freedmen: An Essay Review," *Journal of Southern History*, XXXI (1965), 164-70.

Drake, Richard Bryant, "The American Missionary Association and the Southern Negro, 1861-1888," Ph.D. dissertation, Emory University, 1957.

Eggleston, G. K., "The Work of Relief Societies During the Civil War," *Journal of Negro History*, XIV (1929), 272-99.

Englesman, John C., "The Freedmen's Bureau in Louisiana," *Louisiana Historical Quarterly*, XXXII (1949), 145-224.

Everett, Donald E., "Demands of the New Orleans Free Colored Population for Political Equality, 1862-1865," *Louisiana Historical Quarterly*, XXXVIII (1955), 43-64.

Gara, Larry, "Slavery and the Slave Power: A Crucial Distinction," *Civil War History*, XV (1969), 5-18.

Harrington, Fred Harvey, "The Fort Jackson Mutiny," *Journal of Negro History*, XXVII (1942), 420-31.

Hooper, Ernest Walter, "Memphis, Tennessee: Federal Occupation and Reconstruction, 1862-1870," Ph.D. dissertation, Univ. of North Carolina, 1957.

Jackson, Luther P., "The Educational Efforts of the Freedmen's Bureau and Freedmen's Aid Societies in South Carolina, 1862-1872," *Journal of Negro History*, VIII (1923), 1-40.

————, "The Origin of Hampton Institute," *Journal of Negro History*, X (1925), 131-49.

Johnson, Clifton H., "The American Missionary Association, 1846-1861: A Study in Christian Abolitionism," Ph.D. dissertation, Univ. of North Carolina, 1958.

Jordan, W. J., "The Freedmen's Bureau in Tennessee," *East Tennessee Historical Society Publications*, No. 11 (1939), 47-61.

Low, W. A., "The Freedmen's Bureau and Civil Rights in Maryland," *Maryland Historical Magazine*, XLVII (1952), 29-39.

———, "The Freedmen's Bureau and Education in Maryland," *Journal of Negro History*, XXXVII (1952), 29-39.

Man, Albon P., Jr., "Labor Competition and the New York Draft Riots of 1863," *Journal of Negro History*, XXVI (1951), 375-405.

May, J. Thomas, "Continuity and Change in the Labor Program of the Union Army and the Freedmen's Bureau," *Civil War History*, XVII (1971), 245-54.

———, "The Freedmen's Bureau at the Local Level: A Study of a Louisiana Agent," *Louisiana History*, IX (1968), 5-19.

Morton, Richard L. (ed.), "A 'Yankee Teacher' in North Carolina, by Margaret Newbold Thorpe," *North Carolina Historical Review*, XXX (1953), 564-82.

———, " 'Contraband' and Quakers in the Virginia Peninsula, 1862-1869," *Virginia Magazine of History and Biography*, LXI (1953), 419-29.

———, (ed.), "Life in Virginia, by a 'Yankee Teacher,' Margaret Newbold Thorpe," *Virginia Magazine of History and Biography*, LXIV (1856), 180-207.

Murray, Robert K., "General Sherman, the Negro, and Slavery: The Story of an Unrecognized Rebel," *Negro History Bulletin*, XXII (1959), 125-230.

Noyes, Edward, "The Negro in Wisconsin's Civil War Effort," *Lincoln Herald*, LXIX (1967), 70-82.

Pease, William H. and Jane H. "Antislavery Ambivalence: Immediatism, Expediency, Race," *American Quarterly*, XVII (1965), 682-95.

Prichard, Walter, "The Effects of the Civil War on the Louisiana Sugar Industry," *Journal of Southern History*, V (1939), 315-32.

Riddleberger, Patrick W., "The Radicals' Abandonment of the Negro During Reconstruction," *Journal of Negro History*, XLV (1960), 88-102.

Rosenberg, John S., "Toward a New Civil War Revisionism" *American Scholar,* XXXVIII (1969), 250-72.

Scheips, Paul J., "Lincoln and the Ciriqui Colonization Project," *Journal of Negro History,* XXXVII (1952), 418-53.

Shortreed, Margaret, "The Antislavery Radicals: From Crusade to Revolution 1840-1868," *Past and Present,* XVI (1959), 65-87.

Shugg, Roger Wallace, "Survival of the Plantation System in Louisiana," *Journal of Southern History,* III (1937), 311-25.

Sing-Nan Fen, "Notes on the Education of Negroes at Norfolk and Portsmouth, Virginia During the Civil War," *Phylon,* XXVIII (1967), 197-207.

Smith, Thomas H., "Ohio Quakers and the Mississippi Freedmen—'A Field of Labor,' " *Ohio History,* LXXVIII (1969), 159-71.

Sproat, John G., "Blueprint for Radical Reconstruction," *Journal of Southern History,* XXIII (1957), 25-44.

Taylor, Joe Gray, "Slavery in Louisiana During the Civil War," *Louisiana History,* VIII (1967), 27-33.

Thomas, John L., "Romantic Reform in America, 1815-1865," *American Quarterly,* XVII (1965), 656-81.

Wiley, Bell Irvin, "Vicissitudes of Early Reconstruction Farming in the Lower Mississippi Valley," *Journal of Southern History,* III(1937), 441-52.

Williams, T. Harry, "General Banks and the Radical Republicans in the Civil War," *New England Quarterly,* XII (1939), 268-80.

Wish, Harvey, "Slave Disloyalty Under the Confederacy," *Journal of Negro History,* XXIII (1938), 435-50.

Index

★

Abolitionists, 3, 4, 49; inconsistencies of regarding slave personality, 99-100; role of in Negro affairs, 183; on Sea Islands, South Carolina, 50

Accomac County, Virginia, 22, 24

Algiers, Louisiana, 107

Allen, William F., 158-159, 161-162, 164, 172

American Freedmen's Inquiry Commission (AFIC), 34-35, 78, 99-100

American Missionary Association (AMA), 17-18, 20, 23, 25-27, 31, 37, 47, 51, 56

Andrew, John A., 12

Ann Arbor Cotton Company, 144

Armstrong, Samuel Chapman, 47

Ascension Parish, Louisiana, 92, 105

Assumption Parish, Louisiana, 89, 90

Banks, Gen. Nathaniel P.; attitude of toward black troops, 107, 108; attitude of toward New Orleans, 74; attitude of toward planters, 90-92; blacks protected from fraud by, 86; Butler replaced by, 73; contraband labor organized by, 75-77; and Fort Jackson mutiny, 108-109; and impressment of vagrant contrabands, 107; and labor contract system, 75, 101, 148-149; slave returned by, 92; slavery controls maintained by, 79; slavery suspended by, 78; and wages for contrabands, 79-80

Baton Rouge, Louisiana, 102

247

as Freedmen's Bureau agent,
188, 190; racial attitudes of,
33-34; Radical support sought
by, 49
Winchell, Alexander, 144
Wool, Gen. John E., 19-21
Wright, Elizure, 18

Yeatman, James E., 127, 143,
149, 150, 183; and Davis Bend

colony, 176; leasing reforms
proposed by, 130-133; paternalism of toward contrabands,
129; and plantation system,
131; and Treasury Department
reforms, 138-144
York County, Virginia, 25, 41
Yorktown peninsula. *See* Fortress
Monroe, Virginia
Young's Point, Louisiana, 173